PERFECT
LIGHT
DESSERTS

PERFECT LIGHT DESSERTS

Fabulous Cakes, Cookies, Pies,
and More Made with Real Butter,
Sugar, Flour, and Eggs, All Under
300 Calories per Generous Serving

NICK MALGIERI

and

DAVID JOACHIM

WM
WILLIAM MORROW
An Imprint of HarperCollinsPublishers

HarperCollins books may be purchased for educational, business, or sales promotional use. For information,
please write: Special Markets Department, HarperCollins Publishers, 10 East 53rd Street, New York, NY 10022.

FIRST EDITION

Photographs by Tom Eckerle
Illustrations by Laura Hartman Maestro
Food styling by Cara Tannenbaum, Andrea Tutunjian, and Jeff Yoskowitz
Prop styling by Ceci Gallini
Book design by Joel Avirom and Jason Snyder
Design assistant: Meghan Day Healey

Printed on acid-free paper

Library of Congress Cataloging-in-Publication Data has been applied for.

ISBN-13: 978-0-06-077929-0
ISBN-10: 0-06-077929-2

06 07 08 09 10 ❖/RRD 10 9 8 7 6 5 4 3 2 1

To everyone who enjoys dessert...
but doesn't enjoy dieting

———————————

CONTENTS

INTRODUCTION

About ten years ago, David Joachim approached me about writing a light desserts book. I had a few projects under way at the time, so the idea was put on hold. A few years later, I had the opportunity to develop and test a variety of lightened recipes and, to my amazement, the results were very good. I then approached David and suggested that we write this book together.

David and I decided to create desserts with exceptional flavor and texture but limited to 300 calories per serving. We didn't want to surgically alter any of the desserts or monkey with minuscule portion sizes. Instead, we carefully selected traditional desserts that are naturally low in calories and fat. We also developed new ones that meet the same criteria.

Some recipes have been moderately lightened with simple techniques. We replaced egg yolks with combinations of whole eggs and egg whites to reduce calories, yet still achieve good texture and rich tone. We used buttermilk to create moist and rich texture in desserts that incorporate less butter, such as Devil's Food Cake with Fluffy White Icing (page 24). Many of the cakes and pastry doughs use reduced amounts of butter, but butter and sugar are used throughout the cakes, cookies, and other desserts. We had one abiding rule for the ingredients in these recipes: no artificial anything. We use real sugar, real butter, and real eggs. We even use real heavy cream in moderate amounts. The furthest out the ingredients go is toward the realm of reduced-fat and low-fat milk, sour cream, and other dairy products.

The portion sizes here are generous. They are the same as they would be for full-fat, high-calorie cakes and desserts. These desserts just happen to be lower in calories.

The recipes are generally simple to prepare. There are no elaborate spun sugar cages or difficult preparation techniques. Some recipes seek only to enhance the natural flavor of one or two main ingredients, such as Gratin of Summer Berries (page 200) or Peaches Baked with Macaroon Filling (page 198). Others are more fancy showstoppers like Raspberry Mousse Cake (page 60) and Mary's Cappuccino Brûlé (page 160). But nothing here should scare off the home cook. Every recipe can be made easily with widely available ingredients and equipment.

It was a treat to discover that so many elegant desserts could be made with intense flavor and rich texture without an overload of calories. We hope that you enjoy making these recipes as much as we enjoyed developing them. By the way, when you serve these desserts to guests, don't tell them that they are low-calorie or low-fat. They'll never guess.

Nick Malgieri
David Joachim

INTRODUCTION

INGREDIENTS

All of the ingredients used in this book will be familiar to home cooks and are easy to find in the average supermarket. What follows here is a list of ingredients, like applesauce and all-fruit spread, that bear a brief explanation. The list will point you in the right direction for purchasing and is not meant to be a treatise on the nature of the ingredients themselves.

For the best results, buy from a reliable merchant and get the best-quality ingredients you can. See Sources on page 291 for some of my preferences among purveyors of chocolates, spices, yogurts, and other specialty ingredients.

Flours, Starches, Gelatin, and Filo Dough

ALL-PURPOSE FLOUR: I always use unbleached all-purpose flour. If a recipe just specifies all-purpose flour, you may use bleached or unbleached.

CAKE FLOUR: Any cake flour called for here is the plain type, not self-rising.

CORNMEAL: This is used to make old-fashioned Baked Indian Pudding (page 144). I prefer stone-ground yellow cornmeal because it has a slightly chewier, more pleasing texture than finely milled cornmeal. It also has more corn flavor than degerminated cornmeal.

CORNSTARCH: Plain cornstarch is available in the supermarket.

GELATIN: Here I use powdered gelatin in an envelope, the common form used in the United States. One envelope equals about 2½ teaspoons. For hints on working with gelatin, see the introduction to Chapter 4.

OATS: Old-fashioned rolled oats are called for in a few cookies and crisps. Don't substitute instant or quick-cooking oats. Their texture is too flimsy.

BREAD CRUMBS: I scatter fine, dry bread crumbs onto greased pans instead of using flour. Bread crumbs create a slightly thicker coating, allowing the cake to release more easily. These bread crumbs may be bought in the supermarket. Be sure to buy unflavored ones.

TAPIOCA: The recipe for Coconut Tapioca with Lime and Mint-Scented Pineapple (page 141) calls for pearl tapioca. Make sure you buy small or medium pearl tapioca, not the crushed, granulated, or "instant" kind used to thicken pie fillings.

FILO DOUGH: Sheets of this paper-thin dough are used to make Individual Apple Strudels (page 126) and Lemon Meringue Tartlets (page 128). Look for fresh filo in Greek or Middle Eastern markets. You can also find sheets of frozen filo in the frozen bread section of most supermarkets.

Sugars and Sweeteners

GRANULATED SUGAR: I use plain granulated sugar in all the recipes, never superfine sugar.

BROWN SUGAR: I call for light brown sugar in this book. You may use dark, but remember that dark brown sugar has a more pronounced molasses flavor.

CONFECTIONERS' SUGAR: I use this mainly for sprinkling on finished cakes and pastries, and sometimes as an ingredient in meringues. I never use confectioners' sugar for sweetening whipped cream because it contains cornstarch and imparts a chalky taste to the cream.

CORN SYRUP: Light corn syrup is used to improve the texture of some lean desserts here. Dark corn syrup is occasionally called for to provide a richer flavor.

MAPLE SYRUP: Available in several grades ranging from light to dark. Grade A is the best and most expensive, more delicate in flavor, medium amber in color, and meant to be used as a table syrup. Grade B, however, is stronger flavored, darker amber in color, and much better for baking—and usually a little lower in price.

HONEY: I buy dark, full-flavored honey but not always one with a fancy pedigree.

MOLASSES: I use unsulfured molasses, which tends to be milder in flavor than the other type available, which is usually marked "robust flavor." Sometimes the mild type is labeled "light" molasses, but this does not refer to its nutritional content.

Leaveners

BAKING POWDER: I use double-acting baking powder, the type sold in most supermarkets. Always check the expiration date on the container. Baking powder does lose its leavening power over time. After the expiration date, discard the old baking powder and buy a fresh container.

BAKING SODA: Plain bicarbonate of soda. Be careful to crush any lumps before measuring and adding to other ingredients.

Flavorings

SALT: I usually use fine sea salt for both baking and salting food that I am cooking. When a coarse salt is needed, I use kosher salt, available in the supermarket.

EXTRACTS: Always buy 100 percent pure extracts. Some brands may advertise "pure vanilla extract" in large letters and put "with artificial extract added" in fine print below. The same is true of almond extract.

WHOLE-BEAN VANILLA: Look for the best-quality vanilla beans you can find from a reliable source, such as Nielsen-Massey (see Sources, page 291). If you happen to have some dried-out beans, see the remedy on page 55.

GINGER: Fresh ginger, crystallized ginger, and ground ginger are used in various recipes here. Don't be tempted to substitute one for another. Each has a unique flavor and texture.

LIQUORS: A lesser-quality liquor or liqueur can instantly ruin a fine dessert. Here's my advice: If a large bottle of imported rum or other liquor or liqueur is expensive, buy a smaller bottle, rather than buying a lesser brand. I often use Kirsch, a clear brandy distilled from cherries. The best comes from Switzerland, Alsace in France, Austria, and Germany. It may be labeled as Kirschwasser, but the best types are imported and are never cheap.

CHOCOLATE: Various chocolates are used here, including unsweetened, bittersweet, semisweet, sweet, milk, and white chocolates. See page 6 for a description of each type. Remember that a chocolate dessert will only taste as good as the chocolate used to prepare it. See Sources on page 291 for some of the brands I like best.

COCOA POWDER: I use alkalized (Dutch process) cocoa exclusively and most supermarkets carry it. The package will either have a Dutch-sounding name (Droste, Van Houten, Bensdorp) or will state that it is alkalized. Hershey's European-style cocoa is also alkalized. See page 7 for a more detailed description of cocoa powder.

COCONUT: I call for both sweetened shredded coconut and coconut milk in these recipes. Look for Thai coconut milk, which can be found in Asian grocery stores and most supermarkets. Don't buy coconut cream, which is a thicker mixture used to make blended tropical drinks such as piña coladas.

COFFEE: Either brew triple-strength espresso (3 tablespoons coffee and ¾ cup boiling water) or use instant espresso. The latter's flavor may be improved by dissolving it in brewed coffee instead of in water.

JAM: I use all-fruit spreads here because they are sweetened with fruit juice instead of sugar and have about 80 fewer calories per ½ cup compared with most jams and preserves. But if you don't have all-fruit spreads, your favorite jam or preserves will work just fine.

HERBS AND SPICES: I prefer fresh herbs over dried and, fortunately, fresh herbs are now widely available. Remember that the flavor of dried herbs and spices will dissipate over time. If your spices have been in the spice rack for more than a year, it's probably time to discard them and buy new ones. The Sources section (page 291) will direct you toward some reliable purveyors of herbs and spices.

Nuts and Nut Products

Nutmeats with the skin on are generally referred to as natural or unblanched. Those with the skins removed are referred to as blanched or skinless. Almonds, pistachios, and hazelnuts (also called filberts) are available both natural and blanched. It's easier to buy nuts that are already blanched, but if you can only find natural ones, it's simple to blanch them and remove the skins at home. Put almonds or pistachios in a saucepan and cover with water. Bring to a boil and drain. Rub the nutmeats in a towel to loosen the skins, then check each nut to make sure the skins are separated from the nuts. Place the blanched nuts on a jelly-roll pan and dry them out in the oven for about 10 minutes at 325 degrees, then cool them, especially if you have to grind them afterward. To blanch hazelnuts, put them in a small roasting pan and bake them at 350 degrees for about 15 minutes, or until the skins begin to char slightly and loosen. Rub in a towel and separate from the skins as for almonds. It's not necessary to dry them out after blanching. Pecans and walnuts are not blanched, but the skins are so thin that they're no bother in recipes.

Store nuts in a plastic bag in the freezer. If you need to grind nuts in a food processor, bring them to room temperature before grinding. Cold nutmeats will clump up and never grind finely enough. Warm ones will turn almost immediately to nut butter.

Eggs

All the eggs called for here are large eggs, 24 ounces per dozen. Some recipes, notably those for meringues that are not subsequently baked, call for egg whites that are just heated but not completely cooked. If you are concerned about this, substitute pasteurized egg whites, which are now widely available in supermarkets. You can also buy pasteurized whole eggs if necessary.

Dairy Products

Real butter, milk, and other dairy products are used throughout these recipes. In some cases, reduced-fat or low-fat dairy products are called for to minimize calories. Reduced-fat products are used most often. Know that there can be a big flavor and texture difference between reduced-fat and fat-free foods, particularly among dairy products such as sour cream. Fat-free sour cream tastes like spackling paste, but a good-quality reduced-fat sour cream works perfectly in cakes such as Ginger Lovers' Pound Cake (page 67) and frostings such as the milk chocolate frosting used on Lemon Cupcakes (page 65). Terminology can be confusing, so here are definitions of labels you may see on lower-fat dairy products. These definitions are set by the Food and Drug Administration (FDA) and must be adhered to by food manufacturers in labeling their products.

Light or lite: One-third fewer calories than the original product. Or, less than 50 percent fat per serving, which means that if more than half of the product's calories come from fat, the fat content must be reduced by at least 50 percent to use this label claim.

Reduced-fat: At least 25 percent less fat than the original product.

Low-fat: 3 grams of fat or less per serving.

Fat-free: Less than ½ gram (0.5 gram) of fat per serving with no added fats.

BUTTER: I use unsalted butter in the recipes here. I never use so-called European or extra-anything butters. All the recipes were tested with plain butter available at the supermarket. If you substitute butter with a higher fat content, you might get different results, especially in cookie batters and pastry doughs. They will have a tendency to spread more and be highly fragile after baking. Butter is probably the most important ingredient in fine baking, so it needs to be fresh to be good. Unwrap a stick of butter and scratch the surface with the point of a table knife. If the butter is lighter colored on the inside than on the outside, it has oxidized and become stale. Such butter won't impart anything but a stale flavor to whatever you bake with it. If you stock up on butter during a sale, by all means store it in the freezer. If you intend to keep it for more than a month or so, wrap the packages in plastic wrap and foil to keep them as airtight as possible.

MILK: Whole milk, reduced-fat milk, low-fat milk, and fat-free milk are used in various recipes. Whole milk contains about 3½ percent fat. Reduced-fat milk contains 2 percent fat and is often labeled as 2 percent. Low-fat milk has 1 percent fat and is frequently labeled as such. Fat-free milk has less than 0.5 percent fat and may be labeled skim milk or nonfat milk.

BUTTERMILK: Naturally low in fat yet rich in texture, buttermilk lends moisture and tenderness to desserts made with less butter and eggs. I use low-fat buttermilk, which has about 100 calories and 2 grams of fat per cup. Reduced-fat buttermilk will also work but is slightly more caloric at about 140 calories and 5 grams of fat per cup.

CREAM: I use both heavy whipping cream and half-and-half in these recipes. The heavy cream should have a fat content of 36 percent. If you have 40 percent cream available, you can use it, but know that it will add a few calories and fat grams. When half-and-half is called for, it is traditional half-and-half (half whole milk, half cream). Don't substitute fat-free half-and-half, which has a disagreeable texture and will not perform well in these desserts.

EVAPORATED MILK: I use evaporated skim milk in a few recipes to provide rich texture without piling on the calories.

SWEETENED CONDENSED MILK: Similar to evaporated milk but sweetened and very thick.

NONFAT DRY MILK: Meant to be reconstituted with water to make skim milk. Used in some recipes to boost the solids content of the batter or mixture.

SOUR CREAM: Reduced-fat or low-fat sour cream is called for in these recipes. Avoid fat-free sour cream because the thickeners used to make it will not perform well here.

YOGURT: I call for low-fat or fat-free yogurt. Greek yogurt has wonderful texture and flavor, and it is preferred for all recipes. See Sources (page 291) for purchasing information.

RICOTTA: Part-skim ricotta is used in the recipes here. Buy the best quality you can find. As with other dairy products, don't be tempted to use fat-free. There is a world of difference between part-skim and fat-free ricotta.

CREAM CHEESE: I use both reduced-fat and low-fat cream cheese in these recipes. Again, I recommend avoiding fat-free cream cheese.

Fruit

Before buying fruit, observe it, feel it, and smell it to make sure it is of the best quality. Every recipe specifies how ripe fresh fruit should be. See the chart on page 209 for a list of what fruit is in season when.

APPLESAUCE: A few recipes such as cakes use applesauce to provide moistness and tenderness when less fat is incorporated into the batter. Only use unsweetened applesauce for these recipes. Sweetened applesauce will add calories and could make some recipes taste overly sweet.

BERRIES: I always prefer to use fresh berries. But sometimes you have to work with frozen berries, and I've developed a few recipes such as Cooked Raspberry Sauce (page 283) to make the most of frozen berries. For the best quality, buy bags of individually quick-frozen berries. Squeeze the bag to make sure that the berries are loose and not clumped together.

DRIED FRUIT: Use unsulfured dried fruit whenever possible to avoid the sulfites used as preservatives.

CANNED FRUIT: I generally avoid canned fruit, but there are two exceptions in this book. One: I use canned pumpkin puree because the texture and flavor are more reliable than what you get by cooking and pureeing fresh pumpkins. When making Perfect Pumpkin Pie (page 100), be sure to buy pure pumpkin puree, not pumpkin pie filling or mix, which has sugar and other flavorings added to it. Two: I prepared Apricot Custard Tart (page 119) for a class one year when apricots were out of season. I used canned apricots then and, to my surprise, the tart turned out very well, with a fine apricot flavor.

Oils

VEGETABLE OILS: Canola, corn, or soybean oil will all work fine. I use vegetable oil cooking spray to minimize calories when greasing pans. The spray does a good job of quickly and evenly coating pans.

EQUIPMENT

No highly specialized equipment is needed for the recipes in this book. Most of the cake pans, tart pans, and other bakeware can be easily purchased or may already be stocked in your kitchen. I find it helpful to list the pans, molds, hand tools, and small appliances called for in the recipes so that there are no surprises when you start baking. Having the right equipment, especially the correct pan sizes, makes all the difference with successful results in baking.

Baking Pans

LAYER PANS: These are round pans that are 2 inches deep. For the recipes in this book, I call for 9-inch- and 10-inch-diameter pans.

RECTANGULAR PANS: I use both 10 x 15-inch jelly-roll pans and 12 x 18-inch commercial half-sheet pans. If you don't have the latter, an 11 x 17-inch pan works just as well. Cookie sheets that don't have sides are useful for moving dough and cake layers and for chilling pieces of dough, aside from baking cookies. Insulated cookie sheets are worth the expense if your oven gives strong bottom heat and has a tendency to burn things on the bottom. Only use them in the bottom of the oven, though. You can get the same effect by stacking two uninsulated pans together for baking in the bottom of the oven. A 9 x 13 x 2-inch rectangular pan is called for in some recipes. A metal one doubles as a roasting pan and can be used for the water bath when making baked custards. I also like the glass pans.

SQUARE PANS: A glass or metal 9-inch square pan is useful for brownies and smaller snack cakes.

TUBE PANS: This can be a 1- or 2-piece 12-cup (10-inch) tube pan, or what's commonly referred to as a Bundt pan, also having a 12-cup capacity. Note that angel and chiffon cakes always use the former style of tube pan (not a Bundt pan).

LOAF PANS: I use both 9 x 5 x 3-inch loaf pans and 8½ x 4½ x 2¾-inch pans for the recipes in this book.

SPRINGFORMS: Both 9- and 10-inch springform pans are called for here. There are relatively new ones manufactured by Kaiser (see Sources, page 291) that have a completely flat bottom, so you can slide your cake or pastry off the pan bottom onto a platter. Old-fashioned springform pans have a lip on the pan bottom, which means you have to dig in under it slightly to remove something.

GRATIN DISHES: These wide, shallow dishes are useful for making crisps, pudding cakes, and bread puddings to maximize the amount of topping. I call for 1½- and 2-quart gratin dishes in the recipes.

PIE PANS: I prefer Pyrex for a pie pan and use the standard 9-inch size.

TART PANS: I like to use a removable-bottom tart pan with fluted sides. The recipes call for 9- or 10-inch pans. These are interchangeable, so you only need to have one of each size. There are also individual tart pans with removable bottoms that are about 4½ inches in diameter—perfect for individual tarts.

TARTLET PANS: The ones I use most often are about 2½ inches in diameter, have sloping sides, and are made from tinned base metal. Bake the pans for half an hour at 350 degrees before using them for the first time to season them. You may butter them the first few times you use them, but after that it won't be necessary. Just wipe the pans well with a dry cloth or paper towel after each use. Don't wash them or you'll have to season them again.

MUFFIN AND MINI-MUFFIN PANS: These can be useful as substitutes for individual tart and tartlet pans. Some of the tartlets in Chapter 3 are baked in a muffin pan and the muffin cups are lined with filo dough.

CUPCAKE PANS: I use 12-cavity cupcake pans with paper liners.

RAMEKINS: Straight-sided shallow ramekins are used for cooking some custards and serving some mousses. I generally use 4-ounce ceramic ramekins, but 6-ounce ramekins are called for in Rum Raisin Semifreddo (page 236). Glass custard cups or even heatproof coffee cups make good substitutes.

Pans for Cooking

The cooking here only involves simmering a filling or a sauce, but here are some suggestions for basic cookware.

ENAMELED IRON COOKWARE: I use enameled iron Dutch ovens for poaching fruit and making some compotes. The pans are heavy-bottomed, which makes them heat very evenly without scorching their contents.

BIMETAL COOKWARE: These are stainless steel pans with an aluminum core for even heating. Saucepans are the type used most often in these recipes. Calphalon Tri-Ply is an example of this type of pan and works well for the same purposes as enameled iron.

SAUTÉ PANS: A 10- and a 12-inch sauté pan will be useful for a variety of jobs.

Hand Tools

KNIVES: Three knives are essential in every kitchen: a good paring knife, a chopping (or chef's) knife, and a serrated knife for slicing bread and through cake layers. I like to use an offset serrated knife for a variety of slicing and chopping tasks. In some knife assortments, this type is labeled as a sandwich knife. A thin-bladed slicing knife is also useful for slicing cakes and other desserts at serving time.

SPATULAS: Small and large offset spatulas are essential for evenly spreading out batters before baking, spreading fillings onto dough, and finishing cakes. I also like to use a wide griddle spatula for moving around finished cakes and desserts.

SKIMMER: Skimmers, tongs, and slotted spoons are all useful for a variety of kitchen jobs such as skimming the foam from custard mixtures and removing meringue eggs from their poaching liquid.

GRATERS: A box grater with diagonally set holes, large and small, is better than one that has only holes that look as though they were formed by a nail piercing the sheet metal. Microplane and Cuisipro are two brands of graters that come in all sizes and degrees of fineness for grating citrus zests, nutmeg, cheese, or even shaving chocolate. A zester or zesting tool perfectly removes the zest from citrus in narrow strips without also removing the bitter white membrane beneath the zest. For a picture of this tool, see the illustration on page 143.

WOODEN SPOONS: Useful for stirring sauces and other mixtures. Flat-ended wooden spatulas are even more practical because they can evenly sweep across the bottom of a pan, scraping it efficiently.

PIZZA WHEEL: A plain sharp one and a serrated one (sometimes both come mounted on the same handle) are useful for cutting various doughs.

THERMOMETER: Use the kind of candy and deep-fry thermometer that looks like a ruler, not the one that looks like a stem with a round dial at the top.

INSTANT-READ THERMOMETER: This is useful for monitoring the internal temperature of heated meringue.

ROLLING PIN: I prefer the type without handles that is a straight cylinder of wood, about 16 inches long and about 2 inches in diameter. There are also nylon ones in the same shape that resist dough sticking to them.

PASTRY BRUSH: A natural bristle pastry brush works better than one with synthetic bristles. If you can't find a pastry brush specifically, a small, high-quality, wooden-handled paintbrush works well. Just don't use a basting brush that has already been used for barbecue sauces. Keep pastry brushes and barbecue brushes separately to avoid off flavors.

Papers and Foil

PARCHMENT PAPER: Years of production work in professional kitchens has spoiled me forever into using large sheets of parchment paper (18 x 24 inches) that come in a box of 1,000 sheets. These are easy to obtain from paper wholesalers, and a friendly bakery may even sell you a box. It's the type of thing you can share with several friends who also like to bake, and it's so much more convenient than using that dinky paper on a roll.

ALUMINUM FOIL: I prefer parchment paper, but foil can be substituted in many of the recipes. Extra-wide foil is practical for lining large pans. Nonstick foil makes a good choice when the pan liner will be greased, although I usually coat the nonstick foil with spray to be sure the dessert won't stick.

WAX PAPER: Failing everything else, I have also used buttered wax paper.

CARDBOARDS: These are available in a variety of sizes and shapes. Round ones the same diameter as your cake will make cake finishing a breeze. Rectangular ones can make unmolding large cakes or tarts easy.

Measuring Tools

LIQUID MEASURES: These are usually made from glass or clear plastic and are graduated for fractions of cups. Newer measuring cups make it possible to read the quantity from the top rather than the side of the cup—a definite improvement. I have several each in 1-, 2-, 4-, and 8-cup sizes. Not having to rinse out the cup before measuring another ingredient makes things easier.

DRY-MEASURE CUPS: For measuring dry ingredients such as flour, confectioners' sugar, or cornstarch. Spoon the ingredient into the cup and level it off for accurate measurement. Sugar is the only dry ingredient I scoop when measuring.

MEASURING SPOONS: Graduated metal measuring spoons are essential. I like to have several sets so that if one gets wet measuring liquid ingredients, there is another set of dry ones waiting.

SCALES: There are any number of fairly inexpensive battery-operated scales available. These make quick work of weighing out chocolate or other ingredients measured by weight.

Electricals

STAND MIXER: A heavy-duty mixer such as a KitchenAid is an essential baker's tool. You could use a heavy-duty handheld mixer, but those mixers are much less convenient and always break. If you are investing in a stand mixer, buy an extra bowl and whisk. They will pay for themselves by saving you time when whisking several mixtures for a single dessert.

FOOD PROCESSOR: I always use a food processor for grinding nuts and mixing doughs. All of the pastry doughs here are made in a food processor. Use the metal blade for grinding nuts and mixing pastry doughs.

BLENDER: A blender is useful for pureeing fruit for sauces or fillings. I think it does a faster and more efficient job than a food processor does.

PERFECT
LIGHT
DESSERTS

─────

CHOCOLATE DESSERTS

Chocolate is everybody's favorite ingredient. Nine times out of ten, when someone has a sweet craving, it's for chocolate or something made with it. Chocolate is rich and creamy, yes, but it's that pleasantly bitter note that makes the flavor of chocolate so irresistible. And scientists now say that about an ounce a day of bittersweet chocolate improves heart health. That's got to be the best nutrition news I've ever heard.

Chocolate is so popular that I have grouped all of the chocolate recipes into one chapter. Here you'll find fabulous chocolate cakes, tarts, cookies, cupcakes, brownies, puddings, mousses, and even real chocolate truffles! Except for the truffles, which I consider to be a rare treat, every recipe keeps calories to a minimum by using common ingredients and relatively simple techniques. For instance, Devil's Food Cake with Fluffy White Icing (page 24) tastes as rich and chocolaty as you would expect and it's drenched in thick, sweet icing. Yet the recipe uses no butter or solid chocolate. Instead, naturally low-fat buttermilk creates a rich, moist texture in the cake. The recipe also includes dark corn syrup and a bit of applesauce for sweetness and moistness with relatively few calories. These ingredients enhance the intense chocolate flavor of naturally low-fat, high-quality cocoa powder, which takes the place of higher-fat solid chocolate.

Similar techniques are used throughout the recipes to deliver maximum chocolate flavor without all the calories and fat. The only chocolate recipes not included in this chapter are chocolate ices and sauces, which are included in the Ices chapter (page 211) and Sauces chapter (page 273). You can also find a virtuous chocolate chip cookie recipe on page 256 and instructions for making chocolate shavings on page 286.

Chocolate Types

Several forms of chocolate are used in the recipes, including solid chocolate and cocoa powder, both of which have subtypes. Solid chocolates are generally categorized by the amount of chocolate liquor they contain and the amount of sugar added to them. Chocolate liquor is the term used to describe the basic raw material created after roasting, hulling, and grinding cocoa beans. It's a blend of cocoa solids and cocoa butter, which is the natural fat in cocoa beans. Simply put, the more chocolate liquor that is used to make solid chocolate, the stronger the resulting chocolate flavor will be. When you see a chocolate labeled as 55 percent, 64 percent, or 70 percent, the percentage refers to the amount of cocoa solids in the chocolate. High-cocoa chocolates are great for low-calorie recipes because they have a lower sugar content, packing more chocolate flavor into fewer calories. Here's a quick look at the various forms of solid chocolate used in the recipes, plus a few others for reference.

UNSWEETENED: Also known as baking chocolate or bitter chocolate, this is pure solidified chocolate liquor with no added sugar.

BITTERSWEET: Intensely flavored, yet mellowed with a bit of sugar, bittersweet chocolate contains at least 35 percent chocolate liquor. Bittersweet chocolate is an ideal choice for flavorful, low-calorie desserts because it contains less sugar and more cocoa solids than the more common semisweet chocolate. If you really love strong chocolate flavor, as I do, look for bittersweet chocolate with a high percentage of cocoa solids or chocolate liquor on the label. Less expensive "dark" chocolates use only the minimum 35 percent chocolate liquor. But you'll get more bang for your buck with higher percentages such as 70 to 72 percent chocolate. I prefer 72 percent chocolate and, thankfully, it is becoming more widely available in supermarkets. There's even a health bonus to these high-percentage bittersweet chocolates: They have more heart-protecting antioxidants than any other food—even more than red wine and tea. The darker the chocolate, the better the chocolate flavor *and* the healthier it is. I'm in heaven!

SEMISWEET: Similar to the bittersweet variety, semisweet chocolate is made with a minimum of 35 percent chocolate liquor, but it includes more sugar, so I generally avoid it for low-calorie desserts. Note that semisweet chocolate chips are formulated with less added cocoa butter than bars and squares so that the chips do not lose their shape when baked in chocolate chip cookies. For this reason, semisweet chocolate chips are not recommended for melting.

SWEET: Also known as sweet German chocolate because of a popular brand name, this type contains yet more sugar and even less chocolate liquor—a minimum of 15 percent. It tastes sweeter and less chocolaty than semisweet or bittersweet chocolate.

MILK: Softened by the flavor of milk, this variety is made with a minimum of only 10 percent chocolate liquor and at least 12 percent added milk solids. Some manufacturers make milk chocolate with more chocolate liquor—up to 38 percent—giving it a stronger chocolate flavor. Due to the milk solids and high sugar content, milk chocolate is more sensitive to heat than semisweet and bittersweet chocolate.

WHITE: This type is not considered a "true" chocolate because it doesn't include the chocolate liquor that gives chocolate its distinctive flavor and dark color. However, it still tastes rich and creamy, especially in White Chocolate Raspberry Tartlets (page 32). For the best flavor, look for white chocolate that contains cocoa butter as the only type of fat. Less expensive imitations are made with palm kernel oil or other vegetable fats and little or no real cocoa butter. The lack of cocoa butter makes imitation white chocolate taste much less like chocolate and causes it to melt at a higher temperature.

COCOA POWDER: The difference between cocoa powder and chocolate liquor is that most of the natural cocoa butter has been removed and the remaining cocoa solids are ground to a powder. Removing the cocoa butter drastically lowers the fat and calories. For instance, using 3 tablespoons of unsweetened cocoa powder (about ½ ounce) instead of 1 ounce of unsweetened solid chocolate shaves about 110 calories and 14 grams of fat from recipes.

The two basic styles of cocoa powder are nonalkalized (natural) and alkalized (Dutch process). I often use alkalized (Dutch-process) cocoa powder for its mild flavor and lack of harshness. It provides a smooth chocolate flavor and deep, rich color to recipes. That's because alkalized cocoa has an alkali, such as baking soda, added to it during processing, which helps to soften the natural acidity of cocoa. Natural cocoa, on the other hand, retains its acidity and has a more bitter flavor. All the recipes in this book use Dutch-process cocoa. Avoid substituting one for the other, as the balance of acid and alkali ingredients in the recipes has been calculated using the specified cocoa.

Melting Chocolate

There are several ways to melt solid chocolate. The easiest is to stir the chocolate directly into a hot liquid mixture that has just been removed from the heat, such as a custard. If cut into small pieces, the chocolate will melt in a minute or two. You can also melt chocolate in a heatproof bowl set over a pan of hot water that has been brought to a boil and then removed from the heat. Never melt chocolate over direct heat or it will scorch and acquire a burned taste. A third option, if your oven is preheating anyway, is to melt the chocolate in a heatproof bowl in the oven while the heat is still fairly low (about 250 degrees) for 8 to 10 minutes. Then there is the microwave method—arguably the fastest but also the trickiest method and the one that needs the most attention. To microwave chocolate, put the chocolate in a microwave-safe container and microwave in 30-second increments just until the chocolate is soft enough to be stirred smooth. Don't cook it until completely melted or the chocolate may scorch. Stop and stir every 30 seconds, heating only until the chocolate can be stirred smooth or almost smooth (any small bits will soon melt from residual heat).

Whichever melting method you choose, keep three cardinal rules in mind:

1   Use gentle heat. Low, indirect heat is best, which is why chocolate is frequently melted over a pan of hot water.

2   Make sure everything is dry. Even a small drop of water can make chocolate "seize," or solidify into a stiff, grainy mass. Keep your bowls, stirring spoons, and other utensils bone-dry. A dry environment is one thing the oven method has going for it.

3   Use small pieces. Cutting the chocolate into small pieces helps it to melt quickly.

Using uniform pieces also promotes even melting so that you aren't left with large solid chunks swimming in a pool of otherwise melted chocolate. I usually cut chocolate into ¼-inch pieces before melting.

Technique Tips

When making the chocolate cakes, cookies, and pies in this chapter, take a quick look at the relevant chapter introductions for Cakes (page 43), Cookies (page 241), and Pies and Tarts (page 91). These introductions offer general instructions for finishing cakes, mixing cookie doughs, and handling piecrusts.

Chocolate Spice Cookies

Makes about 36 cookies

These moist, chewy cookies are so good, it's hard to believe that they're low in calories and fat. Many thanks to my friend and cookbook dealer Bonnie Slotnick for sharing the recipe.

1½ cups all-purpose flour (spoon flour into dry-measure cup and level off)

⅓ cup alkalized (Dutch-process) cocoa powder

2 teaspoons ground cinnamon

1 teaspoon ground ginger

1 teaspoon baking soda

½ teaspoon ground cloves

½ teaspoon salt

4 tablespoons unsalted butter, melted

1 cup sugar

¼ cup unsweetened applesauce (see Note on page 87)

¼ cup molasses

2 cookie sheets or jelly-roll pans lined with parchment or foil

1 Set racks in the upper and lower thirds of the oven and preheat to 350 degrees.

2 Sift the dry ingredients into a mixing bowl and set aside.

3 In another mixing bowl, beat the butter and sugar together with a large rubber spatula. Beat in the applesauce and molasses.

4 Stir in the dry ingredients to make a soft dough.

5 Drop tablespoons of the dough (or use a small ice cream scoop) an inch apart on the prepared pans.

6 Bake the cookies for about 10 minutes, changing the position of the pans about halfway through the baking. Exchange the top pan and the bottom and also turn them back to front at the same time. The cookies will still be fairly moist when they are done. Avoid overbaking them or they will be dry and hard.

7 Slide the papers from the pans to racks to cool the cookies.

STORAGE: Keep the cookies between sheets of wax paper in a tin or plastic container with a tight-fitting cover.

Per cookie: 61 calories, 2 g total fat (30% of calories), 1 g saturated fat, 1 g protein, 12 g carbohydrates, 0 g fiber, 3 mg cholesterol, 69 mg sodium

Crisp Chocolate Biscotti

Makes about 60 biscotti

This is a streamlined version of an excellent biscotti recipe shared by my friend cake designer Ellen Baumwoll. Adding walnuts to the dough increases calories but provides richness to what would otherwise be a somewhat plain cookie.

1¾ cups all-purpose flour (spoon flour into dry-measure cup and level off)

⅔ cup alkalized (Dutch-process) cocoa powder

2 teaspoons baking powder

½ teaspoon salt

1¼ cups sugar

⅔ cup (about 3 ounces) walnut pieces, coarsely chopped

6 large egg whites

2 teaspoons vanilla extract

2 cookie sheets or jelly-roll pans lined with parchment or foil

1   Set a rack in the middle level of the oven and preheat to 350 degrees.

2   Sift the flour and cocoa into a medium mixing bowl. Stir in the baking powder, salt, sugar, and nuts.

3   Whisk the egg whites and vanilla together and add to the dry ingredients. Use a large rubber spatula to stir the dough together. At first the dough may seem dry, but as the sugar continues to melt, the dough will become softer and eventually quite sticky.

4   Scrape the dough out onto a lightly floured surface and press it together. Divide the dough into 2 equal pieces and roll each into a log the approximate length of the pan you are using. Arrange the two logs of dough on one pan (the other will be used later for toasting the biscotti). Make sure the logs of dough aren't too close to each other or to the side of the pan. Flatten each log with the palm of your hand.

5   Bake the logs of dough for about 30 minutes, or until they are well risen and firm when pressed with a fingertip. Leave the oven on and place racks in the upper and lower thirds.

6 Cool the baked logs on the pan on a rack.

7 After the logs of dough have cooled completely, place them on a cutting board and use a sharp serrated knife to cut them into straight or diagonal slices ½ inch thick.

8 Arrange the slices, cut side down, on the prepared pans and return them to the oven to toast for about 15 minutes.

9 Cool the toasted biscotti on the pans on racks.

SERVING: Very good on their own or dunked into coffee, these cookies also dress up a plain sherbet or ice milk.

STORAGE: Keep the biscotti between sheets of wax paper in a tin or plastic container with a tight-fitting cover.

Per biscotto: 44 calories, 2 g total fat (41% of calories), 0 g saturated fat, 1 g protein, 8 g carbohydrates, 0 g fiber, 0 mg cholesterol, 38 mg sodium

Italian Cocoa
Honey Spice Cookies

Mostaccioli al Cioccolato

Makes about 40 diamond-shaped cookies

These diamond-shaped cookies are often seen in large sizes covered with a blotchy white sugar icing in grocery stores and pastry shops in southern Italy. I worked out this version after tasting several cookies in Italy years ago. These cookies have virtually no fat in them besides the ground almonds, so be careful not to overbake them or they will become dry and tough.

¾ cup alkalized (Dutch-process) cocoa, sifted after measuring

1½ cups all-purpose flour (spoon flour into dry-measure cup and level off)

⅓ cup sugar

1 cup (about 4 ounces) whole almonds, finely ground in the food processor

1 teaspoon ground cinnamon

½ teaspoon ground cloves

1 teaspoon baking soda

¾ cup honey

⅓ cup water or red wine

2 cookie sheets or jelly-roll pans lined with parchment or foil

1 Set racks in the upper and lower thirds of the oven and preheat to 350 degrees.

2 Combine all the ingredients except the honey and water in a large mixing bowl and stir well to mix.

3 Make a well in the center of the dry ingredients and add the honey and water. Use a large rubber spatula to stir them together and then to gradually draw in the dry ingredients, making a soft dough.

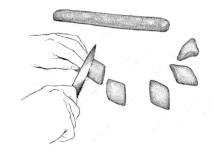

4   Turn the dough out onto a lightly floured work surface
    and divide it into 6 parts. Roll each with lightly floured
    hands to a cylinder about 12 inches long. Press the
    cylinder with your palm to flatten it slightly, then cut
    across it diagonally to make six 2-inch diamonds (see
    illustration, right). Place the cookies on the prepared
    pan, 2 inches apart in all directions, as they are cut.
    Repeat until all the dough has been used. Save all the nondiamonds from the ends
    of the dough and reroll them into a cylinder to cut more cookies.

5   Bake the cookies for about 15 minutes, or until they are well risen and feel firm
    but springy when pressed with a fingertip.

STORAGE: Keep the mostaccioli between sheets of parchment or wax paper in a tin
or plastic container with a tight-fitting cover.

Per cookie: 77 calories, 4 g total fat (47% of calories), 0 g saturated fat, 2 g protein,
13 g carbohydrates, 1 g fiber, 0 mg cholesterol, 35 mg sodium

Chocolate Desserts

Fudgy Brownies

Makes one 9-inch pan, about sixteen 2-inch brownies

Both fudgy and cakey, these brownies are perfect for that snack-craving moment when you need something really chocolaty and satisfying. They also make a great raft for a scoop of ice cream (such as those in Chapter 6) and a spoonful of chocolate sauce (page 276 or page 278). Be sure to test the brownies while they are baking. Overbaking will make them dry and crumbly.

½ cup alkalized (Dutch-process) cocoa powder

1 cup all-purpose flour (spoon flour into dry-measure cup and level off)

1 teaspoon baking powder

½ teaspoon salt

3 tablespoons unsalted butter, melted

1 cup granulated sugar

½ cup dark brown sugar, firmly packed

2 large egg whites

½ cup unsweetened applesauce

2 teaspoons vanilla extract

One 9-inch square pan, sprayed with vegetable cooking spray and the bottom lined with parchment or wax paper

1 Set a rack in the middle level of the oven and preheat to 350 degrees.

2 Sift the cocoa, flour, baking powder, and salt into a bowl.

3 In a medium mixing bowl, beat the butter and sugar together with a large rubber spatula. Beat in the brown sugar, egg whites, applesauce, and vanilla, one at a time, beating until smooth after each addition.

4 Stir in the dry ingredients with a large rubber spatula.

5 Scrape the batter into the prepared pan and bake the brownies for about 30 minutes, or until a toothpick or cake tester inserted in the center emerges with moist crumbs clinging to the tester. Cool in the pan on a rack for about 5 minutes, then invert to a rack and peel off the paper. Invert again and cool completely. Cut the brownies into 2-inch squares.

SERVING: If you're splurging, add a spoonful of real whipped cream to the ice cream with chocolate sauce suggested in the headnote.

STORAGE: Wrap in plastic and store at room temperature. To freeze, double-wrap in plastic, then bring the brownies to room temperature before serving.

Per brownie: 137 calories, 5 g total fat (33% of calories), 1 g saturated fat, 2 g protein, 27 g carbohydrates, 1 g fiber, 6 mg cholesterol, 108 mg sodium

Chocolate Cupcakes
with Brown Sugar Icing

Makes 18 cupcakes

These cupcakes are perfect as individual portions because they pack a strong chocolate punch. I like the brown sugar version of egg-white icing on them, but if you prefer the pure white version, just substitute granulated sugar for the brown sugar in the icing.

CUPCAKE BATTER

2 cups granulated sugar

1½ cups all-purpose flour (spoon flour into dry-measure cup and level off)

½ teaspoon salt

¾ teaspoon baking soda

4 ounces unsweetened chocolate, cut into ¼-inch pieces

1 cup boiling water

2 large eggs

⅓ cup vegetable oil

2 teaspoons vanilla extract

½ cup low-fat sour cream

BROWN SUGAR ICING

2 large egg whites

Pinch of salt

1½ cups dark brown sugar, firmly packed

⅓ cup water

2 teaspoons vanilla extract

Three 6-cavity standard-size muffin pans lined with paper liners

1   For the cupcakes, set a rack in the middle level of the oven and preheat to 350 degrees.

2   Sift the sugar, flour, salt, and baking soda into a bowl and stir well to mix.

3   Put the chocolate into a large mixing bowl and pour the water over it. Let stand for a minute or two so that the chocolate melts, then whisk smooth. Whisk in the eggs, oil, vanilla, and sour cream, one at a time, whisking smooth after each addition.

4   Whisk in the dry ingredients just until the batter is smooth.

5   Evenly divide the batter among the cavities in the prepared pans. Bake the cupcakes for 25 to 35 minutes, or until a toothpick or cake tester inserted in the center of one emerges dry.

6   Cool the cupcakes in the pan on a rack for 5 minutes, then unmold them. Stand them, right side up, on a rack to cool completely.

7   For the icing, half fill a medium saucepan with water and bring it to a boil over medium heat. Regulate the heat so that the water simmers gently but isn't boiling violently. Combine all the icing ingredients in the heatproof bowl of an electric mixer and whisk by hand just to mix. Place the bowl over the pan of water and whisk gently until the egg whites are hot (140 degrees on an instant-read thermometer) and the sugar is dissolved. Place the bowl on the mixer with the whisk attachment and whip on medium speed until the icing is cooled (it doesn't have to come all the way down to room temperature) and increased in volume.

8   Use a small metal spatula to spread a generous crown of icing on each cupcake.

SERVING: Be careful to whom you serve these cupcakes. You'll get requests for them over and over.

STORAGE: Keep the cupcakes under a cake dome after they've been iced. Double-wrap and freeze uniced cupcakes for about a month. Defrost and bring to room temperature before finishing.

Per cupcake (with icing): 280 calories, 9 g total fat (29% of calories), 3 g saturated fat, 3 g protein, 50 g carbohydrates, 1 g fiber, 25 mg cholesterol, 143 mg sodium

19

Chocolate Coffee Cake

Makes one 10-inch tube or Bundt cake, 16 servings

Although not particularly for a special occasion, this cake is perfect for brunch. I like it because you can have a slice with a cup of coffee or tea for a snack and you'll get chocolate cake but not a million calories at the same time. It's my favorite combination of chocolate and virtue.

3 cups all-purpose flour (spoon flour into dry-measure cup and level off)

½ cup alkalized (Dutch-process) cocoa powder

1½ teaspoons baking powder

¼ teaspoon salt

8 tablespoons (1 stick) unsalted butter, softened

1½ cups granulated sugar

¾ cup dark brown sugar

3 large egg whites

2 large eggs

1½ cups buttermilk

⅔ cup cold leftover coffee

One 12-cup tube or Bundt pan, sprayed with vegetable cooking spray and coated with fine, dry bread crumbs

1   Set a rack in the lower third of the oven and preheat to 350 degrees.

2   Sift the flour, cocoa, baking powder, and salt into a mixing bowl.

3   Beat the butter, granulated sugar, and brown sugar in an electric mixer with the paddle on medium speed until well combined. Beat in the egg whites and the eggs, one at a time, beating for 1 minute after each addition.

4   Scrape the bowl and beater.

5   Stir the buttermilk and coffee together in a large measuring cup with a pouring spout.

6   Beat a third of the dry ingredients into the batter on low speed, then beat in half the liquid. Continue beating until the liquid is absorbed. Then repeat with another third of the dry ingredients and the last of the liquid. Stop and scrape the bowl and beater.

7   Beat in the remaining dry ingredients, then scrape the bowl and beater again. Beat the batter for about 3 minutes on medium speed.

8   Scrape the batter into the prepared pan and smooth the top.

9   Bake the cake for 50 to 60 minutes, or until a toothpick or cake tester inserted midway between the side of the pan and the central tube emerges dry.

10 Cool the cake in the pan on a rack for 5 minutes, then invert it to the rack, lift off the pan, and cool completely.

SERVING: If you really want to dress this up, drizzle it with some chocolate sauce (page 276 or page 278), though it's supposed to be a plain coffee cake, not a fancy dessert cake.

STORAGE: Keep the cake under a cake dome at room temperature for about a day. For longer storage, double-wrap in plastic and freeze.

Per serving: 252 calories, 9 g total fat (32% of calories), 4 g saturated fat, 5 g protein, 45 g carbohydrates, 1 g fiber, 16 mg cholesterol, 112 mg sodium

Chocolate Rum Cake

Makes one 10-inch tube or Bundt cake, 16 servings

One of my favorite cakes is Maida Heatter's 86-Proof Cake, one that combines a fine chocolate flavor with a generous dose of good bourbon. Here's a lighter version made with rum. Feel free to substitute bourbon, white rum, or even Scotch for the dark rum used here.

2½ cups all-purpose flour (spoon flour into dry-measure cup and level off)

¾ cup alkalized (Dutch-process) cocoa powder

2 teaspoons baking powder

1 teaspoon baking soda

½ teaspoon salt

4 large egg whites

¾ cup buttermilk

1½ cups dark brown sugar, firmly packed

1 cup unsweetened applesauce (see Note on page 87)

¾ cup dark corn syrup

⅔ cup dark rum (I like Myers's)

2 teaspoons vanilla extract

One 12-cup tube or Bundt pan, sprayed with vegetable cooking spray and coated with fine, dry bread crumbs

1   Set a rack in the lower third of the oven and preheat to 350 degrees.

2   Sift the flour, cocoa, baking powder, baking soda, and salt into a medium mixing bowl. Stir several times to mix.

3   In another bowl, whisk together the egg whites and buttermilk, just to combine. Whisk in the brown sugar, then the applesauce, corn syrup, rum, and vanilla, one at a time, whisking until smooth after each addition.

4   Sift the dry ingredients over the egg-white mixture and gently stir with a large rubber spatula until combined.

5   Scrape the batter into the prepared pan. Bake the cake for 1 hour, or until a toothpick or cake tester inserted midway between the side of the pan and the central tube emerges dry.

6   Cool the cake on a rack for 5 minutes, then unmold it to a rack to cool completely.

SERVING: The rich flavor of this cake can stand on its own with no accompaniments.

STORAGE: Keep the cake under a cake dome at room temperature. Double-wrap in plastic and freeze for up to a month.

Per serving: 248 calories, 4 g total fat (15% of calories), 0 g saturated fat, 4 g protein, 51 g carbohydrates, 2 g fiber, 0 mg cholesterol, 260 mg sodium

Devil's Food Cake
with Fluffy White Icing

Makes one 10-inch tube or Bundt cake, about 16 servings

I love two things about this cake: First, it bakes up beautifully in a tube pan, much better and moister than it would as separate layers. Second, the contrast of the fluffy white icing and the rich chocolate cake has perfect visual and flavor appeal.

CAKE BATTER

1⅔ cups all-purpose flour (spoon flour into dry-measure cup and level off)

½ cup alkalized (Dutch-process) cocoa powder

1½ teaspoons baking powder

1 teaspoon baking soda

½ teaspoon salt

3 large egg whites

¾ cup buttermilk

1 cup dark brown sugar, firmly packed

1 cup unsweetened applesauce (see Note on page 87)

¾ cup dark corn syrup

2 teaspoons vanilla extract

FLUFFY WHITE ICING

2 large egg whites

Pinch of salt

1½ cups granulated sugar

⅓ cup water

2 teaspoons vanilla extract

One 12-cup tube or Bundt pan, sprayed with vegetable cooking spray and coated with fine, dry bread crumbs

1 Set a rack in the lower third of the oven and preheat to 350 degrees.

2 Sift the flour, cocoa, baking powder, baking soda, and salt into a medium mixing bowl. Stir several times to mix.

3 In another bowl, whisk together the egg whites and buttermilk, just to combine. Whisk in the brown sugar, then the applesauce, corn syrup, and vanilla, one at a time, whisking until smooth after each addition.

4   Sift the dry ingredients over the egg-white mixture and gently stir in with a large rubber spatula.

5   Scrape the batter into the prepared pan. Bake the cake for 40 to 50 minutes, or until a toothpick or cake tester inserted midway between the side of the pan and the central tube emerges dry.

6   Cool the cake on a rack for 5 minutes, then unmold it to a rack to cool completely. The cake may be wrapped and frozen for a month before finishing.

7   For the icing, half fill a medium saucepan with water and bring it to a boil over medium heat. Regulate the heat so that the water simmers gently but isn't boiling violently. Combine all the icing ingredients in the heatproof bowl of an electric mixer and whisk by hand just to mix. Place the bowl over the pan of water and whisk gently until the egg whites are hot (140 degrees on an instant-read thermometer) and the sugar is dissolved. Place the bowl on the mixer with the whisk attachment and whip on medium speed until the icing is cooled (it doesn't have to come all the way down to room temperature) and increased in volume.

8   To finish the cake, slide it to a cardboard round or a platter and use an offset metal icing spatula to spread the icing all over the outside of the cake. Swirling the icing in an irregular pattern looks better than spreading the icing flat.

SERVING: This cake doesn't really need any accompaniment, but a few raspberries or sliced strawberries will dress up the white icing.

STORAGE: Keep the cake under a cake dome at room temperature. Don't expect to have a lot of leftovers.

Per serving: 243 calories, 3 g total fat (11% of calories), 0 g saturated fat, 3 g protein, 57 g carbohydrates, 1 g fiber, 0 mg cholesterol, 248 mg sodium

Best and Easiest Chocolate Roll

Makes one 15-inch roll, about 12 servings

This recipe is based on the classic French chocolate roulade introduced to the United States by Dione Lucas in 1947. Lucas was one of the first people, along with James Beard (who also used this recipe), to cook on television, and some of my earliest memories are of seeing their cooking shows. This is the original "convenience" dessert. You probably have all the ingredients in the kitchen, though you might have to run to the store for the cream to fill it. One note of caution: Make sure you use the correct size pan. If you use a larger pan than is called for here, the layer might be too thin to roll without breaking apart.

CHOCOLATE ROLL

6 ounces bittersweet (not unsweetened) chocolate, melted and cooled

3 tablespoons water

5 large eggs, separated

½ cup sugar, divided

Pinch of salt

WHIPPED CREAM FILLING

1 cup heavy whipping cream, very cold

1 tablespoon granulated sugar

1 teaspoon vanilla extract

Confectioners' sugar for sprinkling

One 10 x 15-inch jelly-roll pan, sprayed with vegetable cooking spray and lined, bottom and sides, with parchment or nonstick foil, also sprayed

1   Set a rack in the middle level of the oven and preheat to 375 degrees.

2   Stir the chocolate and water together and set aside.

3   Whisk the egg yolks by hand in the bowl of an electric mixer and whisk in ¼ cup of the sugar in a stream. Whip by machine, using the whisk attachment on medium-high speed, for about 2 minutes, or until the yolks are light and increased in volume.

4   In a clean, dry mixer bowl, combine the egg whites and salt. Whip on medium speed with the whisk attachment until very white, opaque, and able to hold a very soft peak. Increase the speed to medium-high and whisk in the remaining ¼ cup sugar in a stream, continuing to whip the egg whites until they hold a firm peak.

5   Quickly stir the chocolate into the yolks, then fold the whites into the chocolate and yolk mixture.

6   Scrape the batter onto the prepared pan and use a metal offset spatula to spread the batter evenly in the pan.

7   Bake the layer for 15 to 20 minutes, or until it is firm when pressed with a fingertip.

8   Loosen the paper from the pan all around and slide the layer, pulling on the paper, directly to the work surface to cool—this helps to retain moisture in the layer.

9   When the layer is cool, slide a rack or cutting board under it. Sprinkle a little sugar on the top of the layer (this helps to keep it from sticking to the paper) and cover the layer with a piece of parchment or foil and another rack or board. Invert the whole sandwich of the 2 racks with the layer in between and remove the top (originally the bottom) rack. Carefully peel the paper off the layer and replace it with a clean piece of parchment. Replace the rack and invert everything again. Remove the top rack and paper and slide the paper holding the layer off the bottom rack. The layer is now on a clean paper that will be used to roll it.

27

10   For the whipped cream filling, whip the cream with the sugar and vanilla until it holds soft peaks, then spread the cream evenly on top of the chocolate layer.

11   Fold one of the long ends of the layer about ½ inch over the cream, then lift the long edges of the paper and ease the layer into a roll. It should roll itself up very easily. Wrap the paper around the roll and use a piece of stiff cardboard or the side of a cookie sheet to tighten the roll, as in the illustration (right).

12   Trim the ends of the roll so that they are even and slide the roll onto a platter or long wooden board for serving. Sprinkle the roll with a little confectioners' sugar just before serving. For advance preparation, keep the roll in the paper you rolled it in and refrigerate it until you intend to serve it. It will stay well in the refrigerator for several hours, but it shouldn't be made the day before because the whipped cream easily acquires a stale taste when kept for that long.

SERVING: You have two options for slicing: A diagonal slice looks larger in surface area, but a straight cut makes a thicker slice—it's up to you. A few sliced strawberries or lightly sugared raspberries make a pretty garnish.

STORAGE: See step 12 above. Wrap and refrigerate leftovers.

Per serving: 207 calories, 15 g total fat (65% of calories), 8 g saturated fat, 4 g protein, 17 g carbohydrates, 1 g fiber, 115 mg cholesterol, 37 mg sodium

Chocolate Buttermilk Tart

Makes one 10-inch tart, about 8 servings

The tangy flavor of buttermilk perfectly complements the chocolate in this filling. The cocoa crust provides an extra bit of chocolate richness. For full instructions on working with pastry dough and rolling and forming crusts, see page 92.

COCOA DOUGH

1 cup all-purpose flour (spoon flour into dry-measure cup and level off)

3 tablespoons sugar

3 tablespoons alkalized (Dutch-process) cocoa powder

1 teaspoon baking powder

¼ teaspoon salt

3 tablespoons unsalted butter, cold and cut into 8 pieces

1 large egg

1 tablespoon water

CHOCOLATE BUTTERMILK FILLING

4 ounces bittersweet (not unsweetened) chocolate, melted

¼ cup hot tap water

1¼ cups buttermilk, at room temperature (see Note)

⅓ cup sugar

4 large egg whites

2 teaspoons vanilla extract

One 10-inch tart pan with removable bottom

1   For the dough, combine the dry ingredients in the work bowl of a food processor fitted with the metal blade. Pulse several times to mix. Add the butter and pulse repeatedly, about 20 times, to mix it in finely. Add the egg and water and pulse again until the dough forms a ball. Invert the bowl over a lightly floured work surface and carefully remove the blade. Shape the dough into a disk.

2   Set a rack in the lowest level of the oven and preheat to 350 degrees.

3   Roll the dough on a floured surface to an 11-inch disk. Fold the dough in half and place it in the pan, lining up the fold with the diameter of the pan. Unfold the dough into the pan and press it well into the bottom and side of the pan. Cut away any excess dough at the rim of the pan with a bench scraper or the back of a knife.

4   For the filling, combine the chocolate and the water in a large bowl and whisk to mix. Whisk in the buttermilk and the sugar, followed by the egg whites, one at a time, and then the vanilla.

5   Pour the filling into the prepared crust. Bake the tart for about 30 minutes, or until the crust is browned and the filling is set.

6   Cool the tart in the pan on a rack.

7   Unmold the tart and slide it to a platter.

SERVING: This would be marvelous with a spoonful of Maida's Skinny Whipped Cream (page 285). It also makes a good base for a chocolate raspberry tart. Simply cover the filling with concentric circles of raspberries. About two ½-pint baskets should do it.

STORAGE: Keep the tart at room temperature, loosely covered with plastic wrap.

NOTE: Make sure the buttermilk is really at room temperature (about 75 degrees) or the filling will be lumpy and not smooth.

Per serving: 259 calories, 13 g total fat (45% of calories), 6 g saturated fat, 7 g protein, 35 g carbohydrates, 2 g fiber, 40 mg cholesterol, 208 mg sodium

Chocolate Banana Custard Tart

Makes one 10-inch tart, about 8 servings

Bananas and chocolate are one of my favorite rich and creamy combinations. But don't stop there. Think of this tart as a base recipe for different custard tarts using all types of fruit. Apricots, sweet cherries, poached pears, and raspberries are all excellent choices.

1 recipe Cocoa Dough tart crust from Chocolate Buttermilk Tart (page 28)

CHOCOLATE FILLING

¾ cup fat-free milk

¼ cup sugar

1 tablespoon unsalted butter

4 ounces bittersweet chocolate

1 large egg

3 large egg whites

½ teaspoon ground cinnamon

3 ripe bananas, peeled and sliced ½ inch thick

1   Set a rack in the lowest level of the oven and preheat to 350 degrees.

2   For the chocolate filling, combine the milk, sugar, and butter in a saucepan and bring to a simmer over medium heat, whisking occasionally.

3   Remove from the heat and add the chocolate. Let the chocolate melt for a minute, then whisk until smooth. Whisk in the egg, then the egg whites, one at a time. Whisk in the cinnamon.

4   Arrange the banana slices in the tart crust and pour the custard filling over them.

5   Bake the tart for about 35 minutes, or until the crust is baked through and the filling is set. Avoid overbaking the tart or the filling will inflate so much that it might break off at the sides of the tart.

6   Cool the tart on a rack.

SERVING: This tart is rich and satisfying enough to be served on its own. But a dollop of Maida's Skinny Whipped Cream (page 285) wouldn't hurt.

Keep the tart at a cool room temperature (68 to 70 degrees) on the day it is baked. Refrigerate leftovers and bring them to room temperature before serving.

Per serving: 299 calories, 15 g total fat (45% of calories), 7 g saturated fat, 7 g protein, 43 g carbohydrates, 4 g fiber, 68 mg cholesterol, 171 mg sodium

White Chocolate Raspberry Tartlets

Makes twenty-four 2½-inch tartlets

Here is one of my ideal combinations of flavors and textures: sweet white chocolate, tangy raspberries, crumbly cocoa dough, and smooth cream. These individual tarts are tailor-made for teatime or for a lavish dinner when you want to serve something spectacular with coffee after a more simple dessert, such as ice cream.

1 recipe Cocoa Dough from Chocolate Buttermilk Tart (page 28)

WHITE CHOCOLATE FILLING

⅓ cup heavy whipping cream

¼ cup fat-free milk

6 ounces white chocolate, cut into ¼-inch pieces

TOPPING

Two ½-pint baskets fresh raspberries

Confectioners' sugar for finishing

Twenty-four 2½-inch round tartlet pans, sprayed with vegetable cooking spray and lined up on a jelly-roll pan

1 For the tartlet crusts, set a rack in the middle level of the oven and preheat to 350 degrees.

2 Divide the dough into 3 pieces and place one piece on a floured work surface. Roll the dough ⅛ inch thick and use a plain or fluted round cutter to cut the dough into disks. Fit the disks into the prepared pans, pressing them in well.

3 Pierce the tartlet crusts all over with a fork, then bake them for 12 to 15 minutes, or just until the dough looks dull on the surface and is slightly firm. Cool the tartlet crusts in the pan on a rack.

4 For the white chocolate filling, bring the cream and milk to a simmer over medium heat. Remove from the heat, add the chocolate, and allow it to melt for a minute. Whisk until smooth and scrape into a bowl. Refrigerate the filling until it has thickened.

5   To finish the tartlets, remove the tartlet crusts from the pans and line them up on a clean jelly-roll pan. Place a teaspoon of the white chocolate filling into each crust. Arrange 4 or 5 raspberries on the filling, pressing them gently. Just before serving, dust the tartlets with confectioners' sugar.

SERVING: These tartlets don't need anything more than to be arranged on a platter.

STORAGE: The tartlets can be assembled up to 6 hours in advance. You could even prepare all of the elements the day before, then assemble the tartlets on the day you intend to serve them. Keep leftovers, loosely covered, at a cool room temperature (68 to 70 degrees).

Per tartlet: 98 calories, 6 g total fat (55% of calories), 3 g saturated fat, 2 g protein, 12 g carbohydrates, 1 g fiber, 19 mg cholesterol, 54 mg sodium

Easy Chocolate Mousse

Makes about 1½ pints mousse, about six ½-cup servings

Most chocolate mousses are high in calories, but it's quite easy to make a delicious chocolate mousse that contains a fraction of the original calories and fat. The secret is to use high-quality bittersweet chocolate. It packs a strong, lively chocolate flavor and makes up for the fact that the mousse doesn't have a quart of whipped cream in it.

1 envelope unflavored gelatin

¼ cup sweet liqueur, such as Chambord or Triple Sec

1 cup fat-free milk

¾ cup sugar, divided

2 large eggs

4 ounces bittersweet (not unsweetened) chocolate, cut into ¼-inch pieces

4 large egg whites

Large pinch of salt

6 stemmed glasses or ramekins for serving the mousse

1   Sprinkle the gelatin on the liqueur in a small bowl and set aside.

2   Combine the milk and ¼ cup of the sugar in a small saucepan and whisk to mix. Place over medium heat and bring to a simmer.

3   Meanwhile, whisk the eggs in a small bowl. When the milk boils, whisk about a third of the milk into the eggs. Return the remaining milk to a boil over low heat, then whisk in the egg mixture. Continue whisking until the mixture thickens slightly. Don't let it boil or the eggs will scramble. Remove from the heat and quickly whisk in the gelatin mixture.

4   Whisk in the chocolate and continue whisking until the chocolate is melted and the mixture is smooth. Scrape it into a medium bowl and cool it to room temperature.

5   To make the meringue, half fill a medium saucepan with water and bring it to a boil over medium heat. Regulate the heat so that the water simmers gently but isn't boiling violently. Combine the egg whites, salt, and the remaining ½ cup sugar in the heatproof bowl of an electric mixer, whisking by hand just to mix. Place the bowl over the pan of water and whisk gently until the egg whites are hot (140 degrees on an instant-read thermometer) and the sugar is dissolved. Place the bowl on the mixer with the whisk attachment and whip on medium speed until the meringue is cooled (it doesn't have to come all the way down to room temperature) and increased in volume.

6   Fold the meringue into the chocolate mixture.

7   Divide the mousse among the prepared glasses and refrigerate until set, 3 to 4 hours.

SERVING: Serve the mousse alone or with some Maida's Skinny Whipped Cream (page 285). You can also decorate it with a few berries or some chocolate shavings (page 286).

STORAGE: You can prepare the mousse the day before. Keep it covered with plastic wrap if it needs to stay in the refrigerator any more than a few hours after you prepare it.

Per serving: 279 calories, 10 g total fat (32% of calories), 5 g saturated fat, 8 g protein, 41 g carbohydrates, 1 g fiber, 71 mg cholesterol, 80 mg sodium

Old-fashioned Chocolate Pudding

Makes about 1½ pints pudding, about six ½-cup servings

The great thing about traditional chocolate pudding is that it isn't really loaded with fat. It's hardly necessary to trim fat from the basic recipe, though I have made this one as light as possible. Enjoy this creamy pudding on its own or use it as a cake filling, especially if you want to jazz up something really plain like angel food cake or sponge cake.

2 cups fat-free or 1% low-fat milk, divided

⅓ cup sugar

3 tablespoons cornstarch

3 large eggs

4 ounces bittersweet (not unsweetened) chocolate, cut into ¼-inch pieces

2 teaspoons vanilla extract

6 individual glasses or ramekins

1 Combine 1½ cups of the milk and the sugar in a 2-quart saucepan. Whisk once or twice to start dissolving the sugar. Bring to a boil over medium heat, whisking occasionally.

2 Pour the remaining ½ cup milk into a medium mixing bowl and whisk in the cornstarch. Whisk in the eggs, one at a time.

3 When the milk boils, whisk about a third of it into the cornstarch and egg mixture.

4 Return the remaining milk to a boil and whisk in the cornstarch and egg mixture, continuing to whisk until the pudding thickens and comes to a boil. Cook, whisking constantly, for 30 seconds.

5 Remove from the heat, whisk in the chocolate until melted, then whisk in the vanilla.

6 Spoon the pudding into individual glasses or ramekins. Press a piece of plastic wrap directly against the surface of the pudding to prevent a skin from forming on it.

7 Refrigerate the pudding until it is cold.

SERVING: Decorate the top of the pudding with a chocolate shaving or two (page 286), a dollop of Maida's Skinny Whipped Cream (page 285), or both.

STORAGE: You could prepare these a day in advance, especially since they are meant to be served chilled.

Per serving: 221 calories, 11 g total fat (45% of calories), 5 g saturated fat, 7 g protein, 29 g carbohydrates, 1 g fiber, 107 mg cholesterol, 70 mg sodium

Real Chocolate Truffles

Makes about 50 small truffles

Truffles of this kind are usually referred to as Truffes Champagne, not because they contain champagne, the bubbly white wine, but because they are usually flavored with the grade of Cognac known as Fine Champagne. I like to add a little dark rum along with the Cognac for a spicier perfume in the truffles. Of course, these are neither a low-fat nor a low-calorie food, but how many truffles do you eat at one time? I believe it's better to have a good taste of the real thing to satisfy cravings. Constant deprivation leads to cheating . . .

TRUFFLE CENTER MIXTURE

8 ounces high-quality bittersweet (not unsweetened) chocolate

$\frac{1}{2}$ cup heavy whipping cream

1 tablespoon very soft unsalted butter

1 tablespoon light corn syrup

1 tablespoon best Cognac

1 tablespoon dark rum

ENROBING THE TRUFFLES

12 ounces of the same chocolate as the truffle centers, cut into $\frac{1}{4}$-inch pieces

2 cups alkalized (Dutch-process) cocoa powder, sifted (see Note)

1 Bring a small saucepan of water to a boil and remove from the heat. Place the chocolate in a heatproof bowl and set it over the pan of hot water. Stir occasionally until the chocolate is melted. Remove the bowl from the pan, dry the bottom of the bowl, and set aside.

2 In a small saucepan, bring the cream to a simmer. Remove from the heat and set aside for 5 minutes. Whisk the cream into the chocolate, then whisk in the butter, corn syrup, Cognac, and rum, one at a time. Set aside to cool until firm, several hours or overnight.

3 To form the truffles, fit a pastry bag with a $\frac{1}{2}$-inch plain tube, then line a cookie sheet with parchment or wax paper. Using a stand mixer with the paddle attachment or a hand mixer, beat the truffle center mixture for about 30 seconds, or until it lightens visibly in color. Scrape the mixture into the pastry bag and pipe out $\frac{3}{4}$-inch to 1-inch spheres, holding the end of the bag above the pan so a small sphere of the mixture emerges. Chill for 1 hour.

4   While the centers are chilling, melt the remaining chocolate as for the center mixture (see step 1) and cool it to about 90 degrees. Sift the cocoa into a roasting pan or other wide, deep pan.

5   To coat the truffles, dip one hand into the cooled chocolate and pick up a center with your other hand. Place the center in the palm of your chocolate-coated hand and rub the chocolate around the center to cover it. Drop the center into the cocoa and use a fork to push it to the other end of the pan. Repeat with the remaining centers.

6   After all the centers have been coated, chill them in the cocoa for 30 minutes. Carefully lift the truffles from the cocoa and place, a few at a time, in a strainer. Roll them around in the strainer over the pan of cocoa to release excess cocoa from the surface of the truffles.

7   Place the truffles in paper cases or in layers separated by wax paper in a tin or other container with a tight-fitting cover. Store in a cool place and bring to room temperature before serving. The chocolate on the outside of the truffles will keep the centers intact at room temperature. Freeze for longer storage.

NOTE: After you coat the truffles, sift the cocoa to remove any bits of hardened chocolate and reuse the cocoa for any purpose.

Per truffle: 69 calories, 7 g total fat (91% of calories), 2 g saturated fat, 1 g protein, 7 g carbohydrates, 1 g fiber, 4 mg cholesterol, 3 mg sodium

2

CAKES

uests are always impressed when you serve cake. Making a cake requires little more than mixing together butter, sugar, flour, and eggs, but the results are invariably impressive. Whether it's a crumbly coffee cake served at brunch, a prettily iced cupcake at a child's birthday party, or a showstopping filled and frosted layer cake at another special occasion, you can bet it will make a good impression. A wide variety of cakes are included in this chapter.

Many cakes, such as meringue and foam cakes, are quite lean naturally. I've included several of this type, such as Orange Angel Food Cake (page 50), Vanilla Bean Chiffon Cake (page 53), and Coffee Pecan Meringue Cake (page 48).

Even some cakes that are traditionally richer don't have to be sky-high in calories. For instance, the Lemon Cupcakes with Milk Chocolate Frosting (page 65) use only moderate amounts of butter and sugar along with naturally low-fat buttermilk to provide moistness and rich texture. The acidity of buttermilk creates tenderness in cakes such as this one that include very little fat.

Applesauce or other pureed fruit is another ingredient that creates moist and tender cakes when only a small amount of fat is used. Old-fashioned Carrot Cake (page 70) incorporates a bit of applesauce in the batter, along with vegetable oil, to provide moisture and tenderness with minimal calories.

Of course, it helps to use a light hand with the frosting, too. The recipes here use a moderate amount of frosting to avoid piling on the fat and sugar. One of the easiest low-calorie frostings is a simple mixture of melted chocolate and reduced-fat sour cream such as the one on the lemon cupcakes mentioned above. By the way, if you're looking for chocolate cakes, you'll find half a dozen of them in the Chocolate Desserts chapter, beginning on page 3.

Technique Tips

Many of the cake batters here are "creamed" mixtures but contain only a small amount of butter. With so little fat, it's very important to beat the mixture long enough during mixing and again after all the ingredients have been incorporated. Thorough beating aerates the batter, or incorporates air, which helps to create a light, tender texture despite the low amount of fat. Some recipes call for the butter to be softened, and students sometimes ask me how soft the butter should be. The answer: It should be soft enough to be dented with a finger but not lose its shape. Sixty-five degrees is a good softening temperature, or roughly 5 degrees cooler than room temperature.

When choosing pans, be careful to use the size called for in the recipe. If your pan is too small, the cake will overflow and make a mess. If it's too large, the cake may turn out dry, especially if baked for the same amount of time that a smaller (hence thicker) cake would take to bake.

Always test cakes for doneness when about three-quarters of the baking time has elapsed. Ovens may run a little hotter than the temperature on the dial, which could make the cake dry and overbaked if it is left in the oven for the entire time indicated in the recipe before being tested for doneness. Rely on the doneness test rather than relying on a timer.

Most foam cakes such as angel, chiffon, and sponge cakes are based on whipped egg whites, which make them quite delicate. Treat foam cakes carefully to avoid deflating the batter. Fold in the dry ingredients quickly yet gently. Air is dissipating from the batter with every stroke as well as with every extra second it takes to mix the ingredients together. Mixing too vigorously may pop the air bubbles in the whipped egg whites. Mixing too slowly may deflate the batter just because it took too long to mix. Quickly yet gently is the key.

These cakes taste best when served the day they are baked. Serving on the same day retains maximum moisture and tenderness. To prepare the cakes in advance, cool them to room temperature, then double-wrap and freeze. Avoid leaving the cake layers to cool uncovered at room temperature for too long because they will dry out. Similarly, double-wrapping for the freezer is especially important to retain moisture and tenderness because the cakes contain so little fat. Complete storage instructions are included with every recipe.

When frosting these cakes, apply the frosting evenly and thoroughly, since it is used somewhat sparingly to avoid adding extra calories.

Individual Pavlovas with Berries

Makes 8 individual servings

Aside from being the Australian national dessert, a Pavlova also happens to be very low in fat—depending on how much whipped cream you use when serving it. It is usually made as a 9- or 10-inch-diameter cake, but individual Pavlovas are also popular in Australia. A few years ago, I had an excellent one topped with sliced bananas and passion fruit pulp at Geoff Lindsay's Pearl Restaurant in Melbourne. An individual "Pav," as it's referred to Down Under, is the perfect dessert for a dinner party. You can have all the elements ready in advance (bake the meringue bases the day before), so all you need to do is assemble them, not much work at all, right before you serve them.

MERINGUE BASES

4 large egg whites

Pinch of salt

1 teaspoon distilled white vinegar or strained lemon juice

1 cup sugar, divided

1 teaspoon vanilla extract

4 teaspoons cornstarch

BERRY TOPPING

1 pint strawberries, rinsed, hulled, halved, and sliced

3 tablespoons sugar

One ½-pint basket fresh raspberries, picked over but not washed

1 cup blueberries, rinsed, picked over, and drained

WHIPPED CREAM

1 cup heavy whipping cream

2 tablespoons sugar

1 teaspoon vanilla extract

2 cookie sheets or jelly-roll pans lined with parchment or foil

1   Set racks in the upper and lower thirds of the oven and preheat to 275 degrees. Draw four 3- to 3½-inch-diameter circles, well apart from each other, on the paper on each pan. Turn the paper over so that the pencil lead or ink doesn't touch the meringue when it's placed there.

2   To make the meringue bases, combine the egg whites, salt, and vinegar in the bowl of an electric mixer. Whip the whites with the whisk attachment on medium speed until they are white, opaque, and just beginning to hold their shape. Increase the speed to medium-high and whip in ¾ cup of the sugar, a tablespoon at a time, waiting at least 20 seconds between additions. After the sugar has been added whip in the vanilla.

3   In a small bowl, stir the last ¼ cup sugar with the cornstarch and use a large rubber spatula to fold it into the meringue.

4   Divide the meringue equally among the circles on the pans, then use a small metal spatula or a wide-bladed table knife to smooth and shape each one into a disk shape about 1½ inches thick. The easiest way to do this is to spread the top flat first, then position the spatula perpendicular to the pan and smooth the sides.

5   Bake the meringue bases for about 15 minutes, then switch the bottom pan to the top rack and vice versa, turning each pan back to front at the same time. Bake for another 30 minutes or so, or until the meringues are lightly colored and still moist within. Turn off the oven, leave the door ajar (or place a wide spatula between the oven and the oven door frame), and let the meringues cool for an hour. Don't worry if they crack a little.

6   After the meringues have cooled, put them all on one of the pans, cover loosely with plastic wrap or a towel, and reserve at room temperature until you are ready to assemble the dessert.

7   For the berry topping, stir together the strawberries and the sugar in a bowl. Cover and refrigerate for at least a couple of hours. Just before serving, fold in the raspberries and blueberries.

8   For the whipped cream, combine all the ingredients and whip by hand or by machine until soft peaks form. In warm weather, put the cream in the bowl of an electric mixer and put the bowl and whisk in the freezer for 10 minutes before you whip the cream.

9   To assemble, place the meringue bases on dessert plates. Rewhip the cream by hand if you prepared it in advance and refrigerated it, and if it has thinned out. With half the cream, place a spoonful on the top of each meringue base and spread it smooth. Drain the berry mixture and save the juices. Divide the berry mixture evenly among the meringue bases, placing it on the cream. Put a dollop of the remaining cream next to each Pavlova on the plate and drizzle a spoonful of the reserved juices around the outside on each plate.

SERVING: See step 9. It's easiest to use both a fork and spoon to eat these desserts. Hold the meringue base in place with the fork while cutting through it with the spoon, which will prevent the meringue from flying off the plate when you cut into it.

STORAGE: You may keep the meringue bases right on the pan at room temperature for up to a day or so before serving. Just cover loosely with plastic wrap or slide the pan into a large plastic bag. Don't worry if the meringues soften slightly; they're not meant to be dry.

Per serving: 275 calories, 11 g total fat (36% of calories), 7 g saturated fat, 3 g protein, 43 g carbohydrates, 2 g fiber, 41 mg cholesterol, 40 mg sodium

Coffee Pecan Meringue Cake

Makes one thin 10-inch cake, about 12 servings

Like a skinny version of a classic French dacquoise, this dessert works equally well with any type of nutmeats you prefer. I really like the sweetness that pecans impart to the meringue layers, but hazelnuts, almonds, or even walnuts, or a combination, all work well. Please note that the egg whites in the buttercream are not completely cooked; this is a good place to use pasteurized egg whites if you're concerned. Use a generous ½ cup for the 4 egg whites.

PECAN MERINGUE LAYERS

4 large egg whites

Pinch of salt

¾ cup sugar, divided

⅔ cup (about 3 ounces) pecan pieces, finely ground in the food processor

3 tablespoons cornstarch

COFFEE BUTTERCREAM

4 large egg whites

¾ cup sugar

3 tablespoons instant coffee

3 tablespoons brewed coffee or water (see Note)

12 tablespoons (1½ sticks) unsalted butter, cut into 12 pieces and softened

Confectioners' sugar for finishing

2 cookie sheets or jelly-roll pans lined with parchment or foil

1   Set racks in the upper and lower thirds of the oven and preheat to 300 degrees. Trace a 10-inch circle on the paper on each pan and turn the paper over.

2   For the meringue layers, combine the egg whites and the salt in the bowl of an electric mixer and whip with the whisk attachment on medium speed until the egg whites are white, opaque, and beginning to hold their shape. Increase the speed to medium-high and whip in ½ cup of the sugar in a slow stream, continuing to whip until the egg whites hold a stiff peak. Turn off the mixer, add the remaining ¼ cup sugar, the pecans, and the cornstarch without stirring them together first, and use a large rubber spatula to fold them into the egg whites.

3   Divide the pecan meringue equally between the circles on the 2 pans and use an offset metal spatula to spread it evenly to cover the traced circles completely. Don't worry if the sides are not perfect; they'll be trimmed later on.

4   Bake the meringue layers for about 40 minutes, or until they are golden and almost completely firm. Cool them on the pans on racks.

5   While the layers are cooling, make the buttercream. Half fill a medium saucepan with water and bring it to a boil over medium heat. Combine the egg whites and the sugar in the heatproof bowl of an electric mixer and whisk a couple of times to mix. Place the bowl over the pan of boiling water and whisk gently until the egg whites are hot and the sugar is dissolved. Place on the mixer with the whisk attachment and whip on medium-high speed until the egg whites are cooled completely; when you touch the outside of the bowl it will not be at all warm.

6   While the meringue is cooling, stir together the instant and brewed coffees to dissolve. Switch to the paddle attachment and add the butter, one piece at a time, at 10-second intervals until it is all added. Let the buttercream continue whipping until it becomes thick and spreadable; initially it will be very soft and liquid, then it will separate (this is normal, don't panic), and finally it will become emulsified and thick. Only after it has become thick, decrease the speed to medium and add the coffee mixture a tablespoon at a time, beating smooth after each addition. After all the coffee has been added, let the buttercream beat for 2 or 3 minutes so that it becomes very smooth and shiny.

7   To assemble the dessert, use the point of a sharp paring knife to trim each of the meringue layers to an even 10-inch diameter, using a plate or other circular pattern as a guide. Place one of the layers on a platter and scrape all of the buttercream onto it. Spread it evenly with a metal offset spatula. Invert the second meringue layer onto the buttercream so that its smooth underside is upward and gently press to adhere.

8   Dust the top of the dessert with confectioners' sugar immediately before serving.

SERVING: Cut into wedges with a sharp serrated knife. This rich dessert needs no accompaniment.

STORAGE: Sometimes I like to refrigerate layered meringue desserts like this one for a couple of days so that the meringue becomes a bit more tender; the meringue can be somewhat hard when freshly baked. Just double-wrap in plastic first. Remember to bring the dessert to room temperature before serving. Leftovers may be treated in the same way.

NOTE: It's much better to dissolve instant coffee in brewed coffee (rather than in water) for the best flavor. Just save a little leftover coffee in a jar in the refrigerator when you want to make the dessert. Or use freshly made espresso in place of the brewed coffee and coffee granules.

Per serving: 270 calories, 17 g total fat (57% of calories), 8 g saturated fat, 3 g protein, 29 g carbohydrates, 1 g fiber, 30 mg cholesterol, 39 mg sodium

Orange Angel Food Cake

Makes one 10-inch tube cake, about 16 servings

Angel food cake isn't difficult to make and it's perfect if you're watching your calorie and fat intake because it's completely fat-free. That, coupled with the fact that it has a satisfyingly chewy texture, makes angel food cake the ideal healthy dessert. I've added some orange zest and extract to brighten the flavor. If you want a plain cake, leave out the orange zest and extract and substitute 2 teaspoons of vanilla extract, but don't eliminate the lemon juice—it helps to stabilize the egg whites. Make sure there are no specks of yolk in the whites when you separate the eggs. Even the smallest trace of yolk or a wet or greasy bowl or beaters will prevent the egg whites from absorbing maximum air as they are whipped.

The pan is meant to be ungreased so that the cake rises properly during baking. The cake also cools in the pan, but upside down. Use an empty wine or other bottle to suspend the pan upside down. Or use one of those new pans that have little feet at the top to keep the cake elevated when you invert it to cool. The reason for cooling the cake upside down is that it will fall and sink back in on itself if it is left to cool right side up (the way it was baked). If you're using a bottle to invert the pan, make sure it fits by testing it on the tube opening of the pan before you bake the cake.

1½ cups sugar, divided

1 cup bleached all-purpose flour (spoon flour into dry-measure cup and level off)

1½ cups egg whites (from about 12 large eggs)

¼ teaspoon salt

1 tablespoon strained fresh lemon juice

1½ teaspoons orange extract

1 tablespoon finely grated orange zest

One 10-inch two-piece tube pan, ungreased, plus an empty narrow-necked wine bottle or other similar bottle to hang the cake on after it is baked

1   Set a rack in the middle level of the oven and preheat to 325 degrees.

2   Set aside ¾ cup of the sugar to mix in with the egg whites later on. Mix the remaining sugar with the flour and sift it onto a piece of parchment or wax paper.

3   Place the egg whites, salt, and lemon juice in the bowl of an electric mixer. Place the bowl on the mixer with the whisk attachment and whip on medium speed until the egg whites are white, opaque, and beginning to hold their shape. Increase the speed to medium-high and whip in the reserved ¾ cup sugar a couple of tablespoons at a time, continuing to whip until the egg whites hold a soft, glossy peak. Quickly whip in the orange extract and orange zest.

4   Sift a third of the flour and sugar mixture over the whipped egg whites and use a large rubber spatula to fold it in. Repeat with another third of the flour and sugar mixture, and then fold in the rest.

5   Scrape the batter into the ungreased pan, rotating the pan to fill it evenly. Gently plunge the same rubber spatula you used for folding in the flour mixture into the batter at 2-inch intervals with an up-and-down motion to release any large air bubbles. Use the spatula to smooth the top of the batter.

6   Bake the cake for 45 to 55 minutes, or until it is well browned, well risen, and firm to the touch. Invert the central tube of the pan onto the neck of the bottle and allow the cake to cool completely.

7   Use a long, thin knife to loosen the cake from the side of the pan, scraping the knife blade against the pan, not the cake. Pull the cake from the pan by the central tube, then insert the knife between the cake and the pan bottom to loosen it. Use the point of the knife to loosen the cake at the top of the central tube, then invert to a platter. Gently pull the pan base and central tube away from the cake.

SERVING: Even though angel food cake is good on its own, it needs a little something to dress it up. Try it with a spoonful of Maida's Skinny Whipped Cream (page 285). I also like to serve it with some slightly sweetened orange sections or mixed berries.

STORAGE: Keep the cake under a cake dome on the day it is baked. Wrap leftovers in plastic and keep at room temperature. For advance preparation, double-wrap the cake in plastic and freeze it for up to a month. Thaw and bring to room temperature before serving.

Per serving: 116 calories, 0 g total fat, 0 g saturated fat, 4 g protein, 25 g carbohydrates, 0 g fiber, 0 mg cholesterol, 78 mg sodium

Lemon Angel Food Cake Substitute lemon extract and zest for the orange extract and zest.

Spiced Angel Food Cake Omit the orange extract and zest. Stir 1 teaspoon ground cinnamon, ½ teaspoon freshly grated nutmeg, and ¼ teaspoon ground cloves into the flour and sugar mixture before sifting it.

Cocoa-Orange Angel Food Cake Stir 3 tablespoons alkalized (Dutch-process) cocoa powder into the flour and sugar mixture before sifting it. For a pure chocolate flavor without the orange flavor, omit the orange extract and zest and substitute 2 teaspoons vanilla extract.

52

Vanilla Bean Chiffon Cake

Makes one tall 10-inch tube cake, about 16 servings

A chiffon cake is the ideal low-calorie dessert: It's fantastic just the way it is and you don't need to remove any ingredients to make it less fattening. The cake is prepared like an angel food cake—in a tube pan, hanging upside down to cool—but it's both richer and more satisfying than plain angel food because it also contains some egg yolks and a bit of oil. In this recipe, I use a whole vanilla bean instead of vanilla extract because I love the little flecks of vanilla seeds throughout the cake. Sometimes I enjoy a hint of lemon along with the vanilla flavor. To add a subtle lemon flavor, strain 2 tablespoons fresh lemon juice into your measuring cup before measuring the water, then add cold water to equal ¾ cup total liquid. See the introduction to the recipe for Orange Angel Food Cake (page 50) for information about the tube pan and various ways to hang it upside down during cooling.

1½ cups sugar, divided

2¼ cups cake flour (spoon flour into dry-measure cup and level off)

3 teaspoons baking powder

½ cup vegetable oil, such as corn or canola

4 large egg yolks

¾ cup cold water

1 large, plump vanilla bean, split and the seeds scraped out (see Note)

1 cup egg whites (from 7 or 8 large eggs)

Pinch of salt

One 10-inch two-piece tube pan, plus an empty narrow-necked wine bottle or other bottle to hang the cake on after it is baked

1   Set a rack in the middle level of the oven and preheat to 350 degrees.

2   Set aside ¼ cup of the sugar to mix in with the egg whites later on. Mix the remaining sugar with the flour and baking powder and sift it onto a piece of parchment or wax paper.

3   Place the oil, egg yolks, water, and vanilla seeds in a large mixing bowl and whisk well to combine. Sift in the dry ingredients and whisk vigorously for half a minute.

4   Combine the egg whites and salt in the bowl of an electric mixer. Place on the mixer with the whisk attachment and whip on medium speed until the egg whites are white, opaque, and beginning to hold their shape. Increase the speed to medium-high and whip in the reserved ¼ cup sugar, a couple of tablespoons at a time, continuing to whip until the egg whites hold a firm, glossy peak.

5   Using a large rubber spatula, fold the yolk and flour mixture into the whipped egg whites, making sure you scrape the bottom of the bowl every time the spatula passes through so that the batter is thoroughly mixed.

6   Scrape the batter into the ungreased pan, rotating the pan to fill it evenly, and smooth the top.

7   Bake the cake for 55 to 60 minutes, or until it is well browned, well risen, and firm to the touch, and a toothpick inserted halfway between the side of the pan and the central tube emerges clean. Invert the central tube of the pan onto the neck of the bottle and allow the cake to cool completely.

8   Use a long, thin knife to loosen the cake from the side of the pan, scraping the knife blade against the pan, not the cake. Pull the cake from the pan by the central tube, then insert the knife between the cake and the pan bottom to loosen it. Use the point of the knife to loosen the cake at the top of the central tube, then invert to a platter. Gently pull the pan base and central tube away from the cake.

SERVING: Chiffon cake is delicious with a spoonful of Maida's Skinny Whipped Cream (page 285). I also like to serve it with some lightly sweetened mixed berries.

STORAGE: Keep the cake under a cake dome on the day it is baked. Wrap leftovers in plastic and keep at room temperature. For advance preparation, double-wrap the cake in plastic and freeze it for up to a month. Thaw and bring to room temperature before serving.

NOTE: Try to purchase vanilla beans from a reliable source, such as Nielsen-Massey (see Sources, page 291). In any event, if you purchase vanilla beans in a glass or plastic tube, sometimes the beans have dried out and become brittle, making it almost impossible to scrape out the seeds. To remedy this, cut the bean into 2 pieces, place in a small heatproof strainer, and steam it over a covered pan of gently simmering water for about 5 minutes, or until it is moist and flexible. Cool the bean, split the 2 sections, and scrape out the seeds.

Per serving: 226 calories, 8 g total fat (32% of calories), 1 g saturated fat, 4 g protein, 34 g carbohydrates, 0 g fiber, 51 mg cholesterol, 102 mg sodium

VARIATION *Lemon Chiffon Cake* Omit the vanilla bean. Pour ⅓ cup strained lemon juice into a measuring cup before measuring the water, then add water to make ¾ cup total liquid. Add 2 teaspoons lemon extract to the yolk mixture.

Flo's Spectacular Jelly Roll

Makes one 10-inch-long rolled cake, about twelve ¾-inch-thick slices

If you think a jelly roll is boring, you'll rethink your opinion after seeing and tasting this one developed by my friend the cookbook author and cooking teacher Flo Braker. I once saw Flo prepare this roll at a demonstration and I was amazed at both its simplicity and its showstopping appearance. This is so good-looking because a normal rectangular sponge cake sheet is sliced horizontally through the middle (don't worry, it's easier than you think). The two resulting layers are positioned end to end to make a 30-inch-long layer. After the cake is spread with preserves, it's tightly rolled up, then sliced to reveal a stunning spiral design of the thin cake layer and its red jam filling. No one will fail to be impressed when you serve this dessert. Any fruit preserves will work here, but raspberry preserves provide the best color contrast to show off the thin spiral of the cake.

CAKE BATTER

4 large eggs, separated

¾ cup sugar, divided

2 teaspoons vanilla extract

Pinch of salt

1 cup all-purpose flour (spoon flour into dry-measure cup and level off)

½ teaspoon baking powder

FINISHING

1½ cups raspberry all-fruit spread or seedless preserves

Confectioners' sugar for dusting

One 10 x 15-inch jelly-roll pan, sprayed with vegetable cooking spray and lined, bottom and sides, with sprayed foil

1   Set a rack in the middle level of the oven and preheat to 350 degrees.

2   Whisk the egg yolks in a medium mixing bowl, just to break them up. Whisk in half the sugar in a stream, then whisk in the vanilla. Continue whisking for about a minute, or until the yolk mixture is pale and aerated.

3   Combine the egg whites and salt in the bowl of an electric mixer. Whip the egg whites with the whisk attachment on medium speed until they are white, opaque, and just beginning to hold their shape. Increase the speed to medium-high and whip in the remaining half of the sugar in a slow stream, continuing to whip the egg whites until they hold a firm peak.

4   Use a large rubber spatula to fold the yolk mixture into the egg whites.

5   Quickly stir together the flour and baking powder. Sift one-third of the flour mixture over the eggs, then fold in until combined. Repeat with each remaining third of the flour mixture.

6   Scrape the batter onto the prepared pan and use a metal offset spatula to spread it evenly to fill the pan.

7   Bake the cake layer for 15 to 20 minutes, or until it is well risen and firm to the touch. Be careful not to overbake the cake or it may become brittle and difficult to roll.

8   Pulling on the foil in the short end of the pan, drag the layer from the pan to the work surface to cool. Cooling it like this will retain moisture in the cake.

9   After the cake layer has cooled wrap it in plastic (leave the cake stuck to the foil for now) and refrigerate it for at least several hours or, preferably, overnight. This chilling will make the cake easier to cut through without it shredding into a lot of crumbs.

10 When you are ready to assemble the cake, unwrap the layer and invert it to a cutting board. Carefully peel away the foil and discard it. Replace it with a piece of parchment paper. Place another board or the back of a jelly-roll pan against the top of the cake and invert the whole thing. Lift off the pan that's now on top and slide the cake on the parchment paper to the work surface.

11 Use a sharp serrated knife to cut the layer in two horizontally. The easiest way to do this is to make a 1-inch-deep cut all around the perimeter of the cake layer. When you get back to the point where you started cutting, cut another inch deeper into the cake layer all around again. Continue in this way until you have cut all the way through the layer. This method is much easier than trying to cut straight through the cake layer from one side to another. Don't worry if there are a few holes; they won't show once the cake is rolled with the filling.

12 To fill the cake, position the 2 cake layers end to end on a long strip of parchment or wax paper. The two 10-inch-wide short ends should be touching to create one 30-inch-long layer. Stir the preserves smooth. Use a medium soupspoon to dollop spots of the jam all over the cake; this makes it easier to spread than if you just drop all the jam in one place. Use a metal offset spatula to spread an even coating of the jam all over the surface of the cake.

13   To roll the cake, start at one of the 10-inch ends and fold ½ inch of the cake over. Pick up the paper and use it to ease the folded end of the cake toward the length of the cake; it will start to roll itself as you lift the paper and push the rolled part of the cake along.

14   When you reach the other end, tightly wrap the paper around the cake and refrigerate it for an hour or two.

15   To finish the cake, unwrap it and trim the ends even. Pick it up and place the cake, seam side down, on a rectangular or oval platter. Dust with the confectioners' sugar immediately before serving.

SERVING: Cut the cake into ¾-inch slices. Place the cake slices, cut side down, on a plate to show off the spiral pattern. Some slightly sugared berries or a scoop of fruit sherbet would be good next to this on the plate.

STORAGE: Keep the roll tightly wrapped in plastic wrap before and after you serve it. Or double-wrap and freeze the filled roll for up to a month. Bring it to room temperature before serving.

Per slice: 196 calories, 2 g total fat (9% of calories), 1 g saturated fat, 4 g protein, 41 g carbohydrates, 0 g fiber, 71 mg cholesterol, 47 mg sodium

Raspberry Mousse Cake

Makes one 9-inch cake, about 12 generous servings

Save this one for a fancy dinner party. No one will believe that it's a low-calorie dessert. About fifteen years ago, I developed this recipe for a class and it has certainly withstood the test of time. The low-fat ricotta provides some dairy richness that would ordinarily be supplied by a caloric ocean of whipped cream. The lightness comes from a cooked meringue, which is a classic way to lighten a mousse such as this one. Here again, the meringue contains partially cooked egg whites. If you're concerned about this, by all means use pasteurized egg whites instead of fresh ones.

SPONGE CAKE

- 4 large eggs, separated
- ¾ cup sugar, divided
- 1 teaspoon vanilla extract
- 1 teaspoon finely grated lemon zest
- Pinch of salt
- 1 cup all-purpose flour (spoon flour into dry-measure cup and level off)

RASPBERRY MOUSSE

- Two 10-ounce packages frozen raspberries, thawed
- ⅓ cup water
- 1½ envelopes unflavored gelatin
- One 15-ounce container part-skim ricotta
- ⅔ cup egg whites (from 4 to 5 large eggs)
- ¾ cup sugar
- One ½-pint basket fresh raspberries to garnish the dessert (optional)

One 9-inch round cake pan, 2 inches deep, sprayed with vegetable cooking spray, plus a 9-inch springform pan

1   Set a rack in the lower third of the oven and preheat to 350 degrees.

2   For the cake batter, whisk the egg yolks in a medium mixing bowl, just to break them up. Whisk in half the sugar in a stream, then whisk in the vanilla and lemon zest. Continue whisking for about a minute, or until the yolk mixture is pale and aerated.

3   Combine the egg whites and salt in the bowl of an electric mixer. Whip the egg whites with the whisk attachment on medium speed until they are white, opaque, and just beginning to hold their shape. Increase the speed to medium-high and whip in the remaining ⅓ cup sugar in a slow stream, continuing to whip the egg whites until they hold a firm peak.

4   Use a large rubber spatula to fold the yolk mixture into the egg whites. Sift one-third of the flour mixture over the egg mixture, then fold in until combined. Repeat with each remaining third of the flour mixture.

5   Scrape the cake batter into the pan and smooth the top.

6   Bake the cake for about 30 minutes, or until the cake is well risen and firm, and a toothpick inserted in the center emerges clean.

7   Immediately invert the cake to a rack to cool (if you leave a sponge cake of this type in the pan after it's baked, it will shrink and fall). Turn the cake right side up so that the paper is underneath. Cool completely on a rack.

8   While the cake is baking, make the mousse. Puree the raspberries in a food processor. Strain out the seeds over a medium saucepan, letting the raspberry juice collect in the saucepan. Bring the juice to a boil over medium heat, then lower the heat to maintain a steady, gentle simmer. Cook the raspberry juice until it is reduced to 1½ cups.

9   When the cake has cooled, trim the top away and use a long, sharp serrated knife to cut it in half horizontally. Use a plate or other round pattern to trim the layers to an even 8-inch diameter so that their sides won't be visible in the finished cake. Place one of the layers in a 9-inch springform pan.

10 To finish the mousse, put the water into a small heatproof bowl and sprinkle the gelatin on the surface. Allow to soak for 5 minutes, then place the bowl over a small pan of simmering water and allow the gelatin to melt.

11 Combine the cooled raspberry puree, the gelatin, and the ricotta in a food processor or blender and pulse to mix smoothly. Pour the mixture into a large mixing bowl.

12 For the meringue, half fill a medium saucepan with water and bring it to a boil over medium heat. Combine the egg whites and sugar in the heatproof bowl of an electric mixer and whisk by hand a couple of times to mix. Place the bowl over the pan of boiling water and whisk gently until the egg whites are hot and the sugar is dissolved. Place on the mixer with the whisk attachment and whip on medium-high speed until the egg whites are cooled completely. When you touch the outside of the bowl it won't be at all warm.

13 Fold the meringue into the raspberry mixture.

14 Pour half the mousse over the cake layer in the pan. Place the second cake layer on the mousse and pour in the remaining mousse. Smooth the top of the mousse with a metal offset spatula.

15 Chill the dessert to set the mousse, then cover the pan with plastic wrap. You may leave it in the refrigerator for up to a couple of days before serving.

16 To unmold the dessert, insert a sharp paring knife between the mousse and the inside of the pan. Scraping against the pan, not the mousse, run the blade all around the dessert. Undo the clip of the springform side and lift it off. Insert the knife an inch under the dessert to detach it all around from the base. Use a wide spatula to slide the dessert off the springform base onto a platter. Decorate with the raspberries, if using.

62   SERVING: Cut the cake into wedges, using a sharp, thin-bladed knife dipped in hot water and frequently wiped. The cake needs no accompaniment.

STORAGE: Keep the cake refrigerated until you intend to serve it. Wrap leftovers in plastic and refrigerate.

Per serving: 226 calories, 4 g total fat (16% of calories), 2 g saturated fat, 9 g protein, 39 g carbohydrates, 1 g fiber, 85 mg cholesterol, 93 mg sodium

Kyra's Hot Milk Sponge Layer Cake

Makes one 2-layer 9-inch cake, about 10 servings

My friend Kyra Effren, who lives in Dallas, loves to bake. In fact she's usually already in the kitchen by five o'clock every morning, baking the cakes, cookies, pastries, and breads that her former cooking-class students, family, and friends know and love so well. This particular cake derives from Kyra's British upbringing, both in the UK and in South Africa. It's a popular cake for teatime, but it also makes a great dessert. Two very moist and tender sponge cake layers are baked separately, then sandwiched with some jam. Kyra uses raspberry, but any fruit flavor will do. Ginger marmalade transforms this into something spectacular. Just a light dusting of confectioners' sugar completes the cake. Nothing could be simpler—or better.

HOT MILK SPONGE CAKE

- 4 tablespoons (½ stick) unsalted butter

- ½ cup fat-free milk

- 1½ cups bleached all-purpose flour (spoon flour into dry-measure cup and level off)

- 2 teaspoons baking powder

- 3 large eggs

- ¼ teaspoon salt

- 1 cup sugar

- ¾ teaspoon almond extract

- ½ teaspoon vanilla extract

FINISHING

- ½ cup raspberry all-fruit spread or seedless preserves, or any fruit flavor you like

- Confectioners' sugar for dusting

- Two 9-inch round cake pans, 1½ to 2 inches deep, sprayed with vegetable cooking spray and the bottom lined with a disk of parchment paper

1 Set a rack in the middle level of the oven and preheat to 350 degrees.

2 Combine the butter and milk in a small saucepan and cook over low heat until the butter is completely melted. Set aside in the pan.

3 Stir the flour and baking powder together and sift onto a piece of wax paper.

4   In a large mixing bowl, whisk the eggs to break them up, then whisk in the salt. Whisk in the sugar in a stream, then whisk in the extracts. Continue whisking vigorously for about half a minute, or until the mixture is lightened somewhat.

5   Gently whisk in the milk mixture. Use the whisk to fold the flour into the liquid in 4 additions. Using the whisk helps to prevent lumps from forming. Handle the whisk exactly as though you were using a rubber spatula for the folding.

6   Evenly divide the batter between the prepared pans and smooth the tops.

7   Bake the layers for about 20 minutes, or until they are well risen, golden, and firm when touched in the center with a fingertip.

8   Use a sharp paring knife to loosen the layers from the sides of the pans, then invert to racks. Immediately reinvert the layers so that they cool with the paper on the bottom. Cool completely.

9   To assemble the cake, peel the paper off one of the layers and place it, smooth bottom side down, on a platter. Spread the top of the layer with the preserves. Invert the second layer onto the jam and peel off the paper. Dust with confectioners' sugar immediately before serving.

SERVING: This cake is excellent for tea or dessert with no accompaniment.

STORAGE: You may double-wrap the layers and freeze them for up to a month before assembling the cake. Once the cake is assembled, keep it under a cake dome at room temperature.

Per serving: 249 calories, 6 g total fat (22% of calories), 3 g saturated fat, 4 g protein, 44 g carbohydrates, 1 g fiber, 76 mg cholesterol, 168 mg sodium

Lemon Cupcakes with Milk Chocolate Frosting

Makes 18 cupcakes

This is an individual and skinny version of a large cake I developed for my book *Chocolate*. Lemon and chocolate can be excellent together, as long as the lemon flavor is not too harsh. Here, I use only grated lemon zest and lemon extract for flavor rather than lemon juice, which would be too acidic to marry well with the chocolate.

LEMONY WHITE CAKE BATTER

- 2¼ cups cake flour (spoon flour into dry-measure cup and level off)
- 3 teaspoons baking powder
- ½ teaspoon salt
- 6 tablespoons (¾ stick) unsalted butter, softened
- 1¼ cups sugar
- 2 teaspoons finely grated lemon zest
- 1 teaspoon lemon extract
- 4 large egg whites
- 1½ cups low-fat buttermilk

MILK CHOCOLATE FROSTING

- 6 ounces top-quality milk chocolate, cut into ¼-inch pieces
- ½ cup reduced-fat sour cream

Three 6-cavity cupcake pans with paper liners

1. Set a rack in the middle level of the oven and preheat to 350 degrees.

2. Stir together the cake flour, baking powder, and salt and sift them onto a sheet of wax paper.

3. In an electric mixer fitted with the paddle attachment, beat the butter and sugar on medium speed until well mixed, about 2 minutes. Beat in the lemon zest and lemon extract.

4. Thoroughly whisk the egg whites and buttermilk together.

5   Decrease the mixer speed to low and beat a third of the flour mixture into the butter mixture, followed by half the liquid. Stop and use a large rubber spatula to scrape down the bowl and beater. Add another third of the flour mixture, followed by the remaining liquid. Stop and scrape again. Finally, beat in the remaining flour mixture. Beat the batter on low-medium speed for 3 minutes.

6   Evenly divide the batter among the prepared pans. Bake the cupcakes for 20 to 25 minutes, or until they are well risen and a toothpick inserted in the center of one emerges clean.

7   Cool in the pans on racks for 5 minutes, then unmold the cupcakes, stand them right side up on racks, and cool completely.

8   While the cupcakes are baking, prepare the frosting. Half fill a small saucepan with water and bring the water to a boil. Remove the pan from the heat and place the cut-up chocolate in a heatproof bowl. Place the bowl over the pan of hot water and stir often, but not continuously, until the chocolate is melted. Cool the chocolate until it is just lukewarm, about 105 degrees.

9   Quickly whisk the sour cream into the cooled chocolate. Use a small metal spatula or a wide-bladed table knife to spread a thin layer of the frosting on each cupcake.

SERVING: Though they're great for a kids' party, nowadays everyone loves cupcakes again, and of course they're good at any time of the day or night.

STORAGE: Keep the cupcakes at a cool room temperature on the day they are baked. Cupcakes don't make the best leftovers, since they are so small and have a tendency to become dry very easily. If you don't use them all on the day they are baked, wrap them individually in plastic. If you're only going to use a few at a time, double-wrap the remaining cupcakes individually and freeze them. You may freeze the unused frosting, too. Bring both to room temperature and apply the frosting on the day you are going to serve them.

Per cupcake (with frosting): 224 calories, 8 g total fat (32% of calories), 5 g saturated fat, 4 g protein, 34 g carbohydrates, 0 g fiber, 15 mg cholesterol, 177 mg sodium

Ginger Lovers' Pound Cake

Makes one 10-inch tube or Bundt cake, about 12 servings

This excellent recipe comes my way from my friends Andrea Tutunjian and Cara Tannenbaum, two gifted baking teachers who are my colleagues at the Institute of Culinary Education in New York. To trim the fat and calories, I use a bit less butter, fewer eggs, brown sugar instead of white, and reduced-fat sour cream. Don't worry, the three types of ginger provide loads of flavor.

2¼ cups all-purpose flour (spoon flour into dry-measure cup and level off)

2 teaspoons ground ginger

1 teaspoon baking powder

½ teaspoon baking soda

¼ teaspoon salt

8 tablespoons (1 stick) unsalted butter, softened

1½ cups light brown sugar

⅓ cup grated or finely chopped fresh ginger (see Note)

4 large eggs

⅔ cup reduced-fat sour cream

½ cup (about 3 ounces) crystallized ginger, cut into ¼-inch dice

One 12-cup tube or Bundt pan, sprayed with vegetable cooking spray and the sprayed surface coated with fine, dry bread crumbs

1 Set a rack in the middle level of the oven and preheat to 350 degrees.

2 Stir the flour together with the ground ginger, baking powder, baking soda, and salt.

3 In an electric mixer fitted with the paddle attachment, beat the butter and brown sugar on medium speed for about 5 minutes, or until soft and aerated. Beat in the fresh ginger.

4 Beat in the eggs, one at a time, beating smooth after each addition.

5 Decrease the speed to low and beat in a third of the flour mixture; stop and use a rubber spatula to scrape down the bowl and beater. Beat in half the sour cream, followed by another third of the flour mixture. Stop and scrape again. Beat in the remaining sour cream, followed by the remaining flour mixture. Lastly, beat in the diced crystallized ginger.

6   Bake the cake for 50 to 60 minutes, or until a toothpick inserted halfway between the side of the pan and the central tube emerges clean.

7   Cool the cake in the pan on a rack for 5 to 10 minutes, then unmold the cake to a rack to cool completely.

SERVING: This cake would team up well with a small scoop of lemon sherbet.

STORAGE: Keep under a cake dome on the day it is baked. Double-wrap leftovers in plastic. Or double-wrap and freeze for up to a month. Bring to room temperature before serving.

NOTE: To grate fresh ginger for this cake, first peel it with a paring knife or the end of a spoon, scraping away the peel without cutting away too much of the ginger below. Use a grater that has 1/8-inch, diagonally set holes in it. If you use the type of grater that has holes with sharp points that seem to have been made by driving a nail straight through the opposite side of the sheet metal, all you'll get is ginger juice. Also avoid a Microplane grater, which will grate the ginger too finely and produce mostly juice. There should be a little texture to the grated ginger, rather than a puddle of ginger juice. If you do not have the correct type of grater, finely chop the ginger with a stainless steel knife and be sure not to lose any of the juices.

Per serving: 232 calories, 12 g total fat (47% of calories), 7 g saturated fat, 6 g protein, 27 g carbohydrates, 1 g fiber, 96 mg cholesterol, 187 mg sodium

Old-fashioned Carrot Cake

Makes one 10-inch tube or Bundt cake, about 16 servings

There's something homey and satisfying about carrot cake, and this one is very low in calories to boot. I always use fresh carrots sold in a bunch with the greens attached; they seem to taste sweeter than the ones in plastic bags. For a change of pace, try this with half carrots and half shredded zucchini, especially if you are a gardener and are looking for ways to use up that very high-yielding squash.

2¾ cups all-purpose flour (spoon flour into dry-measure cup and level off)

2 teaspoons baking powder

1 teaspoon baking soda

1 teaspoon ground cinnamon

½ teaspoon freshly grated nutmeg

½ teaspoon salt

3 large eggs

2 large egg whites

¾ cup granulated sugar

1 cup dark brown sugar, firmly packed

1 cup unsweetened applesauce (see Note on page 87)

½ cup vegetable oil, such as corn or canola

1 tablespoon finely grated orange zest

2 teaspoons vanilla extract

3 cups peeled, grated carrots

1 cup raisins

One 12-cup tube or Bundt pan, sprayed with vegetable cooking spray and the sprayed surface coated with fine, dry bread crumbs

1 Set a rack in the middle level of the oven and preheat to 350 degrees.

2 Stir together the flour, baking powder, baking soda, spices, and salt. Sift once onto a piece of wax paper.

3 In a large mixing bowl, whisk the eggs and egg whites to break them up. Whisk in the granulated sugar and brown sugar. Whisk in the applesauce and oil, then the orange zest and vanilla.

4 Use a large rubber spatula to fold in the carrots and raisins.

5 Fold in the flour mixture, being careful not to overmix.

6   Scrape the batter into the prepared pan and smooth the top.

7   Bake the cake for about an hour, or until it is well risen and firm, and a toothpick inserted halfway between the side of the pan and the central tube emerges clean.

8   Cool the cake in the pan on a rack for 5 minutes, then unmold it to a rack to cool completely.

SERVING: To add a little richness to this, I spread a slice with some reduced-fat cream cheese, rather than slathering the entire cake with a very caloric cream cheese icing.

STORAGE: Keep the cake under a dome at room temperature on the day it is baked. Wrap leftovers in plastic. For advance preparation, double-wrap the cake in plastic and freeze for up to a month. Bring to room temperature before serving.

Per serving: 290 calories, 8 g total fat (25% of calories), 1 g saturated fat, 5 g protein, 50 g carbohydrates, 2 g fiber, 40 mg cholesterol, 244 mg sodium

Shredded Apple Cake

Makes one 10-inch Bundt or tube cake, about 12 servings

This moist cake packs a lot of apple flavor as well as a hint of spice. It makes a perfect autumn dessert or brunch cake. Many thanks to Ana Rambaldi, who gave me the recipe on which this one is based.

2 cups all-purpose flour (spoon flour into dry-measure cup and level off)

1 teaspoon baking soda

¼ teaspoon salt

1 teaspoon freshly grated nutmeg

½ teaspoon ground cinnamon

½ teaspoon ground cardamom

3 large eggs

¾ cup light brown sugar, firmly packed

⅔ cup vegetable oil, such as corn or canola

3 cups peeled, cored, and coarsely grated Golden Delicious apples (from about 1½ pounds apples)

½ cup dark or golden raisins, optional (see Note)

One 12-cup tube or Bundt pan, sprayed with vegetable cooking spray and the sprayed surface coated with fine, dry bread crumbs

1 Set a rack in the middle level of the oven and preheat to 350 degrees.

2 Stir the flour together with the baking soda, salt, and spices. Sift onto a piece of wax paper and set aside.

3 In a large mixing bowl, whisk the eggs to break them up. Whisk in the brown sugar, followed by the oil.

4 Use a large rubber spatula to fold in half the grated apples, followed by the flour mixture. Fold in the remaining apples along with the raisins, if using.

5 Bake the cake for 45 to 55 minutes, or until a toothpick inserted halfway between the side of the pan and the central tube emerges clean.

6 Cool the cake in the pan on a rack for 10 minutes, then unmold it to a rack to cool completely.

SERVING: This moist cake tastes great as it is. A drizzle of Caramel Sauce (page 279) would also dress it up nicely.

STORAGE: Keep under a cake dome on the day it is baked. Double-wrap leftovers in plastic. Or double-wrap and freeze for up to a month. Bring to room temperature before serving.

NOTE: If the raisins are dry or hard, before you start mixing the cake batter, place them in a small saucepan and cover them with water. Bring to a boil over medium heat. Remove from the heat, drain, and spread out on a plate or pan covered with paper toweling. Allow to cool completely while you are preparing the cake batter.

Per serving: 220 calories, 14 g total fat (57% of calories), 1 g saturated fat, 4 g protein, 20 g carbohydrates, 1 g fiber, 53 mg cholesterol, 181 mg sodium

Holiday Fruitcake

Makes one 10-inch tube or Bundt cake, about 16 servings

Don't get scared, this isn't one of those fruitcakes everyone hates, but a really delicious and delicate cake packed with fresh-tasting dried fruit. Feel free to vary the fruit any way you wish as long as you have 2½ cups total. I always make sure to include some dried cranberries, especially around the holiday season.

FRUIT MIXTURE

½ cup (about 3 ounces) dried cranberries

½ cup (about 3 ounces) dark raisins or currants

½ cup (about 3 ounces) golden raisins

½ cup (about 3 ounces) dried apricots, cut into ½-inch dice (see Note)

½ cup (about 3 ounces) snipped pitted dates

2 tablespoons dark rum (optional)

CAKE BATTER

2 cups all-purpose flour (spoon flour into dry-measure cup and level off)

2 teaspoons baking powder

½ teaspoon salt

1 teaspoon ground cinnamon

½ teaspoon ground ginger

½ teaspoon freshly grated nutmeg

¼ teaspoon ground cloves

1 cup unsweetened applesauce (see Note on page 87)

⅔ cup dark brown sugar, firmly packed

4 tablespoons (½ stick) unsalted butter, melted

1 large egg

1 tablespoon finely grated orange zest

One 12-cup tube or Bundt pan, sprayed with vegetable cooking spray, the sprayed surface coated with fine, dry bread crumbs

1   Set a rack in the middle level of the oven and preheat to 350 degrees.

2   Combine the fruit in a large bowl and mix well. Sprinkle with the rum, if using, and mix again.

3   For the cake batter, stir the flour together with the baking powder, salt, and spices. Sift once onto a piece of wax paper.

4   In a large mixing bowl, whisk the applesauce and brown sugar together until smooth. Whisk in the butter, egg, and orange zest, one at a time, whisking smooth after each addition.

5   Use a large rubber spatula to fold in the flour mixture, followed by the dried fruits.

6   Pack the batter into the prepared pan and smooth the top.

7   Bake the cake for 65 to 75 minutes, or until it is firm and a toothpick inserted halfway between the side of the pan and the central tube emerges clean.

8   Cool the cake in the pan on a rack for 10 minutes, then unmold the cake to a rack and cool completely.

SERVING: Cut thin slices of this rich cake. I think of fruitcake as something to serve with tea or coffee rather than as a dessert to serve after a meal. But it's up to you.

STORAGE: After the cake has cooled completely, double-wrap it in plastic and age it for a few days at a cool room temperature or in the refrigerator. The flavor improves after a couple of days. You may also sprinkle it with a few more tablespoons of dark rum before aging it.

NOTE: Oil your knife blade to make cutting the fruit easier.

Per serving: 186 calories, 3 g total fat (15% of calories), 2 g saturated fat, 3 g protein, 40 g carbohydrates, 2 g fiber, 21 mg cholesterol, 134 mg sodium

Banana Loaf Cake

Makes one 9 x 5 x 3-inch cake, about ten ¾-inch-thick slices

No matter what type of banana cake you're making, one thing is essential: The bananas have to be really ripe or you might as well use potatoes. Of course, many of us don't get the urge to make a banana-flavored cake or bread until we have some overripe bananas hanging around. If you have to buy the bananas especially for a baking project, let them ripen at least until they are covered with spots. I even like them a little beyond that point for a really rich banana flavor. Another key to excellent banana flavor is to mash them with a fork or potato masher instead of pureeing them in a food processor or blender. Hand-mashing leaves behind small pieces of banana that pack a lot of flavor.

2½ cups bleached all-purpose flour
(spoon flour into dry-measure cup
and level off)

2 teaspoons baking powder

1 teaspoon baking soda

½ teaspoon ground cinnamon

3 large egg whites

½ cup granulated sugar

½ cup dark brown sugar, firmly packed

3 tablespoons unsalted butter, melted

1 teaspoon vanilla extract

2½ cups mashed bananas (about
5 large, very ripe bananas, mashed,
then measured)

One 9 x 5 x 3-inch loaf pan, sprayed
with vegetable cooking spray and the
sprayed surface coated with fine, dry
bread crumbs

1   Set a rack in the middle level of the oven and preheat to 350 degrees.

2   Stir together the flour, baking powder, baking soda, and cinnamon.

3   In a medium mixing bowl, whisk the egg whites to break them up, then whisk in the granulated sugar and the brown sugar.

4   Whisk in the butter and vanilla, followed by the mashed bananas.

5   Sift the flour mixture over the banana mixture and thoroughly fold it in.

6   Scrape the batter into the prepared pan and smooth the top.

7   Bake the cake for about 55 to 65 minutes, or until a toothpick inserted in the center emerges clean.

8   Cool the cake in the pan on a rack for 10 minutes, then unmold it and cool completely on a rack.

SERVING: This cake is excellent unadorned, or it can be spread with a little low-fat cream cheese.

STORAGE: Keep the cake wrapped in plastic at room temperature after it has cooled. For longer storage, double-wrap and freeze for up to a month. Defrost and bring to room temperature before serving.

Per slice: 275 calories, 4 g total fat (13% of calories), 2 g saturated fat, 5 g protein, 56 g carbohydrates, 2 g fiber, 9 mg cholesterol, 228 mg sodium

Lower the Carbs—Keep the Flavor

Dieters have maligned carbohydrates for decades. Some health experts say that eating too many carbohydrates can spike your body's insulin response, setting you up for patterns of overeating and weight gain. The good news is that you can reduce carbohydrates (and calories) in desserts without sacrificing texture or flavor.

Most of the carbohydrates in desserts come from sugar and flour. If you're really carbophobic, you may count fruit, too. But there are so many beneficial nutrients in fruit that many nutritionists recommend reducing refined carbohydrates like sugar and flour rather than unrefined carbohydrates like fruit. Here's how to change the amount and/or type of sugar and flour in your favorite dessert recipes to cut back on carbohydrates:

REDUCE SUGAR. If you've been following the same cake recipe for twenty years, chances are the amount of sugar in it is unnecessarily high. In many older recipes (written before the 1970s, when nutritional concerns hit it big in America), the sugar can be reduced by about ½ cup, which drops approximately 96 grams of carbs and 360 calories. To enhance flavor, add grated lemon or orange zest or vanilla. So-called sweet spices like cinnamon, nutmeg, allspice, and cloves may also help to enhance the sweet flavor in desserts made with less sugar.

SWEETEN WITH SPREADABLE FRUIT. In fruit desserts, you can replace some of the sugar with 100 percent fruit spreads. Sweetened with fruit juice instead of sugar, these spreads will lower carbs, increase beneficial nutrients, and boost the fruit flavor. Replace up to half of the sugar with spreadable fruit in crisps and crumbles, fruit pies and tarts, compotes, and fruit soufflés.

USE BROWN INSTEAD OF WHITE SUGAR. Brown sugar is granulated sugar mixed with molasses, which lowers the carbs slightly. For every ½ cup of brown sugar used in place of white, you'll skip 30 grams of carbohydrates. Brown sugar works particularly well in chocolate desserts, as molasses intensifies the flavor of chocolate. It also adds moisture and tenderness to baked desserts such as cookies and cakes that are made with less fat.

Pumpkin Loaf Cake

Makes one 9 x 5 x 3-inch loaf cake, about twelve ¾-inch-thick slices

Here's a perfectly virtuous spice cake you can enjoy at brunch or tea. Pumpkin puree retains moisture and provides tenderness as applesauce does in other recipes.

2¼ cups cake flour (spoon flour into dry-measure cup and level off)

½ teaspoon baking powder

½ teaspoon baking soda

½ teaspoon salt

½ teaspoon ground cinnamon

½ teaspoon ground ginger

½ teaspoon freshly grated nutmeg

1 large egg

⅓ cup granulated sugar

⅓ cup dark brown sugar, firmly packed

3 tablespoons vegetable oil, such as corn or canola

1 cup canned pumpkin puree

½ cup low-fat buttermilk

One 9 x 5 x 3-inch loaf pan, sprayed with vegetable cooking spray

1   Set a rack in the middle level of the oven and preheat to 350 degrees.

2   Stir the cake flour together with the baking powder, baking soda, salt, and spices. Sift once onto a piece of wax paper.

3   In a medium mixing bowl, whisk the egg to break it up, then whisk in the granulated sugar and brown sugar. Whisk for a minute to lighten. Whisk in the oil, pumpkin puree, and buttermilk.

4   Sift the flour mixture over the pumpkin mixture, and use a large rubber spatula to thoroughly fold the two mixtures together.

5   Scrape the batter into the prepared pan and smooth the top.

6   Bake the cake for 55 to 65 minutes, or until it is well risen and a toothpick inserted in the center emerges clean.

7   Cool the cake in the pan on a rack for 10 minutes, then unmold it to the rack and cool completely.

SERVING: This makes an excellent breakfast or brunch cake. Spread a slice with low-fat cream cheese, or serve with a dollop of Maida's Skinny Whipped Cream (page 285).

STORAGE: Keep under a cake dome on the day it is baked. Double-wrap leftovers in plastic. Or double-wrap and freeze for up to a month. Bring to room temperature before serving.

Per slice: 202 calories, 4 g total fat (18% of calories), 0 g saturated fat, 3 g protein, 37 g carbohydrates, 1 g fiber, 18 mg cholesterol, 215 mg sodium

VARIATION: *Pumpkin Spice Muffins* These are wonderful cakey muffins. Line a 12-cavity muffin pan with paper liners. Divide the batter among the cavities in the pan and sprinkle a few hulled pumpkin seeds on each one if you wish. Bake at 375 degrees for about 20 minutes. Serve warm, or wrap in foil and reheat for 10 minutes at 350 degrees before serving.

81

Blueberry Crumb Cake

Makes one 10-inch cake, about 12 servings

I think I could eat anything with a sweet crumb topping, but I especially love it when the crumbs are scattered over spicy blueberries. This moist cake is easy to prepare and quite versatile. If you prefer, you can replace the blueberries with 3 cups of any soft fruit, such as peeled, sliced peaches; unpeeled, quartered apricots or plums; or pineapple, which is great during the winter. I tend not to use apples or pears unless they've been cooked first. Raw apples sometimes don't cook through by the time the cake and crumbs are fully baked, and raw pears are just too watery. Frozen blueberries work fine in this, too. Just add the frozen berries in step 6.

CAKE BATTER

- 6 tablespoons (¾ stick) unsalted butter
- ¾ cup light brown sugar, firmly packed
- 1 teaspoon vanilla extract
- 2 teaspoons finely grated lemon zest
- 2 large eggs
- 1¼ cups all-purpose flour (spoon flour into dry-measure cup and level off)
- 1 teaspoon baking powder
- ½ cup low-fat buttermilk

TOPPING

- 3 cups blueberries, rinsed, drained, and picked over
- 4 tablespoons (½ stick) unsalted butter, melted
- ⅓ cup light brown sugar, firmly packed
- ¾ cup all-purpose flour
- ½ teaspoon ground cinnamon
- ½ teaspoon baking powder

One 10-inch round pan, 2 inches deep, sprayed with vegetable cooking spray and the bottom lined with a disk of parchment paper

1   Set a rack in the middle level of the oven and preheat to 350 degrees.

2   For the cake batter, combine the butter and brown sugar in the bowl of an electric mixer. Beat with the paddle attachment on medium speed until lightened, about 2 minutes.

3   Beat in the vanilla and lemon zest, then beat in the eggs, one at a time, beating smooth after each addition.

4   Quickly stir the flour and baking powder together, decrease the speed to low, and beat in half the flour mixture. Beat in the buttermilk until it is absorbed, stop the mixer, and use a large rubber spatula to scrape down the bowl and beater. Beat in the remaining flour mixture. Use a large rubber spatula to give the batter a final mixing.

5   Scrape the batter into the prepared pan and use a metal offset spatula to spread it evenly.

6   Top the batter with the blueberries, gently pressing them in.

7   For the crumbs, stir the butter and brown sugar together in a bowl. Quickly mix the flour, cinnamon, and baking powder together and use a rubber spatula to stir them into the butter mixture. Use your fingertips to break up the mixture into small crumbs. Evenly scatter the crumbs on the blueberries.

8   Bake the cake for about 55 minutes, or until it is well risen, the crumbs are a deep golden color, and a toothpick inserted in the center emerges clean.

83

9   Cool the cake in the pan on a rack for 5 minutes. Invert the cake to a large plate and remove the pan and paper. Replace the pan with a cooling rack and reinvert. Lift off the plate and cool the cake completely.

SERVING: This is particularly good for brunch or tea. Or serve it as dessert following a very light meal.

STORAGE: Keep the cake under a cake dome at room temperature.

Per serving: 203 calories, 11 g total fat (49% of calories), 6 g saturated fat, 4 g protein, 23 g carbohydrates, 2 g fiber, 61 mg cholesterol, 89 mg sodium

Coconut Poppy Seed Coffee Cake

Makes one 9-inch round cake, about 12 servings

This is a low-fat version of a wonderful cake that appeared in my book *Chocolate*. The original recipe comes from my friend Kyra Effren of Dallas, who brought it back from a visit to South Africa. Please be aware that the poppy seeds add quite a bit of crunch to the cake, which is somewhat of an acquired taste. If you're not sure whether you like poppy seeds, use half the amount specified or omit them.

1 cup all-purpose flour (spoon flour into dry-measure cup and level off)

¼ cup poppy seeds

¾ cup (about 2 ounces) sweetened, shredded coconut, lightly packed

1 teaspoon baking powder

3 large eggs

¾ cup sugar

½ cup vegetable oil, such as corn or canola

½ teaspoon salt

1 cup (8 ounces) plain fat-free yogurt, preferably Greek yogurt (see Sources, page 291)

One 9-inch round pan, 2 inches deep, or a 9-inch springform pan, sprayed with vegetable cooking spray

1. Set a rack in the middle level of the oven and preheat to 350 degrees.

2. Stir the flour together with the poppy seeds, coconut, and baking powder.

3. In another bowl, whisk the eggs to break them up. Whisk in the sugar and continue to whisk for a minute to lighten the mixture. Whisk in the oil and salt.

4. Use a large rubber spatula to fold half the flour mixture into the egg mixture. Fold in the yogurt, followed by the remaining flour mixture.

5. Scrape the batter into the prepared pan and smooth the top.

6. Bake the cake for 30 to 40 minutes, or until a toothpick inserted in the center emerges clean.

7. Cool the cake in the pan on a rack for 5 to 10 minutes, then unmold, turn the cake right side up, and cool completely.

SERVING: This cake doesn't really need any adornment. Although a few times I have dressed it up, splitting the cake in two and filling it with ½ cup seedless raspberry jam.

STORAGE: Keep under a cake dome on the day it is baked. Double-wrap leftovers in plastic. Or double-wrap and freeze for up to a month. Bring to room temperature before serving.

Per serving: 244 calories, 14 g total fat (52% of calories), 3 g saturated fat, 5 g protein, 25 g carbohydrates, 1 g fiber, 53 mg cholesterol, 180 mg sodium

Easy Spice Cake

Makes one 9 x 13 x 2-inch cake, about twenty-four 2- to 3-inch squares

Here's another cake for cool fall days, when apples and warm spices taste so good after a long summer of peaches, plums, and berries. Some recipes for this type of snack cake include raisins, but I prefer to allot those calories to a few more nutmeats, which provide extra flavor and a bit of crunch.

2½ cups all-purpose flour (spoon flour into dry-measure cup and level off)

1 teaspoon baking soda

¼ teaspoon salt

1 teaspoon ground cinnamon

½ teaspoon freshly grated nutmeg

½ teaspoon ground allspice

6 tablespoons (¾ stick) unsalted butter, softened

1¾ cups light brown sugar, firmly packed

2 large eggs

1½ cups unsweetened applesauce (see Note)

⅔ cup (about 3 ounces) pecan pieces, coarsely chopped

One 9 x 13 x 2-inch pan, sprayed with vegetable cooking spray and the sprayed surface coated with fine, dry bread crumbs

1   Set a rack in the middle level of the oven and preheat to 350 degrees.

2   Stir the flour together with the baking soda, salt, and spices.

3   In an electric mixer fitted with the paddle attachment, beat the butter and brown sugar on medium speed until well mixed, about 2 minutes. Beat in the eggs, one at a time, beating smooth after each addition.

4   Decrease the mixer speed to low and beat a third of the flour mixture into the butter mixture, followed by half the applesauce. Stop and use a large rubber spatula to scrape down the bowl and beater. Add another third of the flour mixture, followed by the remaining applesauce. Stop and scrape again. Finally, beat in the remaining flour mixture, followed by the pecans.

5   Scrape the batter into the prepared pan and smooth the top.

6   Bake the cake for about 40 to 50 minutes, or until a toothpick inserted in the center emerges clean.

7   Cool the cake in the pan on a rack for about 10 minutes, then unmold it to a rack to finish cooling.

SERVING: Cut the cake into 2-inch squares to serve. This is particularly good with a dollop of Milk and Honey Yogurt Cream (page 288).

STORAGE: Keep under a cake dome on the day it is baked. Double-wrap leftovers in plastic. Or double-wrap and freeze for up to a month. Bring to room temperature before serving.

NOTE: To make your own applesauce in season, peel, halve, core, and slice 1½ pounds McIntosh apples. Place in a medium saucepan with ⅓ cup water and cook over medium heat until the mixture comes to a boil. Lower the heat and allow the apples to simmer in their own juices for about 20 minutes, stirring occasionally and watching that the apples don't scorch. If the apples become very dry before they have disintegrated, add 2 to 3 tablespoons water and continue cooking until the apples turn into a chunky puree. Use a whisk or potato masher to break up any large chunks. For this cake, it's not necessary to finely puree the applesauce in a food processor or blender. Cool the applesauce and measure the exact amount before using it in the recipe.

Per square: 104 calories, 5 g total fat (43% of calories), 2 g saturated fat, 2 g protein, 13 g carbohydrates, 1 g fiber, 8 mg cholesterol, 87 mg sodium

PIES AND TARTS

The term "pie" has an interesting history related to birds. According to culinary etymologist Mark Morton, the term dates back to England in the early fourteenth century when someone noticed that a pastry shell filled with bits of this and that resembled a magpie's nest. Back then, the magpie was simply called a "pie," thus a filled pastry shell became known thereafter as "pie."

The term "tart" is more complicated, but rest assured it has nothing to do with the sharp taste we refer to as tart. A dessert tart is simply a filled pastry shell with short sides.

Old-fashioned pie recipes, resembling a magpie's intricate nest, typically combined a wide variety of ingredients. Holiday Mincemeat Tart (page 114) is a recipe of this sort, but don't worry, there is no meat in it! I don't believe that meat belongs anywhere near dessert. Rather, the mincemeat filling is a richly spiced mixture of various dried and candied fruits.

As pies evolved, the fillings eventually became simpler, particularly in North America. Height of Summer Blueberry Pie (page 96) typifies this kind of popular dessert. It is a sweet pastry shell filled with mounds of ripe, juicy blueberries, enhanced only with a touch of lemon zest and cinnamon. A lattice-top crust finishes off the pie perfectly.

Other pies and tarts here feature creamy custard fillings, such as caramel-sweet Butterscotch Pie (page 98) and one of my childhood favorites, Italian-American Ricotta Pie (page 102). I've also included a couple of meringue-topped desserts, such as Lemon Meringue Tartlets (page 128), because meringue is so low in calories and so good-tasting. For chocolate pies and tarts, see Chapter 1. Crisps, cobblers, and other simple fruit desserts are in Chapter 5.

Technique Tips

The foundation of any great pie or tart is a good crust. I rely on three crusts for these lower-calorie recipes: Sweet Pastry Dough (page 93), Flaky Pastry Dough (page 94), and Crumb Crust (page 95). Each one is very low in fat and calories. For example, most single pie-crust recipes include about 8 tablespoons of shortening and/or butter. Sweet Pastry Dough uses only 3 tablespoons of butter, an egg, and a bit of sugar to help tenderize the dough. If you're looking for a lower-calorie alternative, use any of the doughs here to replace the higher-fat doughs in your favorite pie and tart recipes.

These doughs are easily made in the food processor. Plus, they include so little fat that you don't have to worry about the butter melting as soon as you touch the dough. Just be careful not to overhandle the dough when rolling it out. Here are some other hints for making perfect pie and tart dough every time.

Use flour sparingly. When rolling out pastry dough, flour the work surface and the dough lightly. Adding too much flour could make the dough overly dry.

For an even layer of dough, roll from the near to the far edge and back again instead of back and forth. Turn the dough or rolling pin clockwise each time you roll to spread the dough out evenly. Take a little pressure off the rolling pin as you reach the edge of the dough to avoid flattening the edges.

When laying pastry dough into a pie or tart pan, handle it gently and avoid pulling or pushing the dough. I like to fold the dough in half after rolling it, then line up the fold with the diameter of the pan. That way you just unfold the dough so it can be eased into the pan. If you pull the dough or stretch it to fit the pan, it will shrink back to its original size during baking and may look misshapen. Here's what to do if the dough doesn't line up evenly in the pan the first time you unfold the dough: Carefully fold it back up, reposition it over the pan, and unfold it again rather than stretching it to fit the pan.

For fruit pies, I like to cook the filling ahead of time to prevent excess water in the fruit from making the crust soggy during baking. You'll see this method at work in Height of Summer Blueberry Pie (page 96) and Individual Apple Strudels (page 126). Use this technique to prevent soggy crusts in your favorite fruit pies.

Sweet Pastry Dough

**Makes about 9 ounces of dough, enough for a 9- or 10-inch tart
or a single 9-inch piecrust, about 8 servings**

I like to use this as an all-purpose tart and pie dough. It works equally well both when you want to bake the raw dough with a filling in it and also as a fully baked empty crust for a creamy or mousselike filling. Though the dough is very low in fat, a bit of sugar helps to tenderize it. Also the presence of the baking powder does several things: First, the leavening action makes the dough fairly light and prevents toughness. Second, baking powder helps the dough to bake through on the bottom, thus avoiding a soggy, underbaked bottom crust, the greatest nightmare of pie and tart baking. Best of all, this dough takes about 5 minutes to make, from when you begin to measure the flour to wrapping it in plastic. The food processor does all the work.

1 cup all-purpose flour (spoon flour into
    dry-measure cup and level off)

3 tablespoons sugar

½ teaspoon baking powder

¼ teaspoon salt

3 tablespoons unsalted butter, cold and
    cut into 6 pieces

1 large egg

1 tablespoon cold water

1 Combine all the dry ingredients in the bowl of a food processor fitted with the metal blade. Pulse 3 or 4 times to mix.

2 Add the butter and pulse about 10 or 12 times to mix the butter in finely.

3 Add the egg and water and pulse repeatedly until the dough forms a ball.

4 Invert the bowl to a lightly floured work surface and carefully remove the blade.

5 Form the dough into a disk and wrap it in plastic.

6 Refrigerate the dough for several hours or up to 3 days. You may also roll out the dough immediately; it will be a little soft but entirely capable of being rolled.

7 Before you use the refrigerated dough, unwrap it and place it on a floured work surface. Gently knead the dough to render it malleable, then form it into a disk again before rolling.

Per serving: 119 calories, 5 g total fat (38% of calories), 3 g saturated fat, 3 g protein, 16 g carbohydrates, 0 g fiber, 38 mg cholesterol, 107 mg sodium

Flaky Pastry Dough

Makes about 8 ounces of dough, enough for a 9- or 10-inch tart
or a single 9-inch piecrust, about 8 servings

This is the perfect dough to use for fruit galettes, as a cobbler topping, or as a baked empty pie or tart shell to pair with fruit or a creamy filling. It has a fine butter flavor, though it doesn't use a lot. The small amount of sugar in the dough doesn't make it particularly sweet, but it does help to keep the dough tender.

1¼ cups all-purpose flour (spoon flour into dry-measure cup and level off)

1 tablespoon sugar

½ teaspoon baking powder

¼ teaspoon salt

3 tablespoons unsalted butter, cold and cut into 6 pieces

2 tablespoons vegetable oil, such as corn or canola

3 tablespoons cold water

1 Combine all the dry ingredients in the bowl of a food processor fitted with the metal blade. Pulse 3 or 4 times to mix.

2 Add the butter and oil; pulse about 10 or 12 times to mix the butter in finely.

3 Add the water and pulse repeatedly until the dough forms a ball.

4 Invert the bowl to a lightly floured work surface and carefully remove the blade.

5 Form the dough into a disk and wrap it in plastic. If you are using the dough to make individual tarts or galettes, form it into a thick sausage, so it can easily be sliced into individual pieces for rolling.

6 Refrigerate the dough for several hours or up to 3 days. You may also roll out the dough immediately; it will be a little soft but entirely capable of being rolled.

7 When you're ready to roll the dough, unwrap it and place it on a floured work surface. Lightly flour the top of the dough, and with a rolling pin, press the dough, using a series of close, parallel strokes. Turn the dough 90 degrees and repeat. This pressing will soften the cold dough enough to roll it without cracking.

Per serving: 142 calories, 8 g total fat (51% of calories), 3 g saturated fat, 2 g protein, 16 g carbohydrates, 1 g fiber, 11 mg cholesterol, 99 mg sodium

Crumb Crust

Makes one 9- or 10-inch tart crust or a 9-inch piecrust, about 8 servings

This recipe is based on one by my late friend and cooking school partner Peter Kump.
It comes from his book *Quiche and Pâté* (Irena Chalmers Cookbooks, 1982), and Peter
called the recipe "Fear-of-Pastry Crust." It's simply a well-buttered pan with a thick
coating of bread crumbs pressed into it. For a sweet version, I add a bit of sugar and
a dash of baking powder, but that's all there is to it. This crumb crust makes a great
alternative to preparing and rolling dough, and is perfect for any tart or pie in which
the filling is baked right along with the dough. There's only one drawback: It won't hold
a liquid filling in a removable-bottom tart pan, so use either a one-piece tart pan or
a pie plate for this crust.

2 tablespoons unsalted butter, softened

1 tablespoon vegetable oil, such as corn
or canola

⅔ cup dry bread crumbs

One 9- or 10-inch one-piece tart pan
or a 9-inch Pyrex pie pan

1   In a small bowl, beat the butter and oil together with a small rubber spatula.

2   Scrape the butter mixture into the pan. Use your fingertips to smear the mixture evenly
    all over the bottom and sides of the pan.

3   Chill the pan for 10 minutes to firm the coating a little.

4   Scatter the bread crumbs all over the buttered surface and gently press them into
    the butter with your fingertips. Avoid pressing too hard, which might make thin spots
    in the crust.

5   Refrigerate the prepared crust until you are ready to fill and bake it.

Per serving: 76 calories, 5 g total fat (59% of calories), 2 g saturated fat, 1 g protein, 6 g carbohydrates,
0 g fiber, 8 mg cholesterol, 66 mg sodium

VARIATION: *Sweet Crumb Crust*   Add 2 tablespoons sugar and ½ teaspoon
baking powder to the bread crumbs. Proceed as described above.

Height of Summer Blueberry Pie

Makes one 9-inch pie, about 8 servings

Nothing says summer to me more than a juicy blueberry pie, brimming with bright flavor and freshness. My technique of cooking some of the berries first with the sugar and thickening the resulting mixture creates a juicy pie that isn't watery or impossible to cut a wedge from. The same technique also works for pie cherries: See the variation at the end of the recipe.

BLUEBERRY FILLING

5 cups (two and a half 1-pint baskets) fresh blueberries, rinsed, picked over, and drained

⅔ cup sugar

3 tablespoons cornstarch

3 tablespoons water

1 teaspoon finely grated lemon zest

¼ teaspoon ground cinnamon

A double recipe of Sweet Pastry Dough (page 93), divided into 2 equal pieces

One 9-inch Pyrex pie pan

1 For the filling, combine a cup of the blueberries with the sugar in a medium saucepan. Place over low heat and stir occasionally until the sugar melts and the mixture comes to a boil.

2 In the meantime, place the remaining blueberries in a large heatproof bowl and whisk together the cornstarch and water in another heatproof bowl.

3 When the blueberry and sugar mixture comes to a boil, whisk about a third of it into the cornstarch and water. Return the remaining blueberry mixture to a boil and whisk in the cornstarch mixture. Continue whisking until the mixture thickens, becomes clear, and comes to a boil. Cook, whisking constantly, for about 15 seconds; it will be very thick.

4 Scrape the cooked blueberry mixture over the remaining blueberries in the bowl. Add the lemon zest and cinnamon and use a large rubber spatula to fold everything together evenly. Set aside while preparing the crust.

5 Set a rack in the lowest level of the oven and preheat to 350 degrees.

6   Place one of the disks of dough on a floured surface and flour it lightly. Roll it to an 11-inch disk and fold it in half. Transfer it to the pie pan, lining up the fold with the diameter of the pan. Unfold the dough into the pan and press it well into the bottom and sides of the pan. Use a bench scraper or the back of a paring knife to trim the dough even with the edge of the pan.

7   Evenly spread the filling in the dough-lined pan.

8   For the top crust, roll the other disk of dough to a 10-inch square and use a serrated cutting wheel or a pizza wheel to cut the dough into 1-inch-wide strips. Moisten the edge of the bottom crust with water, then place a strip of dough on the pie across its diameter, letting the excess hang over the sides of the pan. Position 4 more strips parallel to the first strip and evenly spaced, so that the pie is covered by 5 parallel strips about an inch apart from each other. Turn the pan 45 degrees and repeat with the remaining 5 strips in a crisscross pattern over the other strips to form a diagonal lattice, as in the illustration (right). Use a bench scraper or the back of a paring knife to trim away any excess dough hanging over the edge of the pan. Press the strips well into the edge of the bottom crust using your fingertips.

9   Bake the pie for about 45 minutes, or until the filling is bubbling and the crust is baked through. If the top crust is not coloring sufficiently after about 30 minutes, finish baking the pie in the upper third of the oven.

10   Cool the pie on a rack.

SERVING: This pie needs no adornment. To serve neat slices, make sure the pie has cooled completely or it will still be too juicy to cut. When I want to serve a fruit pie like this for dessert in the evening, I always try to bake it in the morning so the filling has a chance to set completely.

STORAGE: Cover the pie loosely with plastic wrap or a towel on the day it is baked. Store leftovers the same way. I have also successfully frozen this pie before baking. Place the assembled pie in the freezer for a few hours or until it has frozen solid, then double-wrap in plastic. When you want to bake the pie, unwrap it and bring it to room temperature first. Otherwise, the cold pan may crack when it goes into the hot oven.

Per serving: 300 calories, 8 g total fat (24% of calories), 5 g saturated fat, 5 g protein, 56 g carbohydrates, 4 g fiber, 57 mg cholesterol, 161 mg sodium

VARIATIONS

Cherry Pie   Substitute 5 cups pitted sour cherries (about 2 pounds fresh unpitted cherries) for the blueberries. Omit the cinnamon and lemon zest and add ½ teaspoon almond extract to the cherries when you add the cooked cherry mixture in step 4.

Blueberry or Cherry Crumb Pie   Replace the top crust with the crumb topping (minus the berries) from the Blueberry Crumb Cake on page 82.

Butterscotch Pie

Makes one 9-inch pie, 8 servings

I love the caramel-sweet flavor of butterscotch in anything, but this pie is close to the top among my favorites. It has an intense butterscotch flavor, but it's also light in texture and low in calories.

1 recipe Crumb Crust (page 95), Sweet Crumb Crust variation

BUTTERSCOTCH FILLING

2½ cups fat-free milk, divided

⅔ cup dark brown sugar, firmly packed

¼ teaspoon salt

⅓ cup cornstarch

2 large eggs

1 tablespoon unsalted butter, cut into 4 pieces

1 teaspoon vanilla extract

1   Set a rack in the middle level of the oven and preheat to 325 degrees.

2   Bake the crust for about 15 to 20 minutes, or until it is evenly deep golden. Cool the crust on a rack.

3   For the filling, pour ½ cup of the milk into a small mixing bowl and set aside.

4   Combine the remaining milk with the brown sugar and salt in a medium nonreactive saucepan. Whisk for a few seconds to dissolve the sugar and set over low to medium heat. Let the milk mixture come to a boil.

5   Meanwhile, whisk the cornstarch into the reserved ½ cup milk until smooth. Whisk in the eggs.

6   Once the milk mixture boils, whisk about a third of it into the egg mixture. Return the remaining milk mixture to a boil and, beginning to whisk first, pour in the egg mixture in a stream, continuing to whisk constantly until the filling thickens and comes to a full boil. Large, thick, slow-forming bubbles will burst on the surface of the filling. Let the filling cook, whisking constantly, for about 30 seconds. Remove from the heat and whisk in the butter and vanilla.

7   Pour the hot filling directly into the piecrust, scraping the pan clean with a rubber spatula. Use the spatula to smooth the top of the filling.

8   Press plastic wrap directly against the surface of the filling and refrigerate the pie until it is cold.

9   Bring the pie to room temperature for an hour before serving (less time if the room is warm) so that the crust isn't cold and greasy-tasting.

SERVING: A spoonful of Maida's Skinny Whipped Cream (page 285) on each wedge will dress up the pie considerably.

STORAGE: See steps 8 and 9. Wrap leftovers in plastic and refrigerate. Bring to room temperature before serving again.

Per serving: 247 calories, 9 g total fat (33% of calories), 4 g saturated fat, 5 g protein, 35 g carbohydrates, 0 g fiber, 71 mg cholesterol, 220 mg sodium

VARIATION: *Black Bottom Pie* Substitute granulated sugar for the brown sugar in the recipe. When the filling is cooked, scrape half into a bowl and press plastic wrap against the surface. Stir 4 ounces bittersweet (not unsweetened) chocolate, cut into ¼-inch pieces, into the half of the filling still in the pan, until the chocolate is smoothly incorporated. Scrape the chocolate filling into the baked pie shell and smooth the top. Pour the reserved plain filling on top of the chocolate filling, spreading the top until smooth. Proceed with steps 8 and 9. Top with some chocolate shavings immediately before serving.

Perfect Pumpkin Pie

Makes one 9-inch pie, 8 servings

The moist texture and earthy flavor of pumpkin make it possible to prepare a virtually fat-free pie. Not a bad idea considering all the indulging we do at what I call the "year-end eating holidays." I worked out this recipe years ago when I was developing desserts for my book *How to Bake*, but it made it in there as a variation of a standard pumpkin pie. Here, I've dressed up the pie with a sweet crust, but if you want to keep calories to a bare minimum, simply spray the pan with vegetable cooking spray and dust it with fine, dry bread crumbs. By the way, I always use canned pumpkin. It isn't adulterated in any way and is better and thicker than what you can get by using most of the fresh pumpkins that are available. Just be sure to use pure pumpkin puree and not pumpkin pie filling, both of which come in a similar-looking can.

PUMPKIN FILLING

2 cups canned pumpkin puree
(one 16-ounce can)

4 large egg whites

¼ cup granulated sugar

¼ cup light brown sugar

½ teaspoon salt

1 teaspoon ground cinnamon

¼ teaspoon ground ginger

¼ teaspoon freshly grated nutmeg

1¼ cups evaporated skim milk

1 recipe Sweet Pastry Dough (page 93)

One 9-inch Pyrex pie pan

1   Set a rack in the lowest level of the oven and preheat to 350 degrees.

2   For the filling, scrape the pumpkin puree into a bowl and whisk in the egg whites until smooth.

3   Whisk in the granulated sugar, brown sugar, salt, and spices. Whisk in the evaporated skim milk.

4   Set aside the filling while preparing the crust.

5   Place the dough on a floured work surface. Flour the dough and roll it to an 11-inch disk. Fold the dough in half and transfer it to the pan, lining up the fold with the diameter of the pan. Unfold the dough into the pan and press it well into the bottom and sides. Use a bench scraper or the back of a paring knife to trim away all but a ½-inch overhang of excess dough at the rim of the pan. Fold the half inch of dough under the edge of the crust and crimp the edge of the crust, as in the illustration above.

6   Use a rubber spatula to scrape the filling out of the bowl into the dough-lined pan.

7   Bake the pie for about an hour, or until the crust is baked through and the filling is set.

8   Cool the pie on a rack and refrigerate it, loosely covered with plastic wrap, until serving.

SERVING: This pie is fine on its own, but a spoonful of real whipped cream would be just right with it, especially considering that the pie is fat-free apart from the small amount in the crust.

STORAGE: Keep the pie refrigerated as in step 8. Likewise for leftovers.

Per serving: 300 calories, 6 g total fat (18% of calories), 3 g saturated fat, 9 g protein, 53 g carbohydrates, 3 g fiber, 40 mg cholesterol, 477 mg sodium

Italian-American Ricotta Pie

Makes one 9-inch pie, about 8 servings

This is one of the first baked desserts I remember loving as a child. My maternal grandmother, who lived with us, was a great baker, and it was one of her best specialties. Usually we had it only at Easter, but it was worth waiting for. It's pretty easy to make a low-calorie version of this pie using part—skim milk ricotta, and it still tastes very close to the original in flavor and texture. I've left off the top crust to save a few more calories. I think the pie is just as good without it. To add a citrus flavor, stir a couple of teaspoons of grated lemon or orange zest into the filling.

1 recipe Sweet Pastry Dough
(page 93)

1 pound (or a 15-ounce container)
part-skim ricotta

⅓ cup sugar

3 large eggs

2 teaspoons vanilla extract

¼ teaspoon ground cinnamon,
plus more for sprinkling in the filling

One 9-inch Pyrex pie pan

1   Place the dough on a floured work surface. Flour the dough and roll it to an 11-inch disk. Fold the dough in half and transfer it to the pan, lining up the fold with the diameter of the pan. Unfold the dough into the pan and press it well into the bottom and sides. Use a bench scraper or the back of a paring knife to trim away all but a ½-inch overhang of excess dough at the rim of the pan. Fold the half inch of dough under the edge of the crust and crimp the edge of the crust, as in the illustration on page 101. Set aside while preparing the filling.

2   Set a rack in the lowest level of the oven and preheat to 350 degrees.

3   For the filling, scrape the ricotta into a medium mixing bowl and use a large rubber spatula to stir it smooth. When adding the remaining ingredients, just stir them in. It's not necessary to beat air into the filling. Stir in the sugar until it is absorbed, then stir in the eggs, one at a time, stirring smooth after each addition. Stir in the vanilla and cinnamon.

4   Use a rubber spatula to scrape the filling out of the bowl into the dough-lined pan. Sprinkle the top of the filling with cinnamon.

5   Bake the pie for 40 to 45 minutes, or until the crust is baked through and the filling is set. The filling will puff a little while it is baking. Just be sure not to bake it until the filling cracks around the sides and rises from that point, which will cause the pie to fall in the center as it cools.

6   Cool the pie on a rack and refrigerate it, loosely covered with plastic wrap, until serving.

SERVING: This rich pie needs no accompaniment.

STORAGE: Keep the pie refrigerated. Wrap leftovers in plastic and refrigerate.

Per serving: 246 calories, 11 g total fat (40% of calories), 6 g saturated fat, 11 g protein, 27 g carbohydrates, 0 g fiber, 140 mg cholesterol, 111 mg sodium

Pies and Tarts

Plum and Ginger Galettes

Makes 6 individual galettes

If you've never made a galette before, it's easy. It's a free-form individual tart that you assemble on a jelly-roll pan, placing the filling in the center of a disk of dough. Then you fold the uncovered margin of the dough up and over the filling, leaving the very center exposed. I like to use a cooked filling for galettes to eliminate having excess water accumulate and possibly soften the crust while they are baking. These desserts are perfect when served slightly warm. If you prefer, you can easily substitute peeled, cored, and sliced pears or apples for the plums in the recipe.

PLUM AND GINGER FILLING

1½ pounds ripe red or prune plums, rinsed, dried, halved, pitted, and sliced ½ inch thick

¼ cup sugar

½ teaspoon ground ginger

2 teaspoons peeled, grated fresh ginger (see Note on page 68)

Pinch of salt

1 teaspoon vanilla extract

1 recipe Sweet Pastry Dough (page 93), or Flaky Pastry Dough (page 94), formed into a thick sausage shape before it is chilled

FINISHING

Milk for brushing

Sugar for sprinkling

A small roasting pan for cooking the filling and a jelly-roll pan covered with parchment or foil for baking the galettes

1 Set a rack in the middle level of the oven and preheat to 450 degrees.

2 Combine all the filling ingredients in the roasting pan and toss well to mix. Bake the filling for 15 to 20 minutes, or until some of the juices start to evaporate. Scrape the filling from the hot pan to a bowl to cool. You may cover and refrigerate the filling for several days at this point.

3 When you are ready to bake the galettes, set a rack in the lowest level of the oven and preheat to 375 degrees.

4   Unwrap the dough and cut it into 6 equal slices. Place one of the slices on a floured work surface and lightly flour it. Roll the dough to a 5-inch disk, keeping it as perfect a circle as possible. Trim a little if necessary and transfer the disk of dough to the prepared jelly-roll pan.

5   Place a sixth of the filling in the center of the disk of dough, spreading the filling into a 2½-inch circle. A little at a time, fold the margin of dough over and onto the filling all around. The dough will pleat itself occasionally as you are folding; this is normal, as in the illustration (right). Repeat with the remaining dough and filling.

6   Brush the tops of the dough with the milk and sprinkle with the sugar.

7   Bake the galettes for 20 to 30 minutes, or until the dough is baked through and deep golden and the filling is bubbling slightly.

8   Cool the galettes on a pan on a rack and serve them warm if possible.

SERVING: These individual galettes would be good with any of the creams in the Sauces and Garnishes chapter beginning on page 273. If you have baked the galettes in advance and want to serve them warm, reheat them on a jelly-roll pan at 350 degrees for about 10 minutes. Let them cool slightly on the pan and use a wide spatula to transfer them to plates.

Per galette: 198 calories, 5 g total fat (23% of calories), 3 g saturated fat, 4 g protein, 35 g carbohydrates, 2 g fiber, 40 mg cholesterol, 108 mg sodium

VARIATION: If you prefer to make one large galette instead of individual ones, form the dough into a disk before you chill it. Roll the dough to a 12-inch disk and transfer it to a prepared pan—a wide, flat pizza pan is perfect. Arrange the filling in an 8-inch-diameter circle in the center of the dough, then fold and bake as described above.

Rustic Apple Tart

Makes one 9- or 10-inch tart, about 8 servings

This is my favorite kind of low-calorie dessert recipe. Nothing needs to be removed from it or changed to cut the calories. In fact, it's so low in calories on its own that you can afford to serve it with a scoop of one of the ices in the chapter beginning on page 211.

1 recipe Sweet Pastry Dough
(page 93)

APPLE FILLING

3 large (about 1½ pounds)
Golden Delicious apples

2 tablespoons sugar

½ teaspoon ground cinnamon

APRICOT GLAZE

½ cup apricot all-fruit spread
or preserves

2 tablespoons water

One 9- or 10-inch fluted tart pan
with removable bottom

1   Set a rack in the lowest level of the oven and preheat to 350 degrees.

2   Place the dough on a floured work surface. Flour the dough and roll it to a 12-inch disk. Fold the dough in half and transfer it to the pan, lining up the fold with the diameter of the pan. Unfold the dough into the pan and press it well into the bottom and sides of the pan. Sever any excess dough at the rim of the pan with a bench scraper or the back of a paring knife.

3   Peel the apples, halve, and core them. Cut the apples into ¼-inch-thick slices across the core (perpendicular to the stem), but don't separate the slices from each other. It's easier to arrange them when left this way because they will be overlapping. Arrange the apple slices so they overlap in a row all around the edge of the crust closest to the side of the pan, reserving an entire apple half for the center of the tart. Pile any extra slices in the center of the crust. Fan out the reserved apple half and use a metal spatula to transfer the entire fan of slices to the center of the tart over the extra slices.

4   Mix the sugar and cinnamon together and sprinkle evenly over the apples.

5   Bake the tart for 40 to 45 minutes, or until the crust is baked through and golden and the apples are bubbling slightly.

6   Cool the tart in the pan on a rack.

7 While the tart is baking, stir the preserves and water together in a small saucepan. Bring to a boil over low heat and strain the mixture into another small saucepan to remove any solid fruit pieces.

8 When you are ready to glaze the tart, reheat the glaze over low heat and allow it to boil gently until it has thickened slightly, 3 or 4 minutes. Use a pastry brush to paint the glaze onto the apples.

9 To unmold the tart, stand it on a short, round can or other container that is at least 4 inches in diameter. A 28-ounce can of tomatoes is perfect. Let the side of the tart pan drop away. Slide the tart from the metal pan base to a platter, using a metal spatula to ease it along.

SERVING: This tart is good on its own or dressed up with a spoonful of Maida's Skinny Whipped Cream (page 285), or any frozen dessert that appeals to you in Chapter 6 (page 211).

STORAGE: Pastry-based desserts are best served on the day they are baked. Wrap leftovers in plastic and reheat at 350 degrees for a few minutes (or in the toaster oven). Cool to warm or room temperature before serving again.

Per serving: 217 calories, 5 g total fat (21% of calories), 3 g saturated fat, 3 g protein, 42 g carbohydrates, 3 g fiber, 38 mg cholesterol, 111 mg sodium

Banana Walnut Tart

Makes one 9- or 10-inch tart, about 8 servings

Putting the bananas under the walnut filling in this tart not only prevents them from drying out but also helps them to melt to a tender jamlike consistency while the tart is baking. As with all banana recipes in this book, make sure to use ripe ones. The skin should be flecked with black spots for perfect ripeness and flavor.

1 recipe Sweet Pastry Dough
(page 93)

FILLING

2 large ripe bananas (about 1 pound), peeled and sliced ½ inch thick

½ cup light brown sugar, firmly packed

½ cup (about 2 ounces) walnut pieces

4 tablespoons (½ stick) unsalted butter, softened

1 large egg

¼ teaspoon ground cinnamon

½ teaspoon vanilla extract

¼ cup all-purpose flour (spoon flour into dry-measure cup and level off)

½ teaspoon baking powder

1 tablespoon dark rum (optional)

One 9- or 10-inch fluted tart pan with removable bottom

1 Set a rack in the lowest level of the oven and preheat to 350 degrees.

2 Unwrap the dough and place it on a floured work surface. Knead it lightly to soften it slightly, then form it into a disk. Flour the dough and roll it to an 11- to 12-inch disk. Fold the dough in half and transfer it to the pan, lining up the fold with the diameter of the pan. Unfold the dough into the pan and press it well into the bottom and sides. Sever the excess dough at the rim of the pan with a bench scraper or the back of a paring knife.

3 Arrange the sliced bananas all over the bottom of the pastry crust.

4 Combine the brown sugar and walnuts in the bowl of a food processor fitted with the metal blade. Pulse until the nuts are finely ground. Add the butter and egg and pulse again to mix them in smoothly. Pulse in the cinnamon and vanilla.

5 Quickly mix the flour with the baking powder and add to the bowl. Pulse again until completely mixed in.

6 Use a rubber spatula to distribute the filling in little mounds all over the bananas, which makes it easier to spread it out and cover all the bananas. Use a small metal offset spatula to spread the mounds of filling evenly all over the bananas and to the edge of the crust.

7 Bake the tart for about 35 to 40 minutes, or until the crust is baked through and the filling is firm.

8 Immediately after removing the tart from the oven, use a pastry brush to paint the tart with the rum.

9 Cool the tart on a rack and unmold it according to the instructions on page 107.

SERVING: This rich and complex tart needs no accompaniment.

STORAGE: Keep the tart at room temperature, loosely covered with plastic wrap. Wrap leftovers in plastic and keep them at room temperature.

Per serving: 295 calories, 16 g total fat (49% of calories), 7 g saturated fat, 6 g protein, 35 g carbohydrates, 2 g fiber, 78 mg cholesterol, 153 mg sodium

Updated Linzertorte

Makes one 9- or 10-inch tart, about 10 servings

I love Linzertorte, that Viennese cake with its spicy nut dough and jam filling. In fact I love it so much that it appears in one form or another in almost all my books. This pared-down version might raise a few eyebrows in Vienna, but it's very close to the original in taste and texture.

1 cup all-purpose flour (spoon flour into dry-measure cup and level off)

½ cup (about 2 ounces) whole hazelnuts or almonds, finely ground in the food processor

½ cup sugar

¾ teaspoon baking powder

1 teaspoon ground cinnamon

¼ teaspoon ground cloves

6 tablespoons (¾ stick) unsalted butter, softened

1 large egg

⅔ cup raspberry all-fruit spread or preserves

Confectioners' sugar for finishing

One 9- or 10-inch fluted tart pan with removable bottom

1 Set a rack in the middle level of the oven and preheat to 350 degrees.

2 Combine the flour, ground nuts, sugar, baking powder, and spices in a large mixing bowl.

3 Cut the soft butter into 8 pieces and add to the bowl. Use your hands or a pastry blender to incorporate the butter into the dry ingredients completely, though don't mix until the ingredients bind together. Beat the egg with a fork and pour it all over the mixture in the bowl. Use the fork to toss the egg throughout the mixture until it forms a soft dough.

4 Use a rubber spatula to scrape the dough out onto a floured work surface. Form the dough into a thick cylinder, then cut off a third of it for the top crust.

5 Place the larger piece of dough in the tart pan and use your fingertips to press it all over the bottom of the pan and about three-quarters of the way up the sides.

6 Use a small metal offset spatula to spread the preserves in an even layer on the dough.

7   Divide the remaining dough into 10 pieces and roll each piece to a pencil-thick strand. Flour your hands if the dough is sticky, but don't flour the work surface. Place one strand on the tart across its diameter, letting the excess hang over the sides of the pan. Position 4 more strands parallel to the first strand and evenly spaced, so that the tart is covered by 5 parallel strands about an inch apart from each other. Turn the pan 45 degrees and repeat with the remaining 5 strands in a crisscross pattern over the other strands to form a diagonal lattice, as in the illustration on page 97. Use a bench scraper or the back of a paring knife to trim away any excess dough hanging over the edge of the pan. Press the strands gently into the edge of the bottom crust using your fingertips.

8   Bake the Linzertorte for about 35 minutes, or until it is risen and slightly firm. If you bake it until it is fully firm, it will be dry.

9   Cool the Linzertorte on a rack and unmold it according to the instructions on page 107.

10   Immediately before serving, lightly dust the Linzertorte with confectioners' sugar.

SERVING: Linzertorte is better to have with tea or coffee than as a dessert, though you could dress it up with a few fresh raspberries.

STORAGE: Keep under a cake dome at room temperature. Wrap leftovers in plastic and keep at room temperature.

Per serving: 229 calories, 11 g total fat (43% of calories), 5 g saturated fat, 3 g protein, 32 g carbohydrates, 1 g fiber, 39 mg cholesterol, 42 mg sodium

Cranberry Walnut Tart

Makes one 9- or 10-inch tart, 8 generous servings

This is my dear friend Joseph Viggiani's recipe from the days when he was the proprietor of Café Sandalea in Greenwich Village. I adapted it for my first book, *Perfect Pastry*, and am using a streamlined version here. I like the bittersweet, pungent flavor of this filling, but be forewarned: Not everyone does. Cranberries are like marzipan and caviar; people like them or hate them, but no one is wishy-washy about it.

5 cups fresh cranberries (about 1¼ pounds), rinsed, picked over, and drained

1 cup light brown sugar, firmly packed

½ cup fresh orange juice, strained

1 tablespoon finely grated orange zest

2 tablespoons unsalted butter

½ teaspoon ground cinnamon

½ teaspoon ground ginger

½ cup (about 2 ounces) walnut pieces, coarsely chopped

1 recipe Sweet Pastry Dough (page 93)

One 9- or 10-inch fluted tart pan with removable bottom

1   For the filling, combine all the ingredients except the walnuts in a heavy nonreactive pan, such as an enameled iron Dutch oven. Stir well to mix and place over medium heat. Cook, stirring occasionally, until the cranberries begin to pop and the filling comes to a boil. Decrease the heat to low and cook the filling at a very slow boil for about 5 minutes, just to reduce some of the water. Remove from the heat, pour into a glass or stainless steel bowl, and cool to room temperature. After the filling has cooled, stir in the walnuts. I don't recommend preparing the filling so far in advance that you would have to refrigerate it, because the natural pectin in the cranberries will set the filling firm if it's refrigerated and make it difficult to spread in the tart crust.

2   When you are ready to bake the tart, set a rack in the lowest level of the oven and preheat to 350 degrees.

3   Unwrap the dough and place it on a floured work surface. Flour the dough and roll it to an 11- to 12-inch disk. Fold the dough in half and transfer it to the pan, lining up the fold with the diameter of the pan. Unfold the dough into the pan and press it well into the bottom and sides. Sever the excess dough at the rim of the pan with a bench scraper or the back of a paring knife.

4   Fold the walnuts into the filling and evenly spread it in the prepared pastry crust.

5   Bake the tart for about 30 minutes, or until the crust is baked through and the filling just begins to bubble a little. Don't let the filling boil or it will boil out of the crust and make the top edge of the crust sloppy.

6   Cool the tart on a rack and unmold it according to the instructions on page 107.

SERVING: A scoop of Italian Orange Gelato (page 228), combines perfectly with this tart.

STORAGE: Keep the tart at room temperature before and after it is baked. Cover leftovers with plastic wrap. For advance preparation, bake and freeze the tart. Slide it onto a cardboard cake circle and double-wrap in plastic. Freeze for up to a month. Unwrap the tart and slide it from the cardboard to a cookie sheet with no sides or onto the back of a jelly-roll pan. Reheat at 350 degrees for 10 minutes. Cool to room temperature, then slide the tart onto a platter and serve.

Per serving: 247 calories,
13 g total fat (47% of calories),
5 g saturated fat, 4 g protein,
30 g carbohydrates, 3 g fiber,
46 mg cholesterol, 126 mg sodium

Holiday Mincemeat Tart

Makes one 9- or 10-inch tart, about 8 servings

I first became interested in mincemeat when I was developing recipes for my book *How to Bake* in the early 1990s. I had done a very quickly made version for a previous book, but I admit that I became dissatisfied with it. All I knew was that I wanted to do a meatless one. I don't think that meat, no matter how small an amount, has any place in a dessert. Since mincemeat as we know it is British in origin, I consulted the most important book about food in Victorian England, Isabella Beeton's *Book of Household Management*. To my amazement, a meatless mincemeat was already in use in the nineteenth century. It contained no meat, but some beef fat, which I quickly rationalized into butter. I scanned the ingredients list and took note of the proportions, and I was off and running. Feel free to vary the mix of dried and candied fruit any way you want. If you omit an ingredient, make up its volume with another. If you prepare this tart, set aside a ½ cup of the filling to make the Mincemeat Cookies on page 260.

1½ pounds tart apples (see Note)

1 medium orange

1 medium lemon

¾ cup (about 4½ ounces) dark or golden raisins

½ cup (about 2½ ounces) Zante currants

¼ cup (1½ ounces) candied orange peel, cut into ¼-inch pieces

½ cup light brown sugar, firmly packed

2 tablespoons dark rum or brandy

2 tablespoons distilled white vinegar or cider vinegar

1 tablespoon unsalted butter

½ teaspoon freshly grated nutmeg

½ teaspoon ground cinnamon

¼ teaspoon ground cloves

¼ teaspoon ground ginger

1 recipe Sweet Pastry Dough (page 93)

One 9- or 10-inch fluted tart pan with removable bottom

1 For the mincemeat, peel, halve, and core the apples. Grate them coarsely by hand or with a food processor. Scrape the apples into a large, heavy nonreactive pan, such as an enameled iron Dutch oven. Grate the zest off the orange and lemon and add to the pan. Squeeze and strain the juice from the orange and lemon and add to the pan.

2 Stir in the remaining ingredients except the pastry dough.

3   Place the pan over medium heat and cook until the mixture starts to sizzle. Lower the heat and let the mincemeat come to a simmer, stirring occasionally. Cook the mincemeat, stirring more often during the second half of the cooking time, for about 30 minutes, or until it is reduced to a thick, jamlike consistency. Scrape the mincemeat into a glass or stainless steel bowl and cool it to room temperature. Cover the bowl tightly with plastic wrap and refrigerate the mincemeat until you are ready to use it. For longer storage, pack the cooled mincemeat into a plastic container that has a tight-fitting cover, press plastic wrap against the surface of the mincemeat, cover the container, and refrigerate for up to a month. The flavor improves with a bit of aging, just like a fruitcake.

4   When you are ready to bake the tart, set a rack in the lowest level of the oven and preheat to 375 degrees.

5   Place the dough on a floured surface. Flour the dough and roll it to a 12-inch disk. Fold the dough in half and transfer it to the pan, lining up the fold with the diameter of the pan. Unfold the dough into the pan and press it well into the bottom and sides of the pan. Sever the excess dough at the rim of the pan with a bench scraper or the back of a paring knife.

6   Evenly spread the mincemeat in the crust, spreading the top smooth.

7   Bake the tart for about 30 minutes, or until the crust is baked through and dark golden.

8   Cool the tart on a rack and unmold it according to the instructions on page 107.

SERVING: Serve the tart in small wedges, as it is quite rich and satisfying.

STORAGE: Keep the tart at room temperature on the day it is baked. Wrap leftovers in plastic and keep at room temperature.

NOTE: For the very best flavor and texture in the finished mincemeat, use a combination of half tart apples, such as Granny Smiths, and half McIntosh apples. The former will remain in distinct shreds after cooking and the latter will disintegrate completely, binding all the solids in the mincemeat.

Per serving: 300 calories, 7 g total fat (21% of calories), 4 g saturated fat, 4 g protein, 58 g carbohydrates, 6 g fiber, 43 mg cholesterol, 124 mg sodium

VARIATION: *Cranberry Mincemeat Tart*   Omit 1 apple and replace it with 1 cup (4 ounces) fresh cranberries, rinsed and picked over. Distinctive flavor and a vivid color will result.

Strawberry Meringue Tart

Makes one 9- or 10-inch tart, about 8 servings

This is the perfect tart for really ripe, in-season berries. You could do the same thing with raspberries or even figs or a combination. This tart is definitely for meringue lovers, since the meringue provides all the richness to complement the strawberry flavor.

1 recipe Sweet Pastry Dough
(page 93)

TART FILLING

½ cup strawberry all-fruit spread
  or preserves

2 pints strawberries, rinsed, dried, hulled,
  and halved

MERINGUE

3 large egg whites

Pinch of salt

⅔ cup sugar

One 9- or 10-inch fluted tart pan
with removable bottom

1   For the crust, set a rack in the middle level of the oven and preheat to 350 degrees.

2   Place the dough on a floured surface. Flour the dough and roll it to a 12-inch disk. Fold the dough in half and transfer it to the pan, lining up the fold with the diameter of the pan. Unfold the dough into the pan and press it well into the bottom and sides of the pan. Sever the excess dough at the rim of the pan with a bench scraper or the back of a paring knife.

3   Pierce the dough all over with the tines of a fork. Line the crust with a disk of parchment paper and fill up the paper-lined crust with dried beans.

4   Bake the crust for about 15 minutes, or until it is just beginning to color. Open the oven and remove the paper and beans. Continue baking the crust for a few more minutes, or until it is an even golden color. Cool the crust on a rack.

5   When you are ready to assemble the tart, set a rack in the middle level of the oven and preheat to 400 degrees. Spread the preserves evenly on the crust. Arrange the strawberry halves neatly, overlapping them slightly, to fill the crust.

6   For the meringue, half fill a small saucepan with water and bring to a boil over medium heat. Combine the egg whites with the salt and sugar in the heatproof bowl of an electric mixer and whisk by hand for a few seconds to mix. Place the pan over the boiling water and whisk constantly but gently until the egg whites are hot and the sugar is dissolved.

7   Place the bowl on the mixer and whip the meringue until it has risen in volume and almost completely cooled. The outside of the bowl should still feel slightly warm. (If you whip the meringue until it has completely cooled, it may become overwhipped and grainy.)

8   Spread the meringue all over the top of the tart, making sure that it touches the edge of the crust all around, which prevents it from sliding off the tart after it is baked.

9   Bake the tart for about 5 minutes to color the meringue an even golden color.

10   Cool on a rack and chill before serving. Unmold the tart according to the instructions on page 107.

SERVING: This beauty needs nothing else on the plate. Maybe a glass of champagne on the side.

STORAGE: Meringue-topped desserts are not good keepers. If you don't serve the entire tart, loosely wrap the leftovers in plastic and refrigerate. Don't be surprised if both the berries and the meringue become very wet, it's just a consequence of sitting around and nothing can be done to prevent it.

Per serving: 255 calories, 5 g total fat (18% of calories), 3 g saturated fat, 5 g protein, 49 g carbohydrates, 2 g fiber, 38 mg cholesterol, 132 mg sodium

Apricot Custard Tart

Makes one 9- or 10-inch tart, about 8 servings

Ordinarily I don't use canned fruit, but once I had planned to make an apricot tart for a class without realizing that the scheduled date for the class was much too early for fresh apricots, so I bit the bullet and tried the canned kind. To my amazement, the tart turned out very well, with a fine apricot flavor. I only have one beef with canned apricots: If you buy small cans, one can will contain 4 large halves and the next can, 8 tiny ones. Larger cans have the small and large halves mixed together. Fortunately for this recipe, the custard cream successfully covers up the size differences, which are not at all apparent when you slice and serve the tart.

1 recipe Sweet Pastry Dough (page 93)

APRICOT CUSTARD FILLING

⅓ cup sugar

3 tablespoons all-purpose flour

3 large eggs

1 teaspoon vanilla extract

½ teaspoon almond extract

¾ cup half-and-half (coffee cream)

3 cups drained canned apricot halves (see Note)

¼ cup (about 1 ounce) sliced almonds

One 9- or 10-inch fluted tart pan with removable bottom

1 Set a rack in the lowest level of the oven and preheat to 350 degrees.

2 Unwrap the dough and place it on a floured work surface. Knead it lightly to soften it a little, then form it into a disk. Flour the dough and roll it to an 11- to 12-inch disk. Fold the dough in half and transfer it to the pan, lining up the fold with the diameter of the pan. Unfold the dough into the pan and press it well into the bottom and sides. Sever the excess dough at the rim of the pan with a bench scraper or the back of a paring knife. Set aside the crust while preparing the filling.

3 For the filling, combine the sugar and flour in a medium mixing bowl and whisk to mix. Whisk in the eggs, one at a time, whisking smooth after each addition, but without whisking so much that the mixture becomes aerated. You shouldn't see many bubbles. Whisk in the extracts and the half-and-half.

4   Arrange the apricot halves, cut sides up, in the tart crust, crowding them together to fill the crust. Use a large spoon to skim any foam from the top of the custard mixture, then carefully pour the custard over the apricots in the tart crust. Let the filling settle for a few minutes, then scatter the sliced almonds over the surface.

5   Bake the tart for about 45 minutes, or until the crust is baked through and the filling is set and no longer wobbly in the center.

6   Cool the tart on a rack. When it has cooled completely, unmold it according to the instructions on page 107 and slide the tart onto a platter. Cover loosely with plastic wrap.

SERVING: This rich tart stands alone.

STORAGE: Loosely cover the tart with plastic wrap and keep it refrigerated. Bring it to room temperature for an hour before serving. Wrap and refrigerate leftovers and bring to room temperature again before serving.

NOTE: Apricots may come packed in heavy or light syrup, apricot juice, or water. Use either of the last two for this recipe. The ones packed in juice have a more vivid flavor, but also more calories than those packed in water.

Per serving: 272 calories, 11 g total fat (36% of calories), 5 g saturated fat, 7 g protein, 38 g carbohydrates, 2 g fiber, 126 mg cholesterol, 146 mg sodium

Old-fashioned Raspberry Tart

Makes one 9- or 10-inch tart, about 8 servings

Serving this tart is a breeze: Both the dough for the crust and the custard filling may be prepared the day before and refrigerated. On the day you intend to serve the tart, bake the tart shell and leave it at room temperature. A few hours before serving, just spread the custard cream in the tart shell and top with the berries. You may substitute halved strawberries, rinsed and dried blueberries, or a combination of berries for the raspberries.

1 recipe Sweet Pastry Dough
(page 93)

PASTRY CREAM FILLING

1 cup fat-free milk

¼ cup sugar

3 tablespoons all-purpose flour

2 large eggs

1 teaspoon vanilla extract

2 tablespoons unsalted butter, softened

FINISHING

Three ½-pint baskets fresh raspberries, picked over but not washed (see Note)

2 tablespoons confectioners' sugar for dusting the top of the tart

One 9- or 10-inch fluted tart pan with removable bottom

1 Unwrap the dough and place it on a floured work surface. Knead it lightly to soften it slightly, then form it into a disk. Flour the dough and roll it to an 11- to 12-inch disk. Fold the dough in half and transfer it to the pan, lining up the fold with the diameter of the pan. Unfold the dough into the pan and press it well into the bottom and sides. Sever the excess dough at the rim of the pan with a bench scraper or the back of a paring knife. Refrigerate the tart crust until you are ready to bake it.

2 For the pastry cream filling, combine the milk and half the sugar in a small nonreactive saucepan. Bring to a boil over low heat. Combine the remaining sugar and the flour in a small mixing bowl and whisk well to mix. Whisk in the eggs, one at a time. When the milk boils, whisk about a third of it into the egg mixture. Return the remaining milk to a boil over low heat and add in the egg mixture in a stream, whisking constantly until the

pastry cream thickens and comes to a boil—large bubbles will burst slowly on the surface. Cook, whisking constantly, for about 20 seconds. Off the heat whisk in the vanilla and butter. Scrape the pastry cream into a glass or stainless steel bowl and press plastic wrap directly against the surface. Refrigerate the pastry cream until it is time to assemble the tart.

3 To bake the tart shell, set a rack in the middle level of the oven and preheat to 350 degrees. Remove the unbaked tart crust from the refrigerator and pierce it all over at ½-inch intervals with the tines of a fork. Bake the crust for about 15 minutes, or until it is a very light golden color. If you bake the crust too long, it will be very hard.

4 Cool the baked crust on a rack.

5 When you are ready to assemble the tart, spread the chilled pastry cream on the bottom of the tart crust, using a small metal offset spatula. Arrange the raspberries on the pastry cream (I just pile them on every which way rather than making straight rows). Unmold the tart according to the instructions on page 107. Right before serving, dust with all the confectioners' sugar.

SERVING: This beautiful tart needs no further adornment.

STORAGE: For advance preparation, see the headnote. Keep the assembled tart at a cool room temperature for up to several hours before you serve it. Wrap and refrigerate leftovers.

NOTE: Always keep berries refrigerated. Fluctuations in temperature cause condensation and can lead to the berries becoming moldy. I don't wash raspberries, as they become mashed and unappealing.

Per serving: 236 calories, 9 g total fat (34% of calories), 5 g saturated fat, 6 g protein, 35 g carbohydrates, 3 g fiber, 99 mg cholesterol, 138 mg sodium

Lemon Cheese Tart
with Strawberries

Makes one 9- or 10-inch tart, about 8 servings

The filling in this tart is like a thin layer of cheesecake. A traditional cheesecake usually weighs in at 500 to 800 calories a serving, but don't worry. This tart has all the richness of cheesecake at a fraction of the calories. The strawberries dress it up really well. Try raspberries or even figs, cut in quarters, when they are in season. By the way, if you forget to take the cream cheese out of the refrigerator, put it in a glass bowl and microwave it for about 10 seconds at a time until it softens.

1 recipe Sweet Pastry Dough (page 93)

CHEESE FILLING

12 ounces low-fat cream cheese, softened

⅓ cup sugar

1 teaspoon vanilla extract

2 teaspoons finely grated lemon zest

2 large eggs

2 large egg whites

⅔ cup fat-free plain yogurt, preferably Greek (see Sources, page 291)

FINISHING

1 pint strawberries, rinsed, drained, hulled, and halved

Confectioners' sugar for sprinkling

One 9- or 10-inch fluted tart pan with removable bottom

1   Set a rack in the lowest level of the oven and preheat to 350 degrees.

2   Unwrap the dough and place it on a floured work surface. Knead it lightly to soften it slightly, then form it into a disk. Flour the dough and roll it to an 11- to 12-inch disk. Fold the dough in half and transfer it to the pan, lining up the fold with the diameter of the pan. Unfold the dough into the pan and press it well into the bottom and sides. Sever the excess dough at the rim of the pan with a bench scraper or the back of a paring knife. Set aside the crust while preparing the filling.

3   Beat the cream cheese and sugar in the bowl of an electric mixer set on low speed, using the paddle attachment. Beat for about a minute, or until the mixture is smooth. Stop the mixer and scrape down the bowl and beater. Add the vanilla, lemon zest, and one of the eggs. Beat again on low speed until smooth. Scrape down again and add the other egg. Beat and scrape again. Follow the same procedure for adding the egg whites, one at a time. The low-speed beating prevents the filling from absorbing too much air and cracking after it's baked. All the scraping down of the bowl and beater helps to prevent lumps from forming in the filling.

4   Beat in the yogurt smoothly.

5   Use a large rubber spatula to give a final mixing to the filling and scrape it into the prepared pastry crust, smoothing the top.

6   Bake the tart for 25 to 35 minutes, or until the crust is baked through and the filling is set and no longer wobbly in the center.

7   Cool the tart on a rack. When it has cooled completely, unmold it according to the instructions on page 107 and slide the tart onto a platter. Cover loosely with plastic wrap.

8   Right before serving, arrange the strawberry halves in a ring inside the edge of the crust. Sprinkle the berries lightly with confectioners' sugar.

SERVING: You could always add a few more berries on the side of the tart wedge, but it certainly doesn't need anything more than that.

STORAGE: Keep the tart refrigerated and bring it to room temperature for an hour before finishing with the berries and serving. Wrap and refrigerate leftovers and bring to room temperature again before serving.

Per serving: 297 calories, 14 g total fat (42% of calories), 8 g saturated fat, 11 g protein, 33 g carbohydrates, 1 g fiber, 115 mg cholesterol, 276 mg sodium

Individual Apple Strudels

Makes 12 individual strudels

I have to confess that I used to load a ton of butter into any kind of strudel, whether it was made with homemade or packaged dough. And I was always disappointed that the dough wasn't as crisp as I expected it to be. I finally learned why when I asked Michelle Tampakis, our lead chocolate teacher at the Institute of Culinary Education, to show me how to make some traditional Greek filo pastries that are family recipes of hers. Michelle just sprinkled the dough very sparingly with melted butter. The smaller amount of butter made the dough bake up flavorful and perfectly crisp, and with fewer calories than my previous method of drowning the dough in butter. I also like to use a cooked filling for these strudels, which allows them to bake more quickly and stay crisp after baking, since most of the excess water has been eliminated from the filling before it is rolled up in the dough.

APPLE FILLING

3 pounds Golden Delicious apples, peeled, halved, cored, and each half cut into 8 wedges

½ cup light brown sugar

1 tablespoon unsalted butter

1 tablespoon strained fresh lemon juice

½ teaspoon ground cinnamon (or more, if you like cinnamon a lot)

½ cup Zante currants or dark raisins (about 2½ ounces)

½ cup (about 2 ounces) walnut pieces, toasted and coarsely chopped

ASSEMBLING THE STRUDELS

12 sheets packaged filo or strudel dough

6 tablespoons unsalted butter, melted

¼ cup fine, dry bread crumbs (packaged ones are okay)

One jelly-roll pan lined with parchment or foil

1   For the filling, combine all the ingredients except the walnuts in a heavy casserole or Dutch oven with a tight-fitting cover. Cover the pan and place it over medium heat until you can hear the mixture start to sizzle. Decrease the heat to medium-low and cook the apples for about 10 minutes, or until they are swimming in water. Uncover the pan and increase the heat to medium. Continue cooking for another 10 minutes or so, or until the juices have mostly evaporated. About half the apples will disintegrate and the remaining half will remain in soft wedges.

2   Remove from the heat and scrape the filling into a glass or stainless steel pan and cool it to room temperature. After the filling has cooled, fold in the walnuts. The filling may be prepared up to several days in advance; cover with plastic wrap and refrigerate.

3   When you are ready to assemble the strudels, set a rack in the middle level of the oven and preheat to 375 degrees.

4   Place a sheet of dough on the work surface. (Keep the remaining dough covered with plastic wrap and a damp towel.) Sprinkle the dough with some of the melted butter, using a pastry brush. Scatter a few pinches of bread crumbs on the buttered dough.

5   Arrange about ⅓ cup of the filling in a 5-inch length about an inch from the edge of the dough in the center. Loosely fold the uncovered sides of the dough over the filling. Roll the strudel, jelly-roll style, from the filled end, ending with the seam on the bottom. Repeat with the remaining dough and filling. See the illustration below.

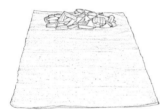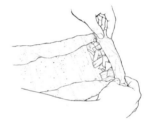

6   As they are made, transfer the strudels to the prepared pan. Brush the tops of the strudels with any remaining butter.

7   Bake the strudels for 25 to 30 minutes, or until they are well browned and crisp.

8   Cool the strudels on the pan on a rack.

SERVING: Serve the strudels at room temperature or warm. If you want to serve them warm, reheat them at 350 degrees for about 10 minutes. In Vienna, strudel is always served with a mountain of Schlag, unsweetened whipped cream. Any of the whipped-cream accompaniments in Chapter 8 would work well.

STORAGE: Keep the strudels at room temperature, loosely covered with plastic wrap. If leftovers become soggy, reheat them as described above to crisp them up.

Per strudel: 236 calories, 11 g total fat (42% of calories), 5 g saturated fat, 3 g protein, 34 g carbohydrates, 5 g fiber, 18 mg cholesterol, 115 mg sodium

VARIATION: *Plum and Ginger Strudels*   Use the filling from the Plum and Ginger Galettes (page 104), instead of the apple filling.

Lemon Meringue Tartlets

Makes 12 individual single-serving tartlets

This recipe uses a simple method for making individual tart shells—in a muffin pan with packaged filo dough. The resulting shells are tender and delicate with a fraction of the calories found in similar tart shells made of puff pastry. The lemon cream filling uses nonfat milk and whole eggs instead of the water and egg yolks that are typically used, contributing richness with very few additional calories from fat. Though you don't have to prepare these at the last minute, don't assemble them more than a few hours in advance or the filo shells will soften and the meringue might start to break down.

TARTLET SHELLS

12 sheets packaged filo or strudel dough

3 tablespoons unsalted butter, melted

2 tablespoons vegetable oil, such as corn or canola

2 tablespoons fine, dry bread crumbs

LEMON CREAM FILLING

2 cups fat-free milk

2/3 cup sugar

1/2 cup strained lemon juice

1/4 cup cornstarch

2 large eggs

1 tablespoon unsalted butter, softened

MERINGUE TOPPING

4 large egg whites

Pinch of salt

3/4 cup sugar

One 12-cavity standard muffin pan and 12 paper muffin cups sprayed with vegetable cooking spray

1   For the tartlet shells, set a rack in the middle level of the oven and preheat to 350 degrees.

2   Place one sheet of the filo dough on the work surface. Keep the others covered with plastic wrap and a damp towel. Mix the melted butter with the oil. To form one of the tartlet shells, sprinkle the sheet of dough with some of the butter and oil mixture, using a pastry brush. Sprinkle with a pinch or two of the bread crumbs.

3   Use a pizza wheel to cut the sheet of dough into two 5-inch squares. Cut the remaining dough outside the squares into 2-inch squares. Place one of the large squares on the other and arrange in one of the cavities of the prepared pan, lining up the center of the square with the center of the muffin cup. Use the small squares of dough to reinforce the bottom of each tartlet shell. Repeat with the remaining pieces of dough.

4   Before baking the shells, invert 12 paper muffin cups and spray them with vegetable cooking spray. Place a cup, right side up, in each of the tartlet shells to help them hold their shape during baking.

5   Bake the tartlet shells for about 20 to 25 minutes, or until they are a deep golden color and very dry and crisp.

6   Cool the shells in the pan on a rack.

7   While the shells are baking, prepare the lemon filling. Combine the milk and sugar in a medium nonreactive saucepan and whisk several times to distribute the sugar. Place over medium heat and bring to a boil. Whisk the lemon juice and cornstarch together in a medium mixing bowl and whisk in the eggs, one at a time. When the milk boils, whisk about a third of it into the cornstarch mixture. Return the remaining milk to a boil over low heat and whisk in the cornstarch mixture, continuing to whisk constantly until the filling comes to a boil (large bubbles will burst slowly on the surface). Continue cooking the filling for about 20 seconds, whisking constantly. Remove from the heat and whisk in the butter.

8   Scrape the filling into a glass or stainless steel bowl and press plastic wrap against the surface. Refrigerate the filling until it has cooled completely. You may prepare the filling the day before, keeping it refrigerated.

9   When you are ready to assemble the tartlets, carefully remove the papers from inside the tartlet shells and lift each shell from the muffin pan, pulling on the paper liner under it. Arrange the shells on a paper- or foil-covered jelly-roll pan. Spoon some of the filling into each shell, dividing it equally among them.

10   Right before you prepare the meringue, set a rack in the middle level of the oven and preheat to 400 degrees.

11 For the meringue, half fill a small saucepan with water and bring to a boil over medium heat. Combine the egg whites with the salt and sugar in the heatproof bowl of an electric mixer and whisk by hand for a few seconds to mix. Place the bowl over the boiling water and whisk constantly but gently until the egg whites are hot and the sugar is dissolved.

12 Place the bowl on the mixer and whip the meringue until it is risen in volume and almost completely cooled. The outside of the bowl will still feel slightly warm. (If you whip the meringue until it has completely cooled, it may become overwhipped and grainy.)

13 Spoon some of the meringue on the filling in each tartlet, dividing it equally among them. Use a small metal spatula to swirl the meringue on each tartlet, making sure that the meringue touches the inside of the crust all around or it may not stay in place after it is baked.

14 Bake the meringue-covered tartlets for about 5 minutes, just enough to color the meringue a light golden brown.

15 Cool the tartlets on a rack and keep them at a cool room temperature until you serve them.

SERVING: A few raspberries or small strawberries would look and taste good with these tartlets.

STORAGE: Keep the tartlets at a cool room temperature until you are ready to serve them, no more than a few hours. The acidity of the lemon juice in the filling will keep it from spoiling even though it is at room temperature. Refrigerate the leftovers, though the meringue will begin to break down before the next day. Meringue-topped desserts are best on the day the meringue is baked.

Per tartlet: 245 calories, 8 g total fat (29% of calories), 3 g saturated fat, 5 g protein, 38 g carbohydrates, 0 g fiber, 46 mg cholesterol, 148 mg sodium

VARIATION: *Lemon Raspberry Tartlets* Omit the meringue and cover the lemon filling with fresh raspberries, mounding them in the tartlet crust. Dust lightly with confectioners' sugar just before serving.

PUDDINGS, CUSTARDS, AND SOUFFLÉS

Most desserts are defined by great flavor. But custards put the emphasis on texture. The creamy richness of custards and puddings and the airy lightness of mousses and soufflés are what make these desserts so irresistible. Among the fancier custards here, you'll find my friend Mary Risley's stunning Cappuccino Brûlé (page 160) enriched with espresso, topped with meringue, and whimsically served in a coffee cup. Some of the more homey desserts include bread pudding, rice pudding, and tapioca, although the tapioca, inspired by the great French pastry chef Pierre Hermé, gets an elegant Asian twist when made with coconut milk and topped with mint and lime-scented pineapple. This chapter also includes my favorite low-calorie dessert, Individual Banana Soufflés (page 170). These single-serving desserts are easy to make, spectacular, and thoroughly satisfying, especially when served with chocolate sauce.

Don't be intimidated by the thought of making custards and soufflés. They're really quite simple if you keep a few things in mind. Even when excess fat is trimmed, custards can still retain their wonderfully rich creaminess. See the technique tips below to find out how.

Tips for Making Creamy Custards

1   Always start with a warm custard mixture. When baked, a warm mixture will set more quickly than a cold one and help to keep the custard from becoming rubbery in texture.

2   Avoid whisking too much. The eggs themselves and the milk that is incorporated should be whisked just enough to blend them. Otherwise, you will create excess foam on the surface, and if the foam is not removed it will make a tough crust on the top of the baked custard and feel grainy when the custard is eaten. Every recipe here directs you to skim any foam from the surface, but it's best to keep the mixture from foaming up in the first place.

3   Always fill molds for baked custards to within ¼ or ⅛ inch of the top. Custards always settle and flatten somewhat when unmolded, so if the molds are not well filled, the custards will be too short when unmolded.

4   Bake custards just until set and no longer jiggly. Be careful that the custards don't puff up in the oven. If they do, they have been overbaked and will separate (leak water) as they are cooling.

5   To gently cook the eggs, bake custards in molds that are set in a larger pan of water, also known as a water bath or bain-marie. Add water to the pan under the custards only to come no more than halfway up the sides of the molds. Too much water in the pan will delay the setting of the custards.

6   Be patient when baking. Custards set when the internal temperature reaches 160 degrees. Right up to that point they may still appear quite liquid. Check custards often, as the setting occurs all at once when it happens.

7   Always cool custards to room temperature before covering and chilling.

8   Always chill custards before serving. Chilling helps to finish setting the custards, and the cool temperature makes them taste light and delicate. Warm custard has an overly rich, eggy taste.

Successful Soufflés

Soufflés seem to intimidate home cooks more than most recipes. The truth is, they are easy to make. They're great for a casual meal, when it's not a bother to whip the egg whites and complete the mixing and baking while guests are at the table. Everything but the egg whites can be made in advance, and the molds can be greased and ready to go. Then it's simply a matter of whipping the egg whites, folding them into the batter, and putting the batter into the molds. Here are a few other hints.

1. A successful soufflé depends a lot on the preparation of the mold. If the mold is not well greased, the soufflé mixture will stick to the side of the mold and rise unevenly.

2. The most important place to grease is the very top rim of the mold. If the soufflé sticks at the top of the mold, the soufflé will develop a rounded top rather than rising high out of the mold with straight sides and a flat top.

3. If possible, make individual soufflés instead of one large soufflé. Individual soufflés always rise well—even if the egg whites are not perfectly whipped. Plus, they look more neat and elegant than a blob of soufflé spooned onto a plate from one large dish. Shallower gratin dishes can also be used for baking a soufflé and this is how the original soufflés were made. Frankly, the deep, wide shape of the classic soufflé dish is impractical for everything but a cheese soufflé, because it is very difficult to get the soufflé to climb so high over such a wide expanse at the same time. When making individual soufflés, fill the molds (4- to 6-ounce capacity are best) to within ¼ inch of the top.

4. Be careful not to overbake a soufflé. You may be tempted to let it rise higher and higher in the oven, but when a soufflé is overbaked it becomes hollow and dry inside like a popover. Fruit and egg-white soufflés will continue to rise so much if overbaked that they will become top heavy and break apart, and pieces will actually fall out of the mold onto the pan or oven floor beneath. Bake a soufflé only until it is well risen and nicely colored. The final test for doneness is to insert the top of a small spatula into the risen soufflé at the side where the soufflé begins rising out of the mold. Individual soufflés should be just slightly undercooked in the center but no more (they will finish cooking out of the oven from the residual heat of the molds). For large soufflés, rely on height, color, and pressing the center with a fingertip. The top should be firm and not feel too jiggly or liquidy underneath.

5. Always serve soufflés within seconds of taking them out of the oven. They begin to deflate immediately.

Working with Gelatin

Some of the desserts in this chapter are made with gelatin to help set the ingredients. Granulated gelatin that comes in an envelope is the common form used in the United States. I usually call for a single envelope, but if you happen to have a larger package of gelatin in your kitchen, one envelope of powdered gelatin equals about 2½ teaspoons. All of the instructions that follow are included in the recipes, but these hints are helpful reminders if you have never worked with gelatin before.

1   Gelatin is extremely sensitive to heat. Never place gelatin over direct heat or it will scorch immediately.

2   Always soak gelatin in cool water before using. Powdered gelatin is never added to a recipe directly from the envelope, except to sprinkle it on the surface of cool or room-temperature liquid to soak. This soaking allows each granule of gelatin to absorb liquid, swell, and soften.

3   After soaking, gelatin needs to be melted. It is typically melted over gently simmering water, then incorporated into the liquid that you want to set. Be careful that the liquid to be set is at room temperature but not cold. If the melted gelatin enters cold liquid, it may wither and set immediately, causing the liquid to form lumps, especially if a meringue is then folded in. Or the gelatin may set in uneven lumps and strands as soon as it is added to the cold liquid. Always incorporate melted gelatin into room-temperature liquid.

4   Sometimes soaked gelatin is added directly to a hot meringue mixture to melt it. In this kind of recipe, the high temperature of the heated egg-white mixture is enough to melt the gelatin. Always whisk in the gelatin thoroughly while the meringue mixture is still over the simmering water, to make sure the soaked gelatin melts.

Blancmange with Yogurt and Honey

Makes 6 servings

Desserts with a history always fascinate me. The traditional French dessert called *blanc-manger* is made from milk cooked with almonds, set with gelatin, with a lot of whipped cream folded in for richness and lightness. It has made a comeback in fancy Parisian pastry shops in the last five years or so, though the twenty-first-century version usually adds some finely diced fruit to the mixture. Hundreds of years ago blancmange was originally a sweet dish of capon cooked with almonds and spices. Late-medieval cooking abounded in recipes that had one foot in the main course and another in dessert. Eventually the capon vanished and unflavored gelatin replaced the jelling power of its bones and cartilage and blancmange became a dessert. My version here takes off in the direction of Greece and uses yogurt sweetened with honey and enriched with chopped, toasted walnuts and some real whipped cream (less than 1½ tablespoons per serving). Plus, it is served in glasses, eliminating the need to unmold it. If possible, use Greek yogurt for this dessert. It has a complex flavor and a creamy texture unequaled by any other kind of yogurt.

2 cups low-fat or fat-free yogurt, preferably Greek, at room temperature (see Note)

⅓ cup dark, flavorful honey, plus more for drizzling on the individual desserts

½ cup (about 2 ounces) walnut pieces, toasted and finely chopped by hand but not ground, divided

⅛ teaspoon ground cinnamon

Pinch of ground cloves

½ cup fat-free milk

1 envelope (about 2½ teaspoons) unflavored gelatin (see Note)

½ cup heavy whipping cream, very cold

6 footed dessert glasses or other stemmed glasses

1 Place the yogurt in a medium mixing bowl and whisk it smooth. Add the honey and whisk it in.

2   Reserve a tablespoon of the walnuts for garnishing the dessert, then stir the rest into the yogurt mixture along with the cinnamon and cloves.

3   Pour the milk into a small heatproof bowl and sprinkle the gelatin on the surface. Let the gelatin soak for 5 minutes.

4   While the gelatin is soaking, whip the cream by hand with a whisk to a soft peak. Set aside.

5   Melt the gelatin in the heatproof bowl over a small pan of simmering water until it is a clear liquid.

6   Stir about ½ cup of the yogurt mixture into the melted gelatin to cool the gelatin, then whisk the gelatin mixture into the yogurt. Quickly fold in the whipped cream.

7   Spoon the dessert into the glasses, dividing it equally among them. Cover the glasses with plastic wrap and chill them until you are ready to serve the dessert.

SERVING: Immediately before serving, drizzle a teaspoon of honey on each dessert and top with ½ teaspoon of the reserved walnuts.

STORAGE: You may prepare these the day before if you wish, but no earlier than that or they might become rubbery.

NOTE: Two things about the yogurt and the gelatin: First, the gelatin is used here mainly to prevent the dessert from separating and having the yogurt leak whey while it is waiting to be served. Also, it's important not to use ice-cold yogurt because the gelatin will set immediately when added to it, and the mixture will get lumpy when you fold in the whipped cream.

Per serving: 256 calories, 14 g total fat (49% of calories), 5 g saturated fat, 7 g protein, 30 g carbohydrates, 1 g fiber, 29 mg cholesterol, 64 mg sodium

Coconut Tapioca with Lime and Mint-scented Pineapple

Makes 6 servings

This is an adaptation of a recipe I saw Pierre Hermé, the top pastry chef in France, prepare at a demonstration class he gave at the Institute of Culinary Education in New York in 1996. It's a thin tapioca pudding, scented with a tiny bit of orange zest and coconut milk, and it serves as a base for a tangy pineapple salad flavored with lime and mint. I was fascinated by his use of homey old tapioca to create such an elegant dessert, but no more so than when it started turning up all over the place in New York. It wasn't until my first visit to Hong Kong in 2005 that I realized that coconut tapioca is a traditional Cantonese dessert, most often served with dices of pomelo, the Asian grapefruit, mixed in as we might mix raisins into a rice pudding. Be careful about cooking the tapioca for this recipe; it's meant to be very soupy so that it retains a delicate texture rather than becoming starchy.

COCONUT TAPIOCA

- ¼ cup (about 1 ounce) pearl tapioca, not the crushed or "instant" kind used in pie filling
- 1 cup whole milk
- 4-inch-long strip of orange zest, removed with a vegetable peeler
- 1 tablespoon sugar
- 1 cup canned Thai coconut milk
- ⅓ cup heavy whipping cream

PINEAPPLE SALAD

- 1 ripe pineapple (about 4 pounds)
- 2 tablespoons sugar
- Zest of 1 lime, removed with a zester (see Note)
- 1 tablespoon strained lime juice
- 6 mint leaves, rolled up and cut into the thinnest ribbons possible
- 6 rimmed soup plates for serving

1 Soak the tapioca in 2 cups cold water for an hour. Pour into a saucepan and cook over low heat, stirring occasionally, until almost all the water has evaporated. Add the milk, orange zest, and sugar and return to a boil. Regulate the heat so that the tapioca boils

very gently. Cook for about 20 minutes, or until the tapioca has thickened the liquid. Add the coconut milk and cream and return to a boil. Remove from the heat, pour the tapioca into a glass or stainless steel bowl, and cool to room temperature, stirring occasionally to prevent a skin from forming. Remove the orange zest. Press plastic wrap against the surface and keep the tapioca at a cool room temperature until serving time.

2 To pare the pineapple, use a sharp knife to cut away the leaves and the bottom. Stand the pineapple on the cut bottom and, following the contour of the pineapple, cut away the skin. Use a melon-ball scoop to remove any remaining "eyes," the recessed areas of skin. Stand the pineapple up on the bottom again and cut in half from top to bottom. Make a cut perpendicular to the first one to cut the pineapple into quarters, as in the illustration below.

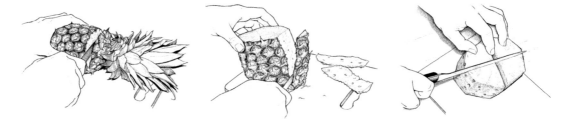

3 Lie one of the pineapple quarters on its rounded side and make a cut about ½ inch deep into the pointed top of the quarter, parallel to the cutting board, to remove the core. Repeat with the remaining quarters and the remaining pineapple. Cut each quarter again lengthwise for a total of 8 pieces, then cut each piece crosswise about ⅜ inch thick. Scrape the pineapple into a bowl and use a large rubber spatula to mix in the sugar, lime zest, lime juice, and mint. Cover and refrigerate until serving time.

4 Just before serving, drain the pineapple in a strainer over a bowl.

SERVING: Divide the tapioca equally among the bowls. Mound the drained pineapple in the center of each. Sprinkle the pineapple in each bowl with a couple of teaspoons of the drained juices. Serve immediately.

STORAGE: You may prepare the tapioca early on the day you intend to serve it if you can keep it at a cool room temperature. If you refrigerate the tapioca it will set quite firmly and the texture of the dessert will be ruined. Don't prepare the pineapple more than an hour or two in advance or the sugar and lime juice will draw all the moisture out of it.

NOTE: A zester is a small hand tool pictured in the illustration (right). It removes the zest from citrus fruit in long, thin strands without removing the bitter white membrane beneath the zest.

Per serving: 257 calories, 14 g total fat (49% of calories), 11 g saturated fat, 3 g protein, 33 g carbohydrates, 2 g fiber, 22 mg cholesterol, 27 mg sodium

Puddings, Custards, and Soufflés

Baked Indian Pudding

Makes 8 servings

An old-fashioned New England favorite, Indian pudding is a classic American dessert that just happens to be low in calories. I remember tasting it for the first time at the original Durgin Park restaurant in Boston back in the 1960s. As with many other starch-based puddings, success with this recipe depends on long, slow cooking. Some modern interpretations add a couple of eggs to help the pudding set quickly, but the real thing is made without eggs.

4½ cups whole milk, divided

3 tablespoons sugar

⅔ cup stone-ground yellow cornmeal

2 tablespoons unsalted butter

½ cup unsulfured molasses

½ teaspoon salt

1 teaspoon ground cinnamon

1 cup half-and-half for serving

One 1½- to 2-quart gratin dish or other baking dish, sprayed with vegetable cooking spray

1 Set a rack in the middle level of the oven and preheat to 325 degrees.

2 Place 3½ cups of the milk and the sugar in a heavy-bottomed pan, such as an enameled-iron Dutch oven. Place over low heat and bring to a simmer.

3 Meanwhile, whisk the cornmeal into the remaining 1 cup milk in a small bowl.

4 Whisk the diluted cornmeal into the hot milk a quarter at a time.

5 Continue cooking the cornmeal over very low heat, stirring often, for about 15 minutes.

6 Remove from the heat and stir in the butter, molasses, salt, and cinnamon.

7 Pour into the prepared pan. Bake the pudding for about 1 hour, or until it is set but still soft.

8 Cool the pudding briefly on a rack and serve immediately.

SERVING: Spoon the warm pudding onto plates or dessert bowls and top each serving with 2 tablespoons of the half-and-half.

STORAGE: This is best made right before serving. To get as much finished in advance as possible, you can prepare the recipe up to the end of step 5. About 2 hours before you intend to serve the pudding, warm up the cornmeal mixture and proceed with the recipe. Wrap leftovers and keep at a cool room temperature. They are best reheated in a microwave oven.

Per serving: 261 calories, 11 g total fat (38% of calories), 7 g saturated fat, 6 g protein, 35 g carbohydrates, 1 g fiber, 32 mg cholesterol, 369 mg sodium

Coach House Bread Pudding

Makes 8 servings

Leon Leonides's restaurant, the Coach House, was a Greenwich Village landmark until, sadly, it closed in 1993. Among the many excellent specialties served there, this bread pudding and a black bean soup were the restaurant's signature dishes. The Coach House was one of James Beard's favorite restaurants and he gave the recipe for its famous bread pudding in his book *American Cookery* (Little, Brown, 1972), from which this recipe is adapted. Unlike typical bread puddings that are mostly bread, which soaks up all the custard while the pudding is baking, this elegant version is made with thin slices of buttered bread which rise to the top when the custard is added and toast appealingly while the pudding is baking, leaving a thick layer of creamy custard beneath.

Sixteen ¼-inch-thick slices (about 8 ounces) crusty French or Italian bread

2 tablespoons unsalted butter, melted

5 cups fat-free milk

¾ cup sugar

3 large eggs

3 egg whites

2 teaspoons vanilla extract

One 2-quart gratin dish or other baking dish, sprayed with vegetable cooking spray and set in a larger pan, such as a roasting pan

1 Set a rack in the middle level of the oven and preheat to 325 degrees.

2 Use a narrow pastry brush (so it doesn't soak up all the butter) to brush one side of the bread slices with the butter. Arrange them slightly overlapping, if necessary, in the bottom of the prepared baking dish.

3 Combine the milk and sugar in a medium saucepan and whisk once or twice to mix. Place over medium heat and bring to a boil.

4 In a large mixing bowl, whisk the eggs and egg whites with the vanilla. Whisk in the milk in a stream, being careful not to overmix and create foam on the surface. Let the custard rest for 5 minutes, then use a ladle or a large kitchen spoon to remove any foam from the surface.

5 Strain the custard over the bread slices in the baking dish, being careful to pour the custard over all the bread slices so that they are evenly moistened.

6   Pour warm water into the larger pan to come about 1 inch up the side of the baking dish.

7   Bake the bread pudding for 45 to 55 minutes, or until the bread is a deep golden color and the custard is set.

8   Remove the pan from the oven and remove the baking dish from the hot water.

SERVING: Serve the bread pudding at room temperature. It's best to bake it and serve it within a few hours.

STORAGE: Keep the bread pudding at a cool room temperature, loosely covered with plastic wrap, for several hours before serving. Wrap leftovers in plastic and refrigerate. Bring to room temperature before serving again.

Per serving: 293 calories, 9 g total fat (28% of calories), 4 g saturated fat, 11 g protein, 40 g carbohydrates, 1 g fiber, 125 mg cholesterol, 291 mg sodium

Panna Cotta

Makes 8 individual servings

If there is one dessert that has taken the American restaurant world by storm in the past ten years, it's definitely panna cotta. It's easy to prepare, light and delicate, and almost infinitely variable with regard to flavoring. Modern panna cotta is made from a mixture of sweetened milk and cream that's set with gelatin to make a custardy dessert with neither eggs nor baking. The Italian name means "cooked cream," and I always assumed that the original version was made by reducing rich cream and pouring it into a mold to set. That may have been the case, but that method would carry the risk of easily scorching the cream and ruining the flavor of the dessert. It wasn't until I watched a BBC cooking show about food in Cornwall, in the south of England, that I found the answer. The show's host visited a farm wife who made clotted cream, that extra-rich, almost solid cream in which a spoon can easily stand on end, that is a specialty of the regions of Cornwall and Devonshire. High butterfat–content unpasteurized cream is poured into a porcelain baking dish, then placed in a large pan half filled with water. After the water comes to a boil, the heat is lowered and the cream is cooked by indirect heat for several hours. Afterward it's left to cool in the water overnight, resulting in a cream that could easily be unmolded, especially if it was cooked in small molds. The version here is the gelatin-based one. I'm sure the original was delicious, but it must have had at least a thousand calories a portion. I've chosen to leave the panna cotta in its mold for serving. This allows you to use much less gelatin than if it had to be unmolded, resulting in a much more delicate texture that isn't rubbery.

3 cups whole milk, divided

1 envelope (about 2½ teaspoons) unflavored gelatin

1 cup half-and-half

¾ cup sugar

Zest of 1 small lemon, stripped off with a vegetable peeler

1 whole vanilla bean

2-inch piece cinnamon stick

Eight 4-ounce ramekins or pot de crème cups, arranged on a jelly-roll pan

1. Early in the day or the day before you intend to serve the dessert, pour 1 cup of the milk into a small bowl and sprinkle the gelatin on the surface. Let the gelatin soak for 5 minutes.

2. Combine the remaining milk with the half-and-half and sugar in a medium saucepan. Whisk a couple of times to mix.

3. Add the lemon zest, vanilla bean, and cinnamon stick. Place the pan over low heat and bring to a simmer, whisking occasionally.

4. Once the mixture is heated, use a slotted spoon to remove the zest, vanilla bean, and cinnamon stick.

5. Scrape the soaked gelatin into the hot liquid and whisk it in. Let stand for 5 minutes, then whisk again.

6. Pour the mixture into the ramekins and refrigerate immediately.

7. After the panna cotta has set, stretch plastic wrap over the surface of the molds to cover them.

SERVING: Serve in the ramekins set on dessert plates. This is excellent with the Strawberries with Balsamic Vinegar and Tarragon on page 178.

STORAGE: If you intend to keep the individual desserts for more than a day, wrap them individually in plastic.

Per serving: 173 calories, 6 g total fat (31% of calories), 4 g saturated fat, 5 g protein, 24 g carbohydrates, 0 g fiber, 20 mg cholesterol, 51 mg sodium

VARIATIONS

Earl Grey Panna Cotta Replace the lemon zest with the zest of a small orange or half the zest of a large one. When you take the milk mixture off the fire, whisk in 1 tablespoon loose Earl Grey tea, which has much better flavor than teabags. (No teabags, please!) Let the tea steep in the hot milk mixture for exactly 5 minutes. Strain the milk mixture before adding the gelatin. Use the same procedure for jasmine tea, or sencha, Japanese green tea, omitting the zest and cinnamon but keeping the vanilla.

Espresso Panna Cotta Substitute ¾ cup strong brewed espresso for ¾ cup of the milk. The rest of the ingredients remain the same.

Viennese Caramel Custard

Makes 8 servings

Usually caramel custard has all the caramel on the outside, but this version has it inside and out. Some of the caramel is used for lining the molds, and the rest is used right in the custard mixture, providing a faint bittersweet flavor and an extra note of creaminess. Normally these are unmolded before serving, but if you want, you may serve them in the ramekins. The caramel will have melted to provide a bit of liquid sauce as you spoon out the custard. Please be aware that hot caramel can give you a bad burn, so be careful when preparing it. Just follow the directions in the recipe exactly and you won't have any problems.

CARAMEL

1¼ cups sugar

½ cup water, divided

CUSTARDS

3 cups whole milk

⅓ cup sugar

3 large eggs

4 large egg whites

1 tablespoon vanilla extract

Eight 4-ounce ramekins or custard cups, set in a small roasting pan or any pan about 2 inches deep

1   For the caramel, combine the sugar and 1 tablespoon of the water in a heavy saucepan. Stir well with a very clean wooden spoon, continuing to stir until the mixture resembles wet sand. Place the pan over low-medium heat and let the sugar start to melt. Gently shake the pan occasionally during the first few minutes of cooking to see if there is a layer of melted, lightly caramelized sugar on the bottom. As soon as the sugar begins to melt, stir occasionally so that the sugar at the bottom of the pan doesn't darken too much and become bitter.

2   Meanwhile, pour the remaining water into a small saucepan and just bring it to a simmer.

3   Once the sugar is about half melted, decrease the heat to low, so that the caramel doesn't cook too quickly. Continue to stir occasionally until the caramel appears deep

amber in the pan. To test for the right color, lift a spoonful of the caramel and look at the color as you let it drop back into the pan. The caramel in the pan always appears darker than it does dripping from a spoon. Once the caramel is a light amber color when dripped from the spoon, remove the pan from the heat and continue testing the color until the caramel appears dark enough. The caramel will continue cooking for a few minutes from the heat retained by the pan.

4   Wearing oven mitts, slowly pour the heated water into the caramel at arm's length, averting your face in case the caramel splatters. After all the water has been added, wait half a minute, then check to see that the caramel is entirely liquid. If there are some lumps of hardened caramel, return the pan to very low heat and stir occasionally to melt the lumps. Remove from the heat and let the caramel cool for a minute.

5   To coat the molds, pour about a tablespoon of caramel into one of the molds. Swirl the caramel around inside the mold, then invert it to a rack set over a piece of wax paper so that the excess drips out. Coat one mold at a time, reheating the caramel as necessary if it becomes too thick. (If you pour the caramel into all the molds, then start to swirl and coat them, the caramel in the first molds will have hardened before you can swirl it around.) Only use about half the caramel to coat the molds; the rest will be used in the custard mixture.

6   Set a rack in the middle level of the oven and preheat to 300 degrees. Arrange the molds in the roasting pan.

7   To make the custard mixture, place the pan of caramel on low heat and let it soften again for a minute. Add the milk and sugar and bring the mixture to a boil, stirring occasionally to make sure that all the caramel has dissolved into the milk.

8   Combine the eggs, egg whites, and vanilla in a mixing bowl and whisk well, but not until the eggs become foamy.

9   When the milk boils, remove the pan from the heat and pour the milk into the egg mixture in a thin stream, whisking constantly but not quickly to avoid creating too much foam.

10   After the milk has been added, let the mixture rest for 5 minutes, then use a ladle or large kitchen spoon to remove any foam from the surface. Pour the mixture into a lipped container, such as a 4-cup liquid measure, and fill the molds almost to the top.

11 Place the pan of molds on the oven rack and immediately pour 3 to 4 cups of warm water into the pan around the molds, so that the water comes about halfway up the sides of each mold. If the molds fit tightly in the pan, it may be necessary to remove one temporarily to have room to pour in the water.

12 Bake the custards for about an hour, or until they are completely set and no longer wobbly in the center.

13 Remove the pan from the oven and place it on a rack for 10 minutes to cool. Then remove the molds from the pan and cool them completely to room temperature. Individually wrap each mold in plastic and chill until you intend to serve them.

SERVING: Serve the custards in the mold or unmold them to dessert plates. To unmold, insert the point of a paring knife about ¼ inch deep between the mold and the custard. Run the knife all around the inside of the mold to loosen the top. Using your fingertips, ease the top of the custard to one side, letting some air into the space you create between the custard and the mold. The loosening is working when you can see some of the caramel in the bottom of the mold. Invert a dessert plate on the mold, then invert it again. Holding both the mold and plate firmly with both hands, quickly raise and lower the stack to unmold the custard. If it does not emerge easily from the mold, repeat the motion several times. Garnish with a dollop of whipped cream if you can afford the calories.

STORAGE: Keep refrigerated at all times. You may prepare these a day or two in advance, but don't keep them for more than 3 days total.

Per serving: 249 calories, 5 g total fat (18% of calories), 2 g saturated fat, 7 g protein, 44 g carbohydrates, 0 g fiber, 88 mg cholesterol, 91 mg sodium

VARIATIONS

Vanilla Caramel Custard Prepare the caramel with half the amount of sugar and water and line the molds with it. Increase the sugar in the custard mixture to ⅔ cup.

Rum Caramel Custard Prepare the custard mixture with or without the caramel in it. Add 2 tablespoons dark rum along with the vanilla.

Coffee Caramel Custard Substitute ¾ cup strong brewed espresso coffee for ¾ cup milk. Prepare the custard mixture with or without the caramel in it, adding a 2-inch piece of cinnamon stick before you bring the milk and coffee mixture to a boil. Remember to remove the cinnamon stick before pouring the custard mixture into the molds.

Get the Most from Spices and Herbs

Herbs and spices offer a quick route to flavor without calories. The usual suspects, like cinnamon, nutmeg, cardamom, cloves, allspice, anise, and vanilla, work well in everything from cakes to custards. Look also to spices like grated fresh ginger for cookies and loaf breads. Or try freshly ground black pepper on strawberry desserts. Whichever spice you choose, the technique used to extract its flavor is a key factor in the taste and look of the final dessert.

FLAVOR BY INFUSION. Steeping whole spices like vanilla beans and cinnamon sticks in hot liquids draws out their flavor while leaving behind the hard shell of the spice itself. This subtle flavoring technique is especially useful in sorbets, custards, and other elegant desserts where you just want the taste of the spice, not the look of it. To infuse, heat whole spices in hot milk, water, sugar syrup, or another liquid called for in the recipe. If the liquid is to be used at room temperature, gently heat the whole spice in the liquid, then let it soak off the heat until the liquid cools. Then remove the spent spice. Use the same technique with citrus zest to infuse the essence of lemon, lime, or orange into liquids.

INTENSIFY BY TOASTING. To extract a stronger flavor from whole spices, first toast them in a dry pan or on a baking sheet in a 300-degree oven. You can use the same pan later in the recipe (if you'll need to make a sauce, for instance) to capture some of the flavor left in the pan. To further intensify that flavor, grind the toasted spice to release its aromas immediately. This technique is useful for frozen desserts and sauces that won't be cooked long enough for the spice to release its essential oils through heating. To achieve a more subtle toasted spice flavor without seeing the spice itself in the dessert, toast whole spices first, then steep them in hot liquids as described above.

BUY WHOLE SPICES INSTEAD OF GROUND. For the most intense flavor, buy whole spices rather than preground ones, which have already released much of their fragrance. Use the spices whole and extract their flavor by infusion or toasting as described above. Or when a ground spice is called for, grind whole spices in a clean electric coffee mill or spice grinder. You can also grind spices with a mortar and pestle. Whole spices like nutmeg can be grated on the fine holes of a box grater.

USE FRESH HERBS. The only fresh herb to gain significant renown in the dessert world is mint. Even then, the herb typically goes uneaten on the dessert plate, relegated to the lonely role of garnish. But herbs have so much more to offer. Fresh basil, for instance, can bring a breath of sweet aroma to cakes, especially those served with a fruit coulis. Lemon verbena or lemon balm can lend the soft kiss of citrus to cakes, custards, and sorbets. The floral perfume of lavender can be gently infused into desserts made with cream or milk. If you don't want to see the herb's color speckled in a dessert such as cake, you can line the bottom of the cake pan with the fresh herb leaves before spooning in the batter. As the cake cooks, the aromatic oils in the leaves will be subtly released throughout the cake. Turn the cake out of the pan and peel off the herbs, leaving behind only the shadow of their bouquet.

Lemon Custard
with Raspberry Sauce

Makes 8 individual servings

A hint of lemon is perfect in a creamy baked custard. This one has no caramel to get in the way of the lemon flavor. Lemon juice would be too overpowering here. Instead, the subtle lemon flavor comes from steeping lemon zest in the milk for the custard mixture. The heat of the milk extracts the essential oil from the lemon zest skin, and the milk absorbs the delicate flavor. The hints of cinnamon and vanilla are there to support the lemon, not obscure it. Raspberry sauce makes a perfect complement. I wouldn't dream of serving the custard without it.

1 quart whole milk

⅔ cup sugar

3 large lemons

1-inch piece cinnamon stick

6 large eggs

2 teaspoons vanilla extract

1 recipe Cooked Raspberry Sauce, page 283

Eight 4-ounce ramekins or custard cups, set in a small roasting pan or any pan about 2 inches deep

1   Set a rack in the middle level of the oven and preheat to 300 degrees.

2   Combine the milk and sugar in a medium saucepan and whisk several times to mix. Bring the mixture to a boil over low to medium heat.

3   Use a vegetable peeler to remove just the yellow zest from the lemons in large strips. Do not include any of the white pith beneath the zest, which would impart a bitter flavor.

4   When the milk boils, remove it from the heat, add the lemon zest and cinnamon stick, and allow to steep for 5 minutes.

5   Combine the eggs and vanilla in a mixing bowl and whisk well, but not so quickly that the eggs become foamy. Strain the milk mixture into a lipped container, such as a 4-cup measure, to remove the strips of zest and the cinnamon stick.

6   Pour the milk into the egg mixture in a thin stream, whisking constantly but not quickly to avoid creating too much foam.

7   After the milk has been added, let the mixture rest for 5 minutes, then use a ladle or large kitchen spoon to remove any foam from the surface. Pour the mixture into the lipped container and fill the molds almost to the top.

8   Place the pan of molds on the oven rack and immediately pour 3 to 4 cups of warm water into the pan around the molds so that the water comes about halfway up the side of each mold. If the molds fit tightly in the pan, it may be necessary to remove one temporarily to have room to pour in the water.

9   Bake the custards for about an hour, or until they are completely set and no longer wobbly in the center.

10 Remove the pan from the oven and place it on a rack for 10 minutes to cool. Then remove the molds from the pan and cool them completely to room temperature. Individually wrap each mold in plastic and chill until you intend to serve them.

SERVING: Serve the custards in the molds or unmold them to dessert plates. To unmold, insert the point of a paring knife about ¼ inch deep between the mold and the custard. Run the knife all around the inside of the mold to loosen the top. Using your fingertips, ease the top of the custard to one side, letting some air into the space you create between the custard and the mold. Invert a dessert plate on the mold, then invert it again. Holding both the mold and plate firmly with both hands, quickly raise and lower the stack to unmold the custard. If it does not emerge easily from the mold, repeat the motion several times. Top each custard with a couple of spoonfuls of the raspberry sauce.

STORAGE: Keep refrigerated at all times. You may prepare these custards a day or two in advance, but don't keep them more than 3 days total.

Per serving: 263 calories, 10 g total fat (34% of calories), 4 g saturated fat, 10 g protein, 34 g carbohydrates, 3 g fiber, 275 mg cholesterol, 108 mg sodium

VARIATION: *Orange Custard* Substitute the zest of 2 large oranges and 1 small lemon for the lemon zest.

Snow Eggs

Oeufs à la Neige

Makes 8 servings

This dessert of individual meringue eggs with a custard sauce is commonly referred to as floating island, though a real floating island, or *île flottante* in French, is a large meringue baked in a caramelized mold, then cut into pieces and served with the custard sauce. Snow eggs are the perfect dessert for an elegant meal. They look appealing and have a combination of lightness and richness from the contrast of the meringue eggs and the custard sauce. I like to use water for poaching the meringue eggs. This is a departure from the classic method, but I don't think that poaching the meringue in milk adds anything to it.

SUGARED ALMONDS

½ cup (about 2 ounces) sliced almonds

2 teaspoons egg white (lightly whisk the egg white to break it up, then measure)

¼ cup sugar

CUSTARD SAUCE

3 cups whole milk

⅓ cup sugar

1 vanilla bean, split lengthwise

4 large eggs

MERINGUE EGGS

⅔ cup egg whites (from 4 to 5 large eggs)

Pinch of salt

¾ cup sugar

Caramel Lace (page 289), to decorate, optional

A small roasting pan for the almonds; a 10- or 12-inch sauté pan, straight-sided if possible, for poaching the meringue eggs; and a jelly-roll pan lined with paper towels for draining the meringue eggs

1   Preheat the oven to 325 degrees. For the sugared almonds, put the sliced almonds in a mixing bowl. Add the egg white and rub the almonds and egg white between the palms of your hands until the pieces of almond are evenly coated with the egg white. Add the sugar and toss the moistened almond pieces with it so that they are evenly coated with sugar.

2   Scrape the sliced almonds into the roasting pan and place them in the oven. Check and stir them with a flat-edged spatula, scraping them up from the bottom of the pan every 5 minutes while they are baking. As soon as the almonds begin to heat up, the sugar will melt and start to slide away from the almonds; be sure to stir often to keep the sugar stuck to the almonds rather than to the bottom of the pan. The almonds will eventually be evenly covered with a sugar crust and will also be toasted within. The whole process should take about 20 minutes.

3   Cool the sugared almonds in the pan and store them at room temperature in a plastic container that has a tight-fitting cover. You may prepare the almonds up to a week in advance.

4   For the custard sauce, combine the milk, sugar, and vanilla bean in a medium saucepan and whisk a couple of times to mix. Place over low heat and bring to a boil. Meanwhile, whisk the eggs in a medium mixing bowl to break them up. When the milk boils, whisk about a third of it into the eggs. Return the remaining milk to a boil and whisk in the egg mixture in a stream, whisking constantly. Cook the custard, whisking constantly, for about 20 seconds, or until it thickens slightly. It won't thicken a lot—most of the thickening takes place as the custard is cooling. If you cook the custard until the temperature gets too close to the boiling point, the eggs will scramble, since there is no starch in the custard to bind them with the milk.

5   Immediately strain the custard into a glass or stainless steel bowl. Cool the custard to room temperature, stirring occasionally to prevent a skin from forming on it. Cover the bowl with plastic wrap and chill the custard. You may prepare the custard the day before serving.

6   For the meringue eggs, bring about 1½ quarts of water to a boil in a sauté pan and turn off the heat under it. Cover the pan to retain the heat.

7   Half fill a saucepan with water and bring it to a boil. Combine the egg whites, salt, and sugar in the heatproof bowl of an electric mixer and whisk a couple of times by hand to mix. Decrease the heat under the saucepan so that it boils gently and place the mixer bowl over the pan. Whisk the egg-white mixture until it is hot and all the sugar has dissolved.

8   Place the bowl on the mixer and whip with the whisk attachment on medium speed until the meringue is cooled and risen in volume. Be careful not to whip the meringue too long or it will become grainy.

9   To form a meringue egg, use a large oval tablespoon to scoop up a spoonful of the meringue. Use another spoon of the same size to ease it off the first spoon and into the heated water in the sauté pan. Fill up the pan with 8 meringue eggs, using half the meringue in the bowl for them. Leave the meringue eggs to cook on the first side for half a minute, then use a wooden spoon to press down on one side of the meringue egg to flip it over. Quickly flip the remaining eggs, then go back to the first one turned over and remove it from the hot water with a slotted spoon, depositing it on the prepared jelly-roll pan. Repeat with the remaining meringue eggs. After poaching the first 8, skim any scraps of meringue from the water, reheat it to boiling, then turn off the heat. Use the second half of the meringue to make 8 more eggs, as for the first 8. Chill the meringue eggs uncovered and away from any foods with strong odors. You may prepare them early in the day for the evening, but not the day before.

SERVING: Pour a scant ½ cup of the custard sauce onto a dessert plate. Remove a meringue egg from the pan with a metal spatula and ease it onto the custard-covered plate a little off center. Set another one next to it so that they are centered on the plate. Sprinkle with a tablespoon of the sliced almonds. Break off a 2-inch piece of the caramel lace, if using, and lean it against the meringue eggs so it is standing up on the plate. Repeat with the remaining sauce, meringue eggs, and almonds.

Per serving: 264 calories, 9 g total fat (31% of calories), 3 g saturated fat, 9 g protein, 39 g carbohydrates, 1 g fiber, 115 mg cholesterol, 101 mg sodium

VARIATION: Substitute another sauce, such as a berry sauce or even a chocolate sauce (see Chapter 8), for the custard sauce.

Mary's Cappuccino Brûlé

Makes 12 servings (recipe may be halved easily)

This spectacular-looking dessert comes from my friend Mary Risley, owner of Tante Marie's Cooking School in San Francisco and author of *Tante Marie's Cooking School Cookbook* (Simon and Schuster, 2003). The premise is simple—a coffee-flavored custard baked in a coffee cup. After the custard is baked and cooled, it is topped with a fluffy meringue and returned briefly to the oven to color. When served, it looks like an inviting cup of cappuccino, complete with a foamy top.

COFFEE CUSTARD

2 cups whole milk

2 cups half-and-half

1 cup sugar

8 large egg yolks

Pinch of salt

1 tablespoon instant espresso coffee

MERINGUE

6 large egg whites

Pinch of salt

1¼ cups sugar

12 ovenproof coffee cups (cups that are low and wide work better than tall, narrow ones), set on a jelly-roll pan

1 Set a rack in the middle level of the oven and preheat to 325 degrees.

2 Combine the milk, half-and-half, and sugar in a medium saucepan and whisk a couple of times to mix. Place over medium heat and bring to a boil.

3 Whisk the egg yolks and salt in a bowl just to break them up.

4 When the milk mixture boils, remove it from the heat and whisk in the instant espresso.

5 Whisk the milk mixture into the egg yolks in a stream, whisking constantly but not quickly to avoid creating too much foam. Let the custard mixture rest for 5 minutes, then use a ladle or large kitchen spoon to remove the foam from the surface.

6 Divide the custard mixture evenly among the cups. Add about a cup of warm water to the pan under the cups.

7 Bake the custards for about 30 minutes, or until they are firm and set.

8   Place the pan on a cooling rack and let the custards cool for about 10 minutes. Remove them from the pan and cool them to room temperature. You can keep them at a cool room temperature for several hours before proceeding. Or cover and refrigerate the custards, but bring them to room temperature again before topping with the meringue. If you put the meringue on the cold custards, the cups might crack when you bake the meringue.

9   To make the meringue, half fill a medium saucepan with water and bring it to a boil over medium heat. Combine the egg whites, salt, and sugar in the heatproof bowl of an electric mixer and whisk once or twice to mix. Place the bowl over the pan of water and whisk constantly but gently until the egg whites are hot and the sugar is dissolved. Place on the mixer with the whisk attachment and whip the meringue until it is risen in volume and cooled. Be careful not to whip too long or the meringue may become grainy.

10 While the meringue is whipping, preheat the oven to 400 degrees.

11 Use a large soupspoon to put some of the meringue on each custard, swirling it upward with the point of the spoon. Make sure the meringue touches the rim of the cup all around to anchor it in place.

12 Return the cups to a dry jelly-roll pan and bake the meringue for 5 to 10 minutes, or until it is touched with golden streaks.

13 Cool on a rack and serve within a couple of hours or the meringue will begin to deteriorate.

SERVING: Place the cups on saucers and serve them with a teaspoon on the saucer.

STORAGE: Like all desserts topped with meringue, these don't keep very well. If you have leftovers, refrigerate them covered with plastic wrap. Condensation will probably develop between the meringue and the custard.

Per serving: 266 calories, 9 g total fat (30% of calories), 5 g saturated fat, 6 g protein, 42 g carbohydrates, 0 g fiber, 155 mg cholesterol, 66 mg sodium

Strawberry Mousse

Makes 8 servings

Excellent when made with flavorful height-of-the-season berries, this mousse may also be made with frozen strawberries or other berries (see the variations at the end of the recipe). I like cooking berries to make this type of mousse. It concentrates the flavor and makes the mousse less watery in general. Dairy richness comes from low-fat ricotta and lightness from a cooked meringue. Remember that the egg whites in the meringue are only partially cooked—if you are concerned about this, by all means use pasteurized egg whites. I haven't used a lot of gelatin here, just enough to keep the elements of the mousse from separating and give it a light set. This dessert is served in a glass and doesn't need to be unmolded, so the small amount of gelatin allows the mousse to retain a creamier and lighter texture.

2 pints strawberries, rinsed, hulled, and pureed in a blender

2 teaspoons strained lemon juice

1 tablespoon Kirsch (optional)

⅓ cup water

1 envelope (about 2½ teaspoons) unflavored gelatin

One 15- or 16-ounce container low-fat ricotta

⅔ cup egg whites (from 4 to 5 large eggs)

Pinch of salt

¾ cup sugar

1 pint strawberries, rinsed, hulled, and sliced, for assembling the dessert

8 medium footed dessert glasses or other stemmed glasses

1 Pour the pureed strawberries into a medium saucepan. Bring to a boil over medium heat and lower to a steady, gentle simmer. Cook the strawberry puree until it is reduced to 1½ cups. Cool the puree to room temperature and stir in the lemon juice and the Kirsch, if using.

2 Put the water into a small heatproof bowl and sprinkle the gelatin on the surface. Allow to soak for 5 minutes, then place the bowl over a small pan of simmering water and allow the gelatin to melt.

3 Combine the cooled strawberry puree, the gelatin, and the ricotta in a food processor or blender and pulse to mix smoothly. Pour the mixture into a large mixing bowl.

4 For the meringue, half fill a medium saucepan with water and bring it to a boil over medium heat. Combine the egg whites, salt, and sugar in the heatproof bowl of an electric mixer and whisk a couple of times to mix. Place the bowl over the pan of boiling water and whisk gently until the egg whites are hot and the sugar is dissolved. Place on the mixer with the whisk attachment and whip on medium-high speed until the egg whites are cooled completely. When you touch the outside of the bowl it won't be at all warm.

5 Fold the meringue into the strawberry mixture.

6 Spoon half the mousse into the glasses, dividing it equally among them. Top with half the sliced strawberries. Top the berries with the remaining mousse. Cover the glasses individually with plastic wrap and refrigerate them until serving time. Reserve the remaining sliced strawberries covered and refrigerated, and divide them equally among the mousses before serving.

SERVING: These mousses would be great with some crisp cookies, such as Almond Tuiles (page 250).

STORAGE: You may prepare the mousses the day before. They'll keep well as long as they remain refrigerated.

Per serving: 181 calories, 4 g total fat (20% of calories), 3 g saturated fat, 8 g protein, 30 g carbohydrates, 2 g fiber, 21 mg cholesterol, 104 mg sodium

VARIATION: *Raspberry, Blueberry, or Blackberry Mousse*

Substitute a quart of raspberries, blueberries, or blackberries for the strawberries. Everything else is the same, including layering the dessert with the same berries that you used to make the mousse. In the case of blueberries, cook the whole berries first with ⅓ cup water so they don't scorch, then puree and measure them. If necessary, you can reduce the puree further to concentrate it to 1½ cups. You can't puree raw blueberries, as they will immediately oxidize and turn brown. When using raspberries or blackberries, strain away the seeds after pureeing the berries.

Lemon Yogurt Mousse

Makes 8 servings

Though I usually like to drain yogurt before using it for a dessert, this mousse is lighter and more pleasant with a liquid yogurt base. There are many brands of fat-free yogurt available, but if you can find the Greek yogurt now being imported, it is the best of all. It has a creamy texture and a rich flavor that make it ideal for this recipe.

1 cup plain fat-free yogurt, preferably Greek (see Note)

1 teaspoon finely grated lemon zest

3 tablespoons strained lemon juice

1 teaspoon vanilla extract

¼ cup water

1 envelope (about 2½ teaspoons) unflavored gelatin

⅔ cup egg whites (from 4 or 5 large eggs)

Pinch of salt

¾ cup sugar

8 medium footed dessert glasses or other stemmed glasses

1   In a medium bowl, whisk together the yogurt, lemon zest and juice, and vanilla. Set aside.

2   Pour the water into a small bowl and sprinkle the gelatin on the surface. Let the gelatin soak while preparing the meringue.

3   For the meringue, half fill a medium saucepan with water and bring it to a boil over medium heat. Combine the egg whites, salt, and sugar in the heatproof bowl of an electric mixer and whisk a couple of times to mix. Place the bowl over the pan of boiling water and whisk gently until the egg whites are hot and the sugar is dissolved. Test the mixture with a fingertip. If it is so hot that you have to withdraw your finger immediately, it is ready. Scrape the soaked gelatin into the hot egg-white mixture and thoroughly whisk it in.

4   Place the bowl containing the meringue mixture on the mixer with the whisk attachment and whip on medium-high speed until the egg whites are cooled completely. When you touch the outside of the bowl it won't be at all warm. If the room is cool, be careful not to whip too long or the gelatin in the meringue might begin to set and cause lumps in the final mixture.

5   Fold the yogurt mixture into the meringue in a stream, folding quickly because the cold yogurt might make the gelatin start to set if you move too slowly or mix for too long.

6   Divide the mousse equally among the dessert glasses, cover each with plastic wrap, and refrigerate until serving time.

SERVING: Serve the mousse chilled and garnish it with a few raspberries or sliced strawberries, if desired, or a spoonful of any of the berry sauces in Chapter 8.

STORAGE: This mousse will keep perfectly well in the refrigerator for a day before serving.

NOTE: Yogurt is no longer packaged in 1-cup containers. Either buy a pint container or larger, or a couple of smaller ones for the recipe.

Per serving: 100 calories, 0 g total fat, 0 g saturated fat, 4 g protein, 22 g carbohydrates, 0 g fiber, 1 mg cholesterol, 47 mg sodium

Thanksgiving Day Pumpkin Mousse

Makes 8 servings

I love pumpkin pie, but this mousse runs a close second. It's perfect for a Thanksgiving dinner whether served alone or in the company of other, richer desserts. Of course, it's also appropriate any time during the fall entertaining season.

PERFECT LIGHT DESSERTS

8 ounces reduced-fat cream cheese, softened (see Note)

2 cups canned pumpkin puree (one 16-ounce can), not pumpkin pie filling

¼ teaspoon salt

1 teaspoon ground cinnamon

¼ teaspoon ground ginger

¼ teaspoon freshly grated nutmeg

⅓ cup water

1 envelope (about 2½ teaspoons) unflavored gelatin

⅔ cup egg whites (from 4 to 5 large eggs)

Pinch of salt

¼ cup granulated sugar

⅓ cup light brown sugar

8 medium footed dessert glasses or other stemmed glasses

1   Beat the cream cheese by machine with the paddle attachment on medium speed until it is soft and fluffy. Beat in the pumpkin puree in 3 or 4 additions, beating smooth after each addition and frequently scraping down the bowl and beater. Beat in the salt and spices.

2   Put the water into a small heatproof bowl and sprinkle the gelatin on the surface. Allow to soak for 5 minutes, then place the bowl over a small pan of simmering water and allow the gelatin to melt.

3   For the meringue, half fill a medium saucepan with water and bring it to a boil over medium heat. Combine the egg whites, salt, and sugars in the heatproof bowl of an electric mixer and whisk a couple of times to mix. Place the bowl over the pan of boiling water and whisk gently until the egg whites are hot and the sugar is dissolved. Place on the mixer with the whisk attachment and whip on medium-high speed until the egg whites are cooled completely. When you touch the outside of the bowl it won't be at all warm.

4   Quickly whisk the warm dissolved gelatin into the pumpkin mixture.

5   Fold the meringue into the pumpkin mixture.

6   Spoon the mousse into the glasses, dividing it equally among them. Cover the glasses individually with plastic wrap and refrigerate them until serving time.

SERVING: These mousses would be great with some crisp cookies, such as Almond Tuiles (page 250).

STORAGE: You may prepare the mousses the day before. They'll keep well as long as they remain refrigerated.

NOTE: If you forget to soften the cream cheese, unwrap it and place it in a microwave-safe bowl. Microwave it for about 10 seconds at a time until it is softened.

Per serving: 165 calories, 5 g total fat (27% of calories), 3 g saturated fat, 6 g protein, 23 g carbohydrates, 2 g fiber, 16 mg cholesterol, 268 mg sodium

167

Puddings, Custards, and Soufflés

Fresh Strawberry Soufflé

Makes 8 generous servings

This dessert would be ideal with ripe, height-of-season berries. But, let's face it, the strawberry season is short and most of the time we have to depend on less flavorful, somewhat bland berries from California or Florida. So I developed this recipe specifically using these year-round berries. The high water content of these berries is what diminishes their flavor, so I have used more of them in the recipe than usual and cooked them down to concentrate the flavor. This method works perfectly, and I'm sure you'll be happy with the results.

3 pints (about 2 pounds) fresh strawberries, rinsed and hulled

¾ cup sugar, divided

1 tablespoon strained lemon juice

1 tablespoon Kirsch

6 large egg whites

Pinch of salt

One 1½- to 2-quart shallow, straight-sided gratin dish or baking dish, sprayed with vegetable cooking spray and the sprayed surface coated with sugar

1   Puree the berries in the blender or food processor.

2   Combine the pureed berries with ½ cup of the sugar in a large saucepan and bring to a boil, stirring occasionally, over medium heat. Decrease the heat to low and let the puree boil gently to reduce to 2 cups.

3   Pour the puree into a glass or stainless steel bowl and cool it to room temperature, stirring occasionally. After the puree has cooled, stir in the lemon juice and Kirsch. You may prepare the puree the day before or early in the day that you intend to serve the soufflé. Cover and refrigerate the puree if you are going to keep it more than a few hours before baking the soufflés. Remember to remove it from the refrigerator and bring it to room temperature for an hour before proceeding.

4   When you are ready to bake the soufflé, set a rack in the middle level of the oven and preheat to 400 degrees.

5   To whip the egg whites, combine them with the salt in the bowl of an electric mixer. Whip the egg whites with the whisk attachment until they are white, opaque, and just beginning to hold their shape. Increase the speed to medium-high and whip in the remaining ¼ cup sugar in a slow stream, continuing to whip the egg whites until they hold a soft, glossy peak.

6   Fold the strawberry puree into the egg whites in a stream, working quickly, but not folding too vigorously or the egg whites will deflate. Gently scrape the soufflé batter into the prepared baking dish.

7   Bake the soufflé for about 20 minutes, or until it is well risen and the top is nicely colored. Serve immediately.

SERVING: Use a large serving spoon to scoop out portions of the soufflé onto dessert plates. Serve with a strawberry sauce or a cream from Chapter 8.

Per serving: 127 calories, 0 g total fat, 0 g saturated fat, 4 g protein, 28 g carbohydrates, 2 g fiber, 0 mg cholesterol, 43 mg sodium

VARIATIONS

Individual Strawberry Soufflés See the recipe for Individual Banana Soufflés on page 170 for instructions and timing for baking individual soufflés.

Raspberry Soufflé Use six ½-pint baskets fresh raspberries or three 10-ounce packages frozen raspberries instead of the strawberries. Puree them and strain away the seeds before cooking down the puree with the sugar.

Blueberry Soufflé Use 2 pints fresh blueberries, rinsed and picked over. Cook the whole berries with the sugar and ¼ cup water until they come to a boil and break apart. Puree in a blender or food processor (be careful handling the hot puree), then return to the heat to continue reducing as above. After the puree cools, stir in ¼ teaspoon ground cinnamon and 1 tablespoon lemon juice. It isn't possible to puree the blueberries before cooking them, since they will oxidize and turn brown.

Individual Banana Soufflés

Makes 8 individual soufflés

This might just be my favorite low-fat and low-calorie dessert. It's brimming with fresh banana flavor and it has a smooth, creamy, and satisfying texture. Make sure to use really ripe bananas for this recipe. They should be speckled with little black spots. If the bananas are not fully ripe, the soufflés will lack flavor and richness.

4 large (about 1¼ pounds) ripe bananas

¼ cup water

¾ cup sugar, divided

⅛ teaspoon ground cinnamon

6 large egg whites

Pinch of salt

8 individual 4-ounce ramekins, sprayed with vegetable cooking spray and the sprayed surface coated with sugar, set on a jelly-roll pan

1 Peel the bananas and cut them into 2-inch chunks. Puree them in a food processor or blender. Measure 2 cups puree and set aside.

2 Combine the water and ½ cup of the sugar in a medium saucepan. Bring to a boil over low heat, stirring occasionally to make sure that all the sugar dissolves. At the boil, cease stirring and continue cooking for about 2 minutes, or until the syrup thickens.

3 Add half the banana puree to the syrup, stirring it in. If the syrup hardens and forms some lumps of sugar, continue stirring until they dissolve. Stir in the remaining puree and increase the heat to medium. Cook the puree, stirring occasionally, until it comes to a full boil. Remove from the heat and stir in the cinnamon.

4 Pour the banana puree into a glass or stainless steel bowl and cool it to room temperature, stirring occasionally. You may prepare the puree the day before or early in the day that you intend to serve the soufflés. Cover and refrigerate if you are going to keep the puree more than a few hours before baking the soufflés. Remember to remove it from the refrigerator and bring it to room temperature for an hour before proceeding.

5 When you are ready to bake the soufflés, set a rack in the middle level of the oven and preheat to 400 degrees.

6   To whip the egg whites, combine them with the salt in the bowl of an electric mixer. Whip the egg whites with the whisk attachment until they are white, opaque, and just beginning to hold their shape. Increase the speed to medium high and whip in the remaining ¼ cup sugar in a slow stream, continuing to whip the egg whites until they hold a soft, glossy peak.

7   Fold the banana puree into the egg whites in a stream, working quickly, but not folding too vigorously or the egg whites will deflate. Evenly divide the soufflé batter among the individual molds.

8   Bake the soufflés for 12 to 15 minutes, or until they are well risen and the tops are nicely colored.

9   Immediately remove the pan from the oven. Use oven mitts to transfer the ramekins to dessert plates and serve the soufflés immediately.

SERVING: Any chocolate sauce from Chapter 8 would make the perfect accompaniment here.

Per serving: 136 calories, 0 g total fat, 0 g saturated fat, 1 g protein, 35 g carbohydrates, 2 g fiber, 0 mg cholesterol, 1 mg sodium

VARIATION: *Chocolate Banana Soufflé* Add 4 ounces bittersweet chocolate, cut into ¼-inch pieces, as you remove the banana puree from the heat. Let stand for a minute to melt the chocolate, then whisk smooth. Proceed as above.

FRUIT DESSERTS

The summer months are a delight for anyone who loves to bake. The bright flavors and vivid colors of sun-drenched foods need little window dressing. When summer fruits are ripe, I try to keep desserts as simple as possible and focus on the flavor of the fruit itself. The recipes in this chapter reflect that philosophy. Some of them avoid cooking altogether and simply enhance the fresh fruit with aromatics. Peaches in Red Wine (page 176) and Strawberries with Balsamic Vinegar and Tarragon (page 178) let you enjoy these summer gems at their peak with no need for a stove or heat source. Other dishes, such as Grilled Curried Mangoes with Ginger Ice Milk (page 186), benefit from briefly cooking the fruit, then dressing it up with flavorful accompaniments. A selection of compotes, a cobbler, and a crisp are also included.

Always use fruit that's in season. There's no sense making pear compote in June or baked peaches in January. Fruit is best enjoyed at the height of ripeness. Not only does it taste better, but according to nutritionists, it's also richer in nutrients than fruit picked before it is fully ripened. Turn to page 209 to see what fruits ripen in what months.

When choosing fruit, look for the best specimens you can find. Most ripe fruit will be quite plump and healthy-looking with no signs of browning, molding, or wrinkling. Smell the fruit before buying it. A rich fragrance lets you know that the fruit is bursting with flavor. If the fruit is rock hard or odorless, pick up and smell a few other pieces.

To hasten the ripening of stone fruits, such as peaches, plums, and apricots, put the fruit in a paper bag along with an apple or banana, each of which emits natural ethylene gas that helps to ripen the fruit. Fold down the top of the bag and leave it at room temperature overnight or until the fruit is no longer hard but firm-tender when touched and fragrant when sniffed.

All of the fruit desserts in this chapter taste good on their own, but some can be paired with other recipes to create more elaborate presentations. The Roasted Pear Compote (page 196) and Italian Poached Whole Oranges (page 188) make good company alongside "plain" cakes, such as Vanilla Bean Chiffon Cake (page 53) and Orange Angel Food Cake (page 50). Or dress up these fruit desserts with a crisp cookie from Chapter 7 or one of the sherbets, gelati, or ice milks in Chapter 6.

Peaches in Red Wine

Makes 4 servings

This preparation is deceptively simple, and if you've never tried the combination, I urge you to do so. When I was growing up, we never had dessert except on special occasions, but after we finished our meal, there would always be a bowl of fruit placed on the table. During the summer we often had melon. My mother would bring the whole melon to the table and my father would ceremoniously halve the melon, scrape out the seeds, and cut the melon into slices for us. We even picked on the seeds afterward, splitting the hull between our front teeth to extract the sweet little "nut" within. But during the height of summer, we would occasionally have a special treat of these peaches macerated in red wine, but only after a special kind of large, very round, yellow, porous-fleshed peach, which we called *precoca* in our southern Italian dialect, became available.

Nowadays I use any perfectly ripe local peaches to make this dessert, and it always brings back memories of the family table during the long summers of my childhood. By the way, as a child I ate the peach slices, but did not drink the wine, not because I wasn't allowed to, but because I just liked the peaches. I've given instructions for preparing these peaches right at the table as we did it back then. If you prepare them too far in advance, they absorb too much wine and all the freshness and simplicity of this dessert vanish.

2 large, perfectly ripe peaches, rinsed and dried

2 teaspoons sugar, divided

8 peach leaves, if available, rinsed and dried

About a pint (2 cups) good red wine, but nothing fancy

4 large stemmed glasses

1   At the table, before you begin your meal, halve and pit the peaches. Cut a peach half into 6 or 8 slices, letting the slices fall directly into one of the glasses. Repeat with the remaining peach halves and glasses.

2   Sprinkle ½ teaspoon sugar over the peach slices in each glass. Add a couple of peach leaves, if you have them.

3   Fill up the glasses with the wine, just to cover the peaches.

SERVING: Place one of the glasses at each guest's or family member's place at the table. After the meal is finished, eat the peaches with a fork, then drink the wine, if you wish.

STORAGE: This dessert is meant to be made and consumed within an hour.

Per serving: 146 calories, 0 g total fat, 0 g saturated fat, 1 g protein, 18 g carbohydrates, 2 g fiber, 0 mg cholesterol, 6 mg sodium

177

Fruit Desserts

Strawberries with Balsamic Vinegar and Tarragon

Makes 4 servings

Strawberries and balsamic vinegar are a classic Italian dessert combination. The addition of the tarragon provides a faintly sweet aniselike note that combines very well with the berries and the sweet rounded flavor of the vinegar. Combining strawberries with tarragon is an idea that comes from my friend Claudia Fleming Hayden, the award-winning former pastry chef of Gramercy Tavern in New York City. She writes about it in her book *The Last Course* (Random House, 2001), where she uses a similar strawberry mixture as a shortcake filling.

Real balsamic vinegar is always expensive and always comes in a very small bottle. Though the kind you can easily find in the supermarket is not bad for adding to a vinaigrette, the real thing is always used alone, and in very small quantities. The presence of the sugar in this recipe could permit you to use a lesser quality of balsamic, but I would be wary of two things when purchasing it: Don't buy anything that wasn't actually made in Modena, in the Emilia-Romagna region of Italy. And please don't use white balsamic vinegar, an aberration developed to cash in on the public's love of all things Italian. The process used to make balsamic vinegar will always yield a dark brown product, so white balsamic vinegar is as impossible and nonsensical as white beef or white cocoa powder.

2 pints (about 1¼ pounds) fresh strawberries, rinsed, hulled, dried, and halved

3 tablespoons sugar

3 large sprigs fresh tarragon, rinsed, stemmed, dried, and gently sliced with a very sharp stainless steel knife into ¼-inch lengths

½ teaspoon balsamic vinegar, the best you can afford

Small sprigs of tarragon as a garnish

1   Place the strawberries in a medium glass or stainless steel bowl and add the sugar. Use a small rubber spatula to fold the berries and sugar together so that the berries are evenly coated.

2   Scatter the tarragon and the vinegar over the surface of the berries and fold them in.

3   Cover and refrigerate the salad until about an hour before you intend to serve it.

4   Remove the salad from the refrigerator as you begin your meal so that it will no longer be ice-cold when you serve it.

5   Divide the salad among glass dessert bowls or short-stemmed glasses, garnish with a small sprig of tarragon if you wish, and serve immediately.

SERVING: You can make this into a fancy dessert by adding an ice from Chapter 6 or one of the creams in Chapter 8, or both. If you do that, serve the salad on a dessert plate with the ice and/or cream on the side.

STORAGE: Please don't make this too far in advance. Freshness matters here. If it is made too far ahead of serving time, the complex flavors at work in this dessert will begin to dissipate. Cover and refrigerate any leftovers, but they won't be as flavorful the next day. Any leftovers are best consumed standing up in front of the refrigerator at 3 A.M.

Per serving: 85 calories, 0 g total fat, 0 g saturated fat, 1 g protein, 21 g carbohydrates, 3 g fiber, 0 mg cholesterol, 2 mg sodium

Not Just Any Fruit Salad

Makes 8 generous servings, about 1 cup each

Fruit salad can be as exciting—or boring—as you want to make it. Here the method for preparing it is simple but a departure from what most people do. First you make a syrup that's scented with vanilla bean, lemon juice, and Kirsch, the cherry brandy that brings out an exquisite perfume in any fruit with which it comes in contact. Then, as the fruit is cut, you add it to the syrup. The syrup sweetens the fruit lightly, and the hints of lemon juice and Kirsch enhance its natural flavor. This salad may be varied infinitely, depending on what type of ripe fruit is available, as long as you use about 8 cups of fruit. In summer, the hardest part may be deciding what not to put into the salad, but during the winter you can prepare a good fruit salad with apples, pears, oranges, pineapple, and seedless grapes.

SYRUP

2 cups water

¾ cup sugar

1 vanilla bean, not split

1 tablespoon strained lemon juice

1 tablespoon Kirsch or white rum

FRUIT MIXTURE

1 tart apple, peeled, halved, cored, and cut into ¾-inch dice

¼ (about 8 ounces) cantaloupe, peeled, seeded, and cut into ¾-inch dice

¼ (about 12 ounces) honeydew, peeled, seeded, and cut into ¾-inch dice

1 ripe freestone peach, peeled, pitted, and cut into ¾-inch dice

2 red plums, halved, pitted, and cut into ¾-inch dice

1 cup (about 6 ounces) seedless grapes (green, red, or a combination), stemmed and halved

½ cup (2 to 3 ounces) blueberries, rinsed and picked over

½ cup (2 to 3 ounces) raspberries, picked over

1 cup strawberries (half of a pint basket, or about 5 ounces), rinsed, hulled, and halved

1 To prepare the syrup, combine the water, sugar, and vanilla bean in a medium saucepan and bring to a boil, stirring occasionally, to make sure all the sugar is dissolved. When the mixture boils, remove from the heat and pour into a large mixing bowl. Cool the syrup to room temperature and stir in the lemon juice and Kirsch.

2 Put the bowl of syrup near your cutting board and add each fruit to the syrup as it is cut. Use a large rubber spatula to fold the mixture together occasionally so that the fruit is coated with the syrup. Add all the fruit to the bowl except the raspberries and strawberries.

3 Cover the bowl with plastic wrap and refrigerate until ready to serve. Refrigerate the raspberries and strawberries·in a separate bowl.

4 When you are ready to serve the fruit salad, use the rubber spatula to gently fold in the raspberries and strawberries.

SERVING: Serve the fruit salad in glass dessert bowls or short-stemmed glasses. The salad is colorful enough that it needs no garnish. Maida's Skinny Whipped Cream (page 285) makes a nice accompaniment.

STORAGE: Keep the fruit salad refrigerated at all times, except when you are serving it.
It will keep for several days.

Per serving: 161 calories, 0 g total fat, 0 g saturated fat, 1 g protein, 40 g carbohydrates, 3 g fiber, 0 mg cholesterol, 14 mg sodium

Fruit Fondue

Makes 12 servings

Everyone loves fruit dipped in chocolate, so here's an easy and fun way to enjoy it. The chocolate fondue part is as simple to prepare as boiling water, and the only other work is cutting and skewering the fruit. Use two short wooden skewers side by side for each piece of fruit to keep it from wobbling and falling into the fondue while you're dipping it. You don't necessarily need lots of special equipment for fondue, but if you want to purchase a fondue pot, see Sources on page 291. Any attractive saucepan, such as one made from copper or enameled iron, would be fine, too. The fruit assortment can easily vary according to the season; just avoid using anything really watery, such as melon or pineapple.

FRUIT ASSORTMENT

- 1 tablespoon strained lemon juice
- 2 tablespoons water
- 1 large eating apple, such as Red Delicious or Braeburn
- 1 large ripe pear, such as Bartlett or Anjou
- 2 firm-ripe freestone peaches
- 2 firm-ripe red plums
- 2 medium seedless oranges or tangerines
- 1 pint strawberries

CHOCOLATE SAUCE

- ½ cup heavy whipping cream
- ¾ cup fat-free milk
- ⅓ cup light corn syrup
- Pinch of salt
- 12 ounces bittersweet chocolate, cut into ¼-inch pieces
- 1 teaspoon vanilla extract

1   For the fruit, combine the lemon juice and water in a large mixing bowl. Halve and core or pit the apple, pear, peaches, and plums. Without peeling them, cut them into 1-inch cubes. As the fruit is cut, add it to the bowl and toss it with the lemon water. Cover the bowl with plastic wrap and refrigerate while preparing the other fruit.

2   For the oranges, cut the peel away completely to expose the flesh, as in the illustration (right). Cut the oranges in half from stem to blossom end, then cut each half again in the same direction. Cut across the first cuts into 1-inch cubes. Place the orange cubes in a bowl, cover, and refrigerate.

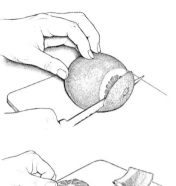

3   Rinse, drain, and hull the strawberries. Place in a bowl, cover, and refrigerate.

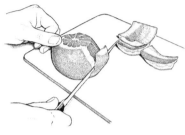

4   At a convenient time before serving, drain the lemon water from the fruit and let the fruit dry for a few minutes on a jelly-roll pan covered with paper toweling.

5   Arrange the cubes of fruit and the strawberries on bamboo skewers, either one fruit or several on each skewer. Arrange the skewered fruit on a platter, cover with plastic wrap, and refrigerate. If using fondue forks, don't bother with the skewers.

6   For the chocolate sauce, combine the cream, milk, corn syrup, and salt in a medium saucepan and whisk several times to mix. Place over medium heat and bring to a boil. Remove from the heat and allow to cool for 5 minutes. Add the chocolate, let stand for 2 minutes for the chocolate to melt, then whisk until smooth. If you prepare the sauce ahead, cover it and leave it at room temperature. Reheat the sauce over low heat, stirring often before serving.

SERVING: Bring the platter of fruit and the pot of sauce to the table at the same time. Invite guests to dip the fruit into the sauce, letting the excess drip back into the pan before removing the fruit from the sauce. If the sauce starts to thicken to the point where it doesn't coat the fruit evenly, gently reheat it over low heat.

Per serving: 264 calories, 16 g total fat (55% of calories), 8 g saturated fat, 3 g protein, 37 g carbohydrates, 5 g fiber, 14 mg cholesterol, 21 mg sodium

Grilled Curried Mangoes with Ginger Ice Milk

Makes 8 servings

Curry powder is a natural with mangoes, since they are both important foods in India. Grilling the mangoes softens them slightly and intensifies their sweetness. The curry powder helps to bring out their heady perfume. This is the perfect dessert for those times when you already have the outdoor grill fired up for cooking your main course.

GRILLED MANGOES

4 large mangoes (or 6 to 8 if they are small)

1 tablespoon light or pure olive oil

¼ teaspoon salt

1 tablespoon best-quality curry powder (see Sources, page 291)

3 tablespoons sugar

FINISHING AND PLATING

1 recipe Ginger Ice Milk (page 233)

½ cup (1 to 1½ ounces) sweetened shredded coconut, lightly toasted

One jelly-roll pan for holding the mango slices before and after grilling

1   Preheat an outdoor grill or stovetop grill pan to medium-high.

2   To cut the mangoes, slice off one of the pointed ends on one of them and stand it up on a cutting board. Using a sharp knife, make a cut from top to bottom, removing one of the wide, rounded sides of the mango from the center pit but keeping the side intact. Repeat with the other side. Also cut away any of the mango flesh around the narrow edge of the pit; reserve that flesh for a fruit salad or another use. See the illustration (right).

3   Peel the two halves removed from the mango, then repeat with the remaining mangoes.

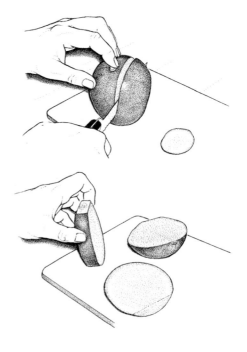

4   Mix the olive oil and salt in a bowl and add the mango halves. Use your hands to mix thoroughly so that all the mango pieces are evenly coated with the mixture.

5   Grill the mango halves for a minute on each side, using a large spatula to turn them. Remove them to the jelly-roll pan.

6   Mix the curry powder and sugar and evenly sprinkle half on the mango halves. Turn the mango halves over and sprinkle the remaining curry mixture on the other side.

7   Return the mango halves to the grill for 30 seconds on each side. Remove the mangoes to the pan again.

8   To assemble the dessert, place a warm grilled mango half on each of 8 dessert plates. Place a scoop of the Ginger Ice Milk next to it, then sprinkle with a tablespoon of the toasted coconut.

SERVING: Serve immediately. For advance preparation, you may do the first grilling before serving time, then add the curry mixture and do the second grilling right before serving.

STORAGE: Cover and refrigerate any leftover mango halves if you are not using all 8. They are also good cold.

Per serving: 189 calories, 5 g total fat (24% of calories), 1 g saturated fat, 4 g protein, 36 g carbohydrates, 2 g fiber, 45 mg cholesterol, 109 mg sodium

Italian Poached Whole Oranges

Makes 8 servings

In Italy, you'll see these oranges on a serving table next to a basket of fresh fruit and a couple of dessert specialties in almost every restaurant you visit. And with good reason: They're flavorful, light, and inexpensive to prepare; all you need is a few oranges and some sugar. I've tried many different ways of flavoring the syrup for cooking the oranges, but I think the supplementary flavors detract from the fresh, clean flavor of the oranges. The most you'll want to add to these is a sprinkling of orange liqueur just before serving. This preparation is perfect for early in the new year when not much fruit is in season besides the new crop of citrus fruit from California and Florida.

8 medium seedless oranges	2 cups sugar
2 cups water	3 tablespoons orange liqueur, such as Cointreau

1   Rinse the oranges, then use a vegetable peeler to remove the zest in long strips. Stack up 3 or 4 of the strips and use a chef's knife to slice the zest into thin julienne strips, as in the illustration below. Place the zest in a small saucepan and cover with water. Place on medium heat and bring to a boil. Pour through a strainer and discard the liquid. Put the zest in a small bowl and cover it with water. Set aside.

2   Place one of the oranges on a cutting board and use a small, sharp knife to cut away the stem and blossom ends. Stand the orange on one of the cut ends and cut from top to bottom, following the contour of the orange and cutting close to the skin to remove all of the skin and expose the flesh below, as in the illustration on page 184.

 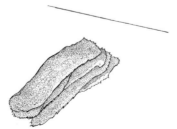 

3　Choose a medium saucepan that will hold 3 or 4 oranges at a time. Combine the water and sugar in the pan and stir well to mix. Place the pan on medium heat and bring the syrup to a boil, stirring occasionally to make sure that all the sugar has dissolved. When the syrup boils, add 3 or 4 of the oranges and continue to cook, gently turning the oranges all around in the syrup occasionally, until the syrup returns to a boil. Lift the oranges out of the syrup with a slotted spoon and put them in a single layer in a shallow bowl. Repeat with the remaining oranges until all of them have been poached.

4　Keep the syrup over the heat and add the blanched orange zest. Return the syrup to a gentle boil and cook the zest in the syrup for about 2 minutes.

5　Pour the syrup and the zest over the cooked oranges. Cover them (even if they are still warm) and cool to room temperature. After the oranges have cooled, refrigerate until serving time.

6　Just before serving the oranges, arrange them on a round or oval platter. Use a slotted spoon to remove the zest from the syrup and scatter it over the oranges. Pour about a third of the remaining syrup over the oranges and sprinkle with the orange liqueur.

SERVING: Serve the oranges in dessert bowls or on plates. Spoon some of the syrup on the platter over each orange. There may be a temptation to add cream or ice cream, but this dessert doesn't really need anything that would detract from the fresh flavor of the oranges.

STORAGE: See step 5 above. Cover and refrigerate leftovers.

Per serving: 287 calories, 0 g total fat, 0 g saturated fat, 1 g protein, 73 g carbohydrates, 7 g fiber, 0 mg cholesterol, 1 mg sodium

Fruit Desserts

Poached Pineapple with Kirsch

Makes 8 servings

Nothing brings out the flavor of pineapple better than Kirsch. Even though Kirsch is made from cherries, it has a natural affinity for pineapple, and while it doesn't make the pineapple taste like cherries, it emphasizes pineapple's intrinsic flavor.

It's much easier now than it used to be to find a good, ripe pineapple. Even so, the ripest ones still benefit from a gentle poaching and the addition of a couple of aromatic elements, such as the vanilla and Kirsch used here. Great on its own with some crisp cookies, this can also be transformed into a more elaborate dessert with the addition of an ice from Chapter 6.

2 large pineapples (about 4 pounds each)

4 cups water

1½ cups sugar

1 vanilla bean, not split

3 tablespoons Kirsch

One 5- or 6-quart enameled iron Dutch oven or other wide pan with a tight-fitting cover

1 To pare the pineapples, use a sharp knife to cut away the leaves and the bottom of each fruit. Stand the pineapple on the cut bottom and, following the contour of the pineapple, cut away the skin. Use a melon-ball scoop to remove any remaining "eyes," the recessed areas of skin. Stand the pineapple up on the bottom again and cut in half from top to bottom. Make a cut perpendicular to the first one to cut the pineapple into quarters, as in the illustration on page 142.

2 Lay one of the pineapple quarters on its rounded side and make a cut about ½ inch deep into the pointed top of the quarter, parallel to the cutting board, to remove the core. Cut into large dice. Repeat with the remaining pineapple quarters.

3   Combine the water, sugar, and vanilla bean in the pan and bring to a boil over medium heat, stirring occasionally to make sure all the sugar dissolves. At the boil, add the pineapple. If the pineapple is not covered completely by the syrup, add a little water to cover it. Invert a small heatproof plate, such as a salad plate, on the pineapple to keep it submerged in the syrup. Return the syrup to a boil, reduce the heat slightly, and let it boil for 1 minute. Cover the pan and allow the pineapple to cool in the liquid.

4   After the pineapple has cooled, use a slotted spoon to remove the pieces to a shallow bowl. Add the vanilla bean to the bowl and sprinkle with the Kirsch. Add only enough of the syrup to cover the pineapple halfway. Cover the bowl with plastic wrap and refrigerate.

5   To serve, place some pineapple in a dessert cup and top it with a spoonful of the syrup.

SERVING: An ice or crisp cookies would be good with this.

STORAGE: You may keep the pineapple as in step 4 until serving time, but no longer than a day. For longer storage, put the pineapple into a plastic container with a tight-fitting lid and fill the container with the remaining syrup. It will keep well for 4 or 5 days in the refrigerator.

Per serving: 118 calories, 0 g total fat, 0 g saturated fat, 1 g protein, 29 g carbohydrates, 2 g fiber, 0 mg cholesterol, 2 mg sodium

Strawberry Rhubarb Compote with Sugared Pecans

Makes about 10 servings

This was one of the desserts on the lunch menu for the opening of Windows on the World in 1976. We would put big crystal bowls of the compote and the sugared pecan topping on the buffet table every day; if it was a slow day, maybe some of the compote would come back with the other leftovers, but the sugared pecans never did. We suspected that the dining room staff made quick work of any remaining at the end of lunch. This compote is a good way to make a fine strawberry dessert when there are no sweet local strawberries and all you can get are hothouse berries that have less flavor.

COMPOTE

- 2 cups water
- 1 cup sugar, divided
- 1 vanilla bean, left whole (see Note)
- 1-inch length cinnamon stick
- 1 medium lemon
- 3 pints (about 2 pounds) strawberries, rinsed and hulled
- 2 pounds fresh rhubarb, leaves removed, rinsed, and cut into 1½-inch pieces

SUGARED PECANS

- 1 cup (about 4 ounces) pecan pieces
- 1 tablespoon egg white
- ½ cup sugar

A small roasting pan or other baking dish for baking the sugared pecans

1 For the compote, combine the water and ½ cup of the sugar in a large pan that has a tight-fitting cover, such as an enameled iron Dutch oven. Add the vanilla bean and cinnamon stick and bring the syrup to a full rolling boil over medium heat.

2 Using a vegetable peeler, remove the zest from the lemon in large strips.

3   Remove the pan from the heat and add the strips of lemon zest and the strawberries. Gently shake the pan to make sure that the berries are submerged. Cover the pan and leave it at room temperature. The strawberries will cook from the heat left in the syrup and the pan. Check the strawberries after about an hour; they should be sufficiently softened.

4   Set a rack in the middle level of the oven and preheat to 325 degrees.

5   While the strawberries are cooling, prepare the sugared pecans. Put the pecans in a mixing bowl. Beat the egg white lightly with a fork and add to the pecans. Rub the pecans and egg white between the palms of your hands until the pecans are evenly coated with the egg white. Add the sugar and toss the moistened pecans with it so that they are evenly coated with it.

6   Scrape the pecans into the roasting pan and place them in the oven. Check and stir them with a flat-edge spatula, scraping them up from the bottom of the pan every 5 minutes while they are baking. As soon as the pecans begin to heat up, the sugar will melt and start to slide away from the pecans; be sure to stir often to keep the sugar stuck to the pecans, rather than to the bottom of the pan. The pecans will eventually be evenly covered with a sugar crust and will also be toasted within. The whole process should take about 20 or 30 minutes.

7   Cool the sugared pecans in the pan. Store them in a plastic container with a tight-fitting cover at room temperature until you are ready to use them. Or freeze for longer storage.

8   When the strawberries have softened, lift them out of the syrup to a large, shallow bowl or dish (the idea is to have the berries in as thin a layer as possible so that they don't all sit atop each other and get crushed). Cover and refrigerate.

9   Remove the strips of lemon zest and cinnamon stick from the syrup left in the pan, but leave in the vanilla bean. Add the remaining ½ cup sugar and stir well to mix. Place the pan over medium heat and bring to a full rolling boil. Stir in the rhubarb and cook on medium heat for 10 seconds. Remove from the heat, cover the pan, and let the rhubarb cool in the syrup. Check the rhubarb after an hour; if it is tender, pour it, syrup and all, into a shallow bowl and let it cool to room temperature. If it is not tender, reheat the rhubarb and syrup mixture just until it reaches 160 degrees, then remove it from the heat and let cool again. Avoid overcooking the rhubarb or it will break up into strings in the syrup.

10   After the rhubarb and syrup are completely cooled, remove the vanilla bean and add the strawberries. Cover and chill.

SERVING: Pour the chilled compote into a large glass bowl and the sugared pecans into a smaller one. Use a large serving spoon or ladle to serve portions of the compote into dessert bowls. Top each serving with a spoonful of the sugared pecans.

STORAGE: Keep the compote refrigerated at all times, except when serving. The compote is good for up to about 5 days. Keep the sugared pecans at room temperature. Freeze any leftover sugared pecans if you don't have another immediate use for them.

NOTE: After you have removed the vanilla bean from the syrup, rinse it off and let it dry at room temperature for a couple of hours. Wrap in plastic, freeze, and use again.

Per serving: 240 calories, 8 g total fat (30% of calories), 1 g saturated fat, 2 g protein, 42 g carbohydrates, 5 g fiber, 0 mg cholesterol, 8 mg sodium

Fruit Desserts

Roasted Pear Compote

Makes 8 generous servings

This compote is loosely based on a component of a dessert that the great Parisian pastry chef Pierre Hermé prepared when he visited the Institute of Culinary Education to give a demonstration class in 1996. Lightly sweetened pears are combined with aromatic flavorings and roasted until tender. You can approach this preparation in a couple of ways: as the main component of a simple fruit dessert, served with one of the garnish creams in Chapter 8 or one of the ices in Chapter 6; or as an accompaniment to a plain cake, such as Orange Angel Food Cake (page 50), or Vanilla Bean Chiffon Cake (page 53). Either way it is delicious and satisfying. If you're going to serve this as a simple fruit dessert, cut the pears into wedges as described below. If you want to use it to accompany a cake, then cut the pears into 1-inch dice. You'll get twice as many portions from the recipe if you use it as an accompaniment.

½ cup apricot preserves

½ cup white wine or vermouth

2 tablespoons dark, flavorful honey

2 tablespoons unsalted butter, cut into 8 pieces

1 teaspoon grated orange zest

1 teaspoon grated lemon zest

¼ teaspoon ground cinnamon

⅛ teaspoon ground ginger

4 large (1½ to 2 pounds) ripe Bartlett pears

¼ cup pine nuts or coarsely chopped walnut pieces

One 9 x 13 x 2-inch Pyrex baking dish or another of similar size, sprayed with vegetable cooking spray

1   Set a rack in the middle level of the oven and preheat to 375 degrees.

2   Combine the preserves, wine, and honey in a large mixing bowl and use a large rubber spatula to mix them together.

3   Add all the remaining ingredients except the pears and the pine nuts and stir well to mix.

4   Peel one of the pears with a vegetable peeler, halve it, and use a melon-ball scoop to remove the core, blossom end, and the interior stem that runs between the core and the top of the pear. Cut each pear in half lengthwise into 3 equal wedges. Add the wedges to the bowl containing the seasonings. Repeat with the remaining pears.

5   Gently fold the pear wedges and the seasonings together so that the pears are evenly coated. Scrape the mixture into the prepared baking dish and scatter the pine nuts on top.

6   Bake the compote for 45 minutes to an hour, or until the pears are tender and the juices have reduced and thickened slightly. Use a wide metal spatula to move the compote around and to scrape the sides of the pan clean several times during baking. Be gentle or the pear wedges will break apart.

7   Cool the compote in the pan on a rack.

8   Scrape the cooled compote into a glass or stainless steel bowl and cover it tightly with plastic wrap. Refrigerate if not serving within a few hours, but bring to room temperature before serving.

SERVING: See suggestions in the headnote.

STORAGE: This keeps well in the refrigerator for 4 days or so.

Per serving: 183 calories, 6 g total fat (30% of calories), 2 g saturated fat, 1 g protein, 31 g carbohydrates, 2 g fiber, 8 mg cholesterol, 8 mg sodium

VARIATIONS

Roasted Apple or Peach Compote   Substitute tart, firm apples, such as Golden Delicious or Granny Smith, or firm-ripe peaches, for the pears. Cut the apple or peach halves into quarters, rather than thirds.

Roasted Pear Tart   Dice the pears instead of cutting them into wedges and make sure that the juices are well reduced by the time the pears are cooked. Substitute the diced-pear compote for the mincemeat in the Holiday Mincemeat Tart on page 114. Or use the apple or peach variation above, making sure that you dice the fruit before cooking it.

Peaches Baked
with Macaroon Filling

Makes 5 servings (2 peach halves per serving)

This is a classic Italian dish often known as Pesche alla Piemontese, peaches in the style of the Piedmont, though I'm not sure exactly why. Piemonte is where the rare and costly white truffles come from, but I've never read or heard that it is a peach-growing area. And as far as the macaroon filling is concerned, hazelnuts would be more like it: Piemonte is covered with hazelnut trees. In any case, this is an easy, light, and excellent summer dessert for the middle to the end of the season when you feel like doing something more than just eating a perfectly ripe, juicy peach as is. You can turn this into an elegant plated dessert with a cream or sauce from Chapter 8 and/or an ice from Chapter 6. You'll need some packaged Italian amaretti (macaroon cookies) for the filling, and they're pretty easy to find. If you don't see the most common brand, Lazzaroni, packed in bright red tins, there are other brands available, packaged in cellophane bags.

6 large, medium-ripe freestone peaches (1½ pounds), rinsed, halved, pitted, but not peeled

¼ cup sugar

10 packaged amaretti, finely crushed

1 large egg yolk

2 tablespoons unsalted butter, melted

One 2- to 2½-quart enameled iron gratin dish or other similar-size baking dish, sprayed with vegetable cooking spray

1   Set a rack in the middle level of the oven and preheat to 350 degrees.

2   Arrange 10 of the peach halves in the prepared pan, rounded side down.

3   Coarsely dice the 2 remaining peach halves and place them in a food processor fitted with the metal blade. Pulse to chop finely, but stop before the peaches become a smooth liquid.

4   Scrape the chopped peaches into a medium mixing bowl. Stir in the sugar, crushed amaretti, and egg yolk.

5   Cover the cut side of each peach half with some of the amaretti mixture, distributing it among the peaches with a large spoon. The mixture is a little runny (more so if the peaches are more pureed than chopped). Don't worry if some of the topping runs off the peaches.

6   Use a small pastry brush to sprinkle the melted butter over the topping on each peach half.

7   Bake the peaches for about 45 minutes, or until the peaches have softened and the topping is a deep golden color.

8   Cool on a rack.

SERVING: Serve the peaches warm, at room temperature, or lightly chilled. See also the serving suggestions in the headnote.

STORAGE: Keep at room temperature until you intend to serve the peaches, or cover with plastic and refrigerate until about an hour before serving. Cover and refrigerate leftovers.

Per serving: 290 calories, 10 g total fat (31% of calories), 7 g saturated fat, 3 g protein, 51 g carbohydrates, 2 g fiber, 55 mg cholesterol, 85 mg sodium

VARIATION: *Pere alla Piemontese*   Substitute ripe Bartlett pears for the peaches, leaving the skin on the pears, but removing the core, blossom end, and inner and outer stems with a melon-ball scoop.

Gratin of Summer Berries

Makes about 6 servings

Here's a simple, elegant way to transform a few baskets of berries from the supermarket or farmers' market into something memorable. If you can find gooseberries and/or red currants, by all means add them to the mix. As long as you use 5 or 6 cups of berries for this dessert, you can vary them any way you want.

BERRIES

1 pint strawberries, rinsed, hulled, and sliced

1 pint blueberries, rinsed and picked over

Two ½-pint baskets raspberries

SABAYON TOPPING

5 large egg yolks

½ cup sugar

¼ cup orange juice

2 tablespoons orange liqueur, such as Cointreau

½ cup (about 1½ ounces) sliced almonds

One 1½-quart gratin dish or other baking dish, sprayed with vegetable cooking spray

1 Set a rack in the upper level of the oven and preheat to 400 degrees.

2 Gently toss the berries together in a large bowl without breaking them up and place in the prepared gratin dish.

3 For the sabayon, whisk together the egg yolks, sugar, orange juice, and liqueur in a heatproof bowl and place over a small pan of simmering water. Whisk the mixture until it thickens slightly. Remove from the heat and continue whisking for about 1 minute.

4 Evenly nap the berries with the sabayon. Sprinkle with the almonds.

5 Bake the sabayon for 5 to 10 minutes, or until the topping is well colored.

6 Serve immediately.

SERVING: Spoon this out into dessert bowls or onto dessert plates. If you have individual gratin dishes or shallow ramekins, use them instead of the large gratin dish to make individual servings; reduce the baking time by about a minute or so. This dessert could also be cooled and chilled before serving. Some crisp cookies such as Almond Tuiles (page 250) make a wonderful accompaniment.

STORAGE: See Serving, above. Cover leftovers with plastic wrap and refrigerate them.

Per serving: 226 calories, 8 g total fat (32% of calories), 2 g saturated fat, 5 g protein, 38 g carbohydrates, 6 g fiber, 171 mg cholesterol, 8 mg sodium

Apple and Blackberry Cobbler

Makes 8 generous servings

This is a simplified version of the famous British pie for which I gave the classic recipe in my book *A Baker's Tour*. But the one here is faster and easier to prepare. Use this recipe for any combination of fruits you like—peaches and raspberries, apricots and sweet or sour cherries, two or three different varieties and colors of plums, or just blueberries.

FILLING

3 pounds tart apples, such as Granny Smith, peeled, halved, and cored, and each half sliced into 8 or 10 wedges

3 tablespoons all-purpose flour

¾ cup sugar

½ teaspoon ground cinnamon

2 cups (about 10 ounces) fresh or individually frozen blackberries

BISCUIT TOPPING

2 cups cake flour (spoon flour into dry-measure cup and level off)

1 tablespoon baking powder

½ teaspoon salt

⅓ cup sugar

1 large egg

1 cup low-fat buttermilk

Sugar for sprinkling the top crust

One 2- to 2½-quart enameled iron gratin dish or other baking dish, sprayed with vegetable cooking spray

1 Set a rack in the upper third of the oven and preheat to 375 degrees.

2 Place the sliced apples in a bowl. Mix together the flour and sugar and scatter a couple of tablespoons in the bottom of the prepared baking dish. Toss the rest of the flour and sugar mixture in with the apples, mixing well to coat all the apples.

3 Scrape the apples into the baking dish and gently press them into an even layer. Sprinkle with the cinnamon, then with the blackberries.

4   For the topping, sift the cake flour, baking powder, and salt into a mixing bowl and use a large rubber spatula to stir in the sugar. Quickly beat the egg and buttermilk together with a fork, then use the spatula to fold the liquid into the flour mixture and make a soft batter.

5   Use a large spoon to deposit spoonfuls of the batter all over the top of the fruit mixture. Use a small metal offset spatula to connect all the puddles of batter and spread the top smooth. Sprinkle the top with sugar, using no more than a couple of teaspoons.

6   Bake the cobbler for about 35 minutes, or until the topping is a deep golden color and the fruit is bubbling.

SERVING: Serve the cobbler warm or at room temperature, but not hot. Use a large serving spoon to scoop it out of the baking dish, making sure to transfer it to the plate with the topping where it belongs—on top of the fruit. Spoon any extra fruit next to the portion, not on top of it.

STORAGE: Keep at room temperature for a few hours after it is baked, but this dessert is meant to be served on the day it is baked. Cover leftovers with plastic wrap and keep at room temperature.

Per serving: 295 calories, 1 g total fat (3% of calories), 0 g saturated fat, 5 g protein, 67 g carbohydrates, 8 g fiber, 28 mg cholesterol, 337 mg sodium

Blueberry Slump

Makes 8 servings

A traditional New England recipe, this dessert may be made with an equal quantity of peeled, sliced apples or peaches, or even sour cherries. After the fruit and sugar come to a boil in a pan that has a tight-fitting cover, the surface is topped with baking powder biscuits. You then cover the pan and the fruit continues to cook while the biscuits steam from the heat trapped in the pan, somewhat like a cobbler made on the stovetop instead of in the oven, a technique that probably dates from the time when not everyone had an oven in their kitchen. Nowadays, it's still a practical way to make it because you can avoid turning on the oven on a hot day.

BERRY MIXTURE

3 pints blueberries, rinsed and picked over

¾ cup sugar

½ cup water

1 teaspoon ground cinnamon

BISCUITS

1 ¾ cups all-purpose flour (spoon flour into dry-measure cup and level off)

3 teaspoons baking powder

½ teaspoon salt

4 tablespoons (½ stick) unsalted butter, cold and cut into 8 pieces

¾ cup whole milk or buttermilk

One 2- or 3-quart enameled iron Dutch oven or other wide pan with a tight-fitting cover

1   For the berry mixture, combine the berries with the remaining ingredients in the Dutch oven and stir well to mix. Place over low heat, stirring occasionally, and bring to a boil.

2   While the berries are beginning to cook, prepare the biscuits. Put the flour, baking powder, and salt in the bowl of a food processor fitted with the metal blade. Pulse 3 or 4 times to mix. Add the butter and pulse repeatedly until the butter is finely mixed with the dry ingredients. Add the milk and only pulse 5 or 6 times to form a soft dough.

3   Invert the bowl to a floured work surface and carefully remove the blade. Use your hands to press the dough into a 9-inch square, about ½ inch thick. Use a bench scraper or a knife to cut the dough into nine 3-inch squares. Cut one of the squares into 8 equal pieces and stick one of those pieces to the bottom of each of the 8 other 3-inch squares.

4   When the berry mixture starts to simmer, arrange the biscuits on the surface. Regulate the heat so that the berry mixture simmers very gently, then cover the pan. Allow the slump to continue cooking for about 25 minutes to steam the biscuits. After a few minutes, check to make sure that the berry mixture isn't simmering too quickly or it may scorch. After 20 minutes or so of steaming, test one of the biscuits with a toothpick, which should emerge dry. If it is not dry, continue cooking for another 5 to 10 minutes.

5   Remove the pan from the heat and place it on a rack. Cool to lukewarm or room temperature.

SERVING: Bring the pan to the table and use a large spoon to scoop out one of the biscuits. Top it with some of the berry mixture. Serve one of the creams in Chapter 8 on the side.

STORAGE: This dessert is really meant to be made and served within a short time; it doesn't keep well. If you have leftovers, place the biscuits in a bowl and pour the remaining berry mixture over them. Cover and keep at room temperature no longer than overnight.

Per serving: 289 calories, 7 g total fat (22% of calories), 4 g saturated fat, 5 g protein, 56 g carbohydrates, 4 g fiber, 16 mg cholesterol, 322 mg sodium

Springtime Rhubarb Crisp

Makes about 12 generous servings

Back when produce was only available in season, rhubarb was the first thing to arrive in the early spring. I love eating strictly according to the season, and I always enjoy cherry-red rhubarb when it starts to appear in the market, a sure sign that winter is on its way out. Of course, hothouse rhubarb is available 12 months a year, but I still prefer to eat rhubarb only in the early spring. One note of caution: If the rhubarb stalks have any remnants of the leaves on them, cut off the leaves and discard them. The leaves contain oxalic acid, which can be toxic in high amounts. But don't worry: The stalks do not contain oxalic acid. This dessert may be adapted for almost any fruit you wish to use—see the variations at the end of the recipe.

RHUBARB MIXTURE

2½ pounds fresh rhubarb, preferably field grown, not hothouse (see Note)

½ cup granulated sugar

½ cup light brown sugar

⅓ cup all-purpose flour

1 tablespoon finely grated orange zest

TOPPING

2 cups all-purpose flour (spoon flour into dry-measure cup and level off)

1 cup rolled oats (regular oatmeal)

½ cup (about 2 ounces) walnut or pecan pieces, coarsely chopped

1 cup light brown sugar

1 teaspoon ground cinnamon

8 tablespoons (1 stick) unsalted butter, melted

One 2½-quart baking dish or gratin dish, or a 9 x 13 x 2-inch Pyrex baking dish sprayed with vegetable cooking spray

1 Set a rack in the middle level of the oven and preheat to 375 degrees.

2 Rinse the rhubarb and cut it into 1-inch chunks. Place in a large bowl and add the sugar, brown sugar, flour, and orange zest. Toss well with both hands and scrape into the prepared baking dish.

3 For the topping, combine the flour, oatmeal, nuts, brown sugar, and cinnamon in a large bowl. Use a large rubber spatula to mix well. Stir in the butter and continue stirring for half a minute or so to make sure that it is completely incorporated. The mixture will be quite dry.

4 Evenly scatter the topping over the rhubarb in the pan.

5 Bake the crisp for about 45 minutes, or until the topping is deep golden and the rhubarb is bubbling.

6 Cool the crisp on a rack.

SERVING: Serve the crisp warm or at room temperature, but not hot. Use a large serving spoon to scoop it out of the baking dish, making sure to transfer it to the plate, with the topping where it belongs—on top of the rhubarb. Spoon any extra rhubarb next to the portion, not on top of it.

STORAGE: Keep the crisp uncovered at room temperature until you are ready to serve it. Cover leftovers with plastic wrap and keep them at room temperature.

Per serving: 275 calories, 12 g total fat (39% of calories), 5 g saturated fat, 5 g protein, 39 g carbohydrates, 4 g fiber, 20 mg cholesterol, 20 mg sodium

VARIATIONS

Apple or Pear Crisp Substitute 3½ pounds apples or pears, peeled, halved, cored, and cut into 1-inch dice, for the rhubarb. Add a teaspoon of cinnamon to the apples, and 2 teaspoons vanilla extract to the pears. Substitute 2 teaspoons finely grated lemon zest for the orange zest.

Peach Crisp Substitute 3 pounds freestone peaches, peeled (see instructions on page 220), halved, pitted, and cut into wedges, for the rhubarb. Add ½ teaspoon freshly grated nutmeg and ½ teaspoon almond extract. Omit the orange zest.

NOTE: Field-grown rhubarb is bright red and has thick stalks and dark green leaves. Hothouse rhubarb has thin stalks, is pink, as opposed to red, and has pale green leaves.

Eat Fruit in Season

Nowadays, most fruits are available year-round in supermarkets. But strawberries in January just can't compare with the succulence of rich, red strawberries picked at the peak of ripeness in June. For the best flavor and the best price, buy fruit in season. Regional weather and climates may vary, but the chart below will give you a good idea of what fruits to buy in any given month of the year. Citrus and dried fruits are included for the winter months.

MONTH	FRUIT THAT'S IN SEASON
January	grapefruits, oranges, tangerines, dried berries, raisins, other dried fruits, such as dates
February	grapefruits, oranges, dried berries, raisins, other dried fruits, such as dates
March	bananas, grapefruits, oranges, pineapples
April	bananas, grapefruits, pineapples, rhubarb
May	bananas, mangoes, pineapples, rhubarb, strawberries
June	apricots, bananas, blackberries, cherries, lemons, limes, mangoes, pineapples, raspberries, rhubarb, strawberries, watermelon
July	apricots, blackberries, blueberries, cantaloupes, cherries, grapes, honeydew melons, lemons, limes, mangoes, peaches, raspberries, strawberries, watermelons
August	apples, blackberries, blueberries, cantaloupes, grapes, honeydew melons, limes, mangoes, peaches, pears, raspberries, watermelons
September	apples, blueberries, cantaloupes, figs, grapes, mangoes, peaches, pears, plums, watermelons
October	apples, grapes, figs, pears, dried berries, raisins, other dried fruits, such as dates
November	apples, grapefruits, tangerines, lemons, limes, dried berries, raisins, other dried fruits, such as dates
December	grapefruits, tangerines, dried berries, raisins, other dried fruits, such as dates

6

ICES AND
FROZEN DESSERTS

Students sometimes ask me to explain the difference between sherbet and sorbet. The answer: There is no difference. Both of these terms refer to a water-based frozen dessert. The difference comes in when cream is used instead of water as the base of the dessert. Cream-based frozen desserts are what we call ice cream. Here's a brief glossary to clarify the terminology commonly used.

ICE: General term that incorporates all the other terms below. Churned ices are made in an ice cream machine that incorporates air as the mixture is freezing.

ICE CREAM: Cream-based ice made with or without eggs.

ICE MILK: Milk-based ice containing little or no cream.

SHERBET: Water-based ice, often flavored with fruit. Some sherbets may also contain milk or cream.

SORBET: French word for sherbet. Period. The term does not connote any special type of sherbet. Some sorbets in France may also contain milk or cream, so that's not the dividing point.

SORBETTO: Italian word for sherbet. More rare in Italy, since most fruit flavors are usually made with milk-based gelato mixtures.

GELATO: General Italian term for ice, as described above. Gelato can be ice cream, a variation of ice milk, or even sherbet. What we think of as gelato is the modern, lower-fat kind of ice made without eggs (gelato isn't deliberately dietetic; it just happens to be less caloric). A typical gelato formula comprises the following ingredients: milk; cream (10 percent to 20 percent of total liquid); sugar; liquid sugar, such as glucose and/or invert sugar for smoothness (I use corn syrup for home recipes); nonfat dry milk to boost the solids content of the mix in the absence of eggs; stabilizer (plain old gelatin works fine in home recipes); and flavoring, which can be as simple as vanilla extract, or it could be a fruit puree added to the milky mixture.

GRANITA: Italian water ice, frozen without incorporating air so that it has a grainy texture. Some granitas may also have milk or cream added, but the defining characteristic of granita is its texture. In home recipes, the mixture is put into a pan and stirred and scraped while it is freezing, giving the ice a "grainy" quality. *Granita* is the Italian word for grainy. Commercially, granita is made in an ice cream freezer but taken out while it's still slushy.

Technique Tips

Most of the recipes in this chapter are water-based ices, such as sherbet. These ices are naturally lower in calories than cream-based or milk-based ices, although I did manage to sneak in a wonderful—and only mildly caloric—Milk Chocolate Ice Milk (page 235) from my friend Maida Heatter. Best of all, the recipe has only two ingredients.

Water-based ices are deceptively simple to make. You make a syrup of sugar and water, stir in some flavorings, and put the mixture into an ice cream machine. All but two of the recipes here—Italian Coffee Granita (page 226) and Rum Raisin Semifreddo (page 236)—call for churning the ice in an ice cream maker to develop a smooth and light texture. See page 215 for information on various types of ice cream makers. Here are some other hints for making perfect homemade ices.

1. Always start with a well-chilled mixture. If it's not well chilled, it will take longer to freeze in the ice cream machine and it may separate.

2. If you are making a large batch, divide it into two or three smaller batches for freezing in your ice cream machine. Smaller batches will freeze more quickly and develop a smoother texture.

3. Always be sure to freeze the container that will store the ice for at least 15 minutes before putting the freshly churned ice into it. A well-chilled storage container will help to prevent the ice from melting and developing an unpleasantly hard, icy texture.

4 To further prevent ice crystals from forming, press plastic wrap directly and thoroughly over the ice in the storage container to create an airtight seal while the ice is in the freezer.

5 Try to serve ices on the day they are churned. They will have the smoothest and lightest texture when served within 24 hours of churning. This is especially important in the case of the lighter ices in this chapter.

Ice Cream Machines

If you're in the market to buy an ice cream maker, I highly recommend it. Homemade ices are a luxurious indulgence even if you only make them a few times a year. Ice cream machines for home use range in price from $30 to upwards of $1,000—depending on how much convenience you'd like to pay for—but all will work equally well for the recipes in this book.

There are a few basic options among machines. Choose the one that best meets your needs. The most expensive—and most convenient—are the automatic electric models with built-in refrigeration. They do all the churning and freezing for you. The only drawback is that they generally yield only about 1 to 2 pints of ice cream at a time. And they cost several hundred dollars. Top-of-the-line models cost more than $1,000.

A less expensive option (about $50 to $100), and arguably the practical choice for most home cooks, is a modern electric model without built-in refrigeration. These machines have a canister whose walls are filled with a coolant-type gel. You store the canister in the freezer until frozen, then fill it with the ice mixture. The machine electrically churns the ice mixture and typically has a capacity of 1 to 1½ quarts.

If you like to make more than a quart or so of ice mixture at a time, the old-fashioned ice cream makers requiring rock salt and ice have the largest capacity. These may be either hand-cranked or electrically cranked. They are the least expensive, but the least convenient because of the rock salt and ice.

Grapefruit and Campari Sherbet

Makes 10 servings

A standard on restaurant menus in the past ten years or so, this sherbet deserves to be better known. The combination of tart-sweet grapefruit juice and bittersweet Campari is perfect.

¾ cup sugar

½ teaspoon unflavored gelatin

⅓ cup water

2 tablespoons light corn syrup

4 cups freshly squeezed grapefruit juice, white or pink, strained

¼ cup Campari

1 Combine the sugar and the gelatin in a medium saucepan and stir well to mix.

2 Whisk in the water and the corn syrup.

3 Bring the syrup to a boil, stirring occasionally.

4 Pour the hot syrup into a bowl and cool it to room temperature. Cover the bowl with plastic wrap and chill the syrup until it is very cold.

5 If there is a film on the syrup, ignore it and stir the grapefruit juice and the Campari into the syrup.

6 Freeze the mixture in an ice cream maker according to the manufacturer's directions.

7 While the sherbet is churning, place a bowl or other container in the freezer. Empty the churned sherbet into the bowl as you remove it from the ice cream maker. Press plastic wrap against the surface and freeze the sherbet. Remove the bowl from the freezer to add the remaining sherbet when it is ready.

SERVING: Serve the sherbet in chilled dessert bowls or glasses. A garnish of fresh berries or other fruit makes a good accompaniment. Or use this sherbet when an ice is suggested for serving in the cake and fruit desserts chapters.

STORAGE: Keep the sherbet in the freezer. It certainly won't spoil if you keep it frozen for a long time, but its texture will be best if you serve it within 24 hours of churning it.

Per serving: 126 calories, 0 g total fat, 0 g saturated fat, 1 g protein, 27 g carbohydrates, 0 g fiber, 0 mg cholesterol, 5 mg sodium

Earl Grey Sherbet

Makes about 6 servings

This fine and delicate sherbet would be the ideal finish for a special dinner. It's low enough in calories that you can easily accompany it with some crisp cookies, such as Almond Tuiles (page 250). But please, please, do not use tea bags or the sherbet will have a very dull flavor.

¾ cup sugar

½ teaspoon unflavored gelatin

2 cups water

⅓ cup light corn syrup

¼ cup (about ¾ ounce) loose Earl Grey tea (not tea bags)

Zest of 1 orange, stripped off with a vegetable peeler

1 Combine the sugar and gelatin in a medium saucepan and stir well to mix.

2 Add the water and corn syrup and whisk to mix. Bring to a boil over medium heat, stirring occasionally.

3 Remove the pan from the heat and whisk in the tea; stir in the orange zest. Cover the pan and allow the tea to steep in the syrup for about 4 minutes, but no longer or it will become bitter and tannic.

4 Strain the mixture into a bowl, then pass it through a coffee filter set in a strainer.

5 Cover the bowl with plastic wrap and chill the mixture until it is very cold.

6 Freeze the mixture in an ice cream maker according to the manufacturer's directions.

7 While the sherbet is churning, place a bowl or other container in the freezer. Empty the churned sherbet into the bowl as you remove it from the ice cream maker. Press plastic wrap against the surface and freeze the sherbet. Remove the bowl from the freezer to add the remaining sherbet when it is ready.

SERVING: Serve the sherbet in chilled dessert bowls or glasses. A garnish of orange slices makes a good accompaniment. Or use it when an ice is suggested for serving in the cake and fruit desserts chapters.

STORAGE: Keep the sherbet in the freezer. It certainly won't spoil if you keep it frozen for a long time, but its texture will be best if you serve it within 24 hours of churning it.

Per serving: 150 calories, 0 g total fat, 0 g saturated fat, 0 g protein, 39 g carbohydrates, 0 g fiber, 0 mg cholesterol, 13 mg sodium

Dorie's Blueberry Sherbet

Makes 10 servings

A gift from my friend Dorie Greenspan, author of the award-winning *Baking with Julia* (Morrow, 1996), this recipe uses frozen berries, but if you prefer to use fresh ones, add them to the sugar syrup and bring them to a boil. If you try to puree raw fresh blueberries they will oxidize and turn brown.

1 cup water	3 tablespoons light corn syrup
1 cup 2% reduced-fat milk	⅓ cup strained lemon juice
1½ cups sugar	1-pound bag frozen blueberries, thawed

1. Combine the water, milk, sugar, and corn syrup in a medium saucepan and whisk to mix. Place over medium heat and bring to a boil, stirring occasionally.

2. Pour the syrup into a bowl and cool it to room temperature. Cover the bowl with plastic wrap and chill the syrup until it is very cold.

3. Stir the lemon juice and blueberries into the syrup.

4. Puree the mixture in batches in a blender. Strain the mixture to remove the skins and seeds.

5. Freeze the mixture in an ice cream maker according to the manufacturer's directions.

6. While the sherbet is churning, place a bowl or other container in the freezer. Empty the churned sherbet into the bowl as you remove it from the ice cream maker. Press plastic wrap against the surface and freeze the sherbet. Remove the bowl from the freezer to add the remaining sherbet when it is ready.

SERVING: Serve the sherbet in chilled dessert bowls or glasses. A garnish of fresh berries or sliced fruit such as peaches makes a good accompaniment. Or use it when an ice is suggested for serving in the cake and fruit desserts chapters.

STORAGE: Keep the sherbet in the freezer. It certainly won't spoil if you keep it frozen for a long time, but its texture will be best if you serve it within 24 hours of churning it.

Per serving: 170 calories, 1 g total fat (5% of calories), 0 g saturated fat, 1 g protein, 42 g carbohydrates, 1 g fiber, 0 mg cholesterol, 14 mg sodium

Creamy Peach Sherbet

Makes 10 servings

This is a perfect example of an old-fashioned American sherbet enriched with cream for flavor and smoothness. Make sure the peaches are perfectly ripe and juicy-sweet or the sherbet will lack flavor.

⅓ cup sugar

¼ teaspoon unflavored gelatin

½ cup water

2 tablespoons light corn syrup

1¼ pounds ripe freestone peaches

1 cup half-and-half

1 teaspoon vanilla extract

¼ teaspoon almond extract

1   Combine the sugar and gelatin in a medium saucepan and stir well to mix. Stir in the water and corn syrup.

2   Bring the syrup to a boil over medium heat, stirring occasionally.

3   Pour the syrup into a bowl and cool it to room temperature.

4   Bring a large pan of water to a boil. Cut a cross in the blossom end of each peach and drop the peaches in the water. Leave the peaches in for about 20 seconds, then use a slotted spoon to lift them out to a bowl of cold water. If the peaches are perfectly ripe, the skins will slip off as soon as you supply gentle pressure with your fingertips. If the peaches don't peel easily, use a paring knife to remove any peel that remains stuck to them. Halve the peaches, remove the pits, and slice each half. You should have 2 cups of peach slices.

5   Mix the syrup with the peach slices and puree the mixture in batches in a blender.

6   Pour the peach mixture into a bowl, cover it with plastic wrap, and chill it until it is very cold.

7   Right before freezing the sherbet mixture, whisk in the half-and-half, vanilla, and almond extract.

8   Freeze the mixture in an ice cream maker according to the manufacturer's directions.

9   While the sherbet is churning, place a bowl or other container in the freezer. Empty the churned sherbet into the bowl as you remove it from the ice cream maker. Press plastic wrap against the surface and freeze the sherbet. Remove the bowl from the freezer to add the remaining sherbet when it is ready.

SERVING: Serve the sherbet in chilled dessert bowls or glasses. A garnish of raspberries or blueberries makes a good accompaniment. Or use this sherbet when an ice is suggested for serving in the cake and fruit desserts chapters.

STORAGE: Keep the sherbet in the freezer. It certainly won't spoil if you keep it frozen for a long time, but its texture will be best if you serve it within 24 hours of churning it.

Per serving: 85 calories, 3 g total fat (32% of calories), 2 g saturated fat, 1 g protein, 14 g carbohydrates, 1 g fiber, 10 mg cholesterol, 13 mg sodium

VARIATIONS

Creamy Apricot Sherbet Replace the peaches with 4 cups sliced, pitted apricots. There is no need to peel them.

Creamy Plum Sherbet Replace the peaches with 4 cups sliced, pitted plums. Use a paring knife to remove the skin from half the plums before you slice them. I like to use large, black Friar plums, but locally grown small green or yellow plums in season are also good. Omit the almond extract.

Bittersweet Chocolate Sherbet

Makes 6 servings

I first learned about this excellent sherbet when I visited the French National Pastry School in Yssingeaux to observe a class taught by Denis Ruffel, the brilliant chef of the Pâtisserie Millet in Paris. Among the specialties he prepared was this elegant and easy sherbet, brimming with chocolate flavor but very light at the same time. It immediately became one of my favorite ice recipes.

2 cups water

½ cup sugar

½ cup light corn syrup

3 ounces unsweetened chocolate, cut into ¼-inch pieces

⅔ cup (about 2 ounces) alkalized (Dutch-process) cocoa powder

2 teaspoons vanilla extract

1 Combine the water, sugar, and corn syrup in a medium saucepan and whisk several times to mix. Bring to a boil over medium heat, stirring occasionally.

2 Remove from the heat and whisk in the chocolate until the mixture is smooth.

3 Sift the cocoa into a bowl and whisk the chocolate syrup into the cocoa a little at a time to prevent lumps from forming. Whisk in the vanilla.

4 Strain the mixture into a bowl and cool it to room temperature.

5 Cover the bowl with plastic wrap and chill the mixture until it is very cold.

6 Immediately before freezing, whisk the mixture. Freeze the mixture in an ice cream maker according to the manufacturer's directions.

7 While the sherbet is churning, place a bowl or other container in the freezer. Empty the churned sherbet into the bowl as you remove it from the ice cream maker. Press plastic wrap against the surface and freeze the sherbet. Remove the bowl from the freezer to add the remaining sherbet when it is ready.

SERVING: Serve the sherbet in chilled dessert bowls or glasses. A garnish of raspberries or other fruit makes a good accompaniment. Or use it when an ice is suggested for serving in the cake and fruit desserts chapters.

STORAGE: Keep the sherbet in the freezer. It certainly won't spoil if you keep it frozen for a long time, but its texture will be best if you serve it within 24 hours of churning it.

Per serving: 241 calories, 8 g total fat (30% of calories), 5 g saturated fat, 4 g protein, 48 g carbohydrates, 5 g fiber, 0 mg cholesterol, 36 mg sodium

Yogurt Sherbet

Makes about 6 servings

This interesting twist on frozen yogurt is an adaptation of a recipe by Sam Mason, the talented young pastry chef of Wylie Dufresnes's restaurant WD-50 on Manhattan's Lower East Side. Sam uses it as a component of complex plated dessert presentations, but it's also excellent on its own or as an accompaniment to cakes or fruit desserts. See the vanilla variation at the end of the recipe.

The gelatin and cornstarch in the recipe replace the ice cream stabilizer typically used by pastry chefs in the preparation of ices made without eggs. The stabilizer's job is to keep the elements in the formula from separating, leaking whey, and consequently forming hard ice crystals in the sherbet. Gelatin and cornstarch perform the same function in this recipe.

¾ cup fat-free milk, divided

½ teaspoon unflavored gelatin

½ teaspoon cornstarch

⅓ cup light corn syrup

¼ cup sugar

2 cups low-fat or fat-free yogurt, preferably Greek yogurt (see Sources, page 291)

1   Pour ½ cup of the milk into a small bowl and whisk in the gelatin and the cornstarch. Set aside for the gelatin to soften.

2   Combine the remaining ¼ cup milk, the corn syrup, and the sugar in a saucepan and whisk several times to mix. Place over medium heat and bring to a boil.

3   Remove from the heat, whisk in the soaked gelatin and cornstarch mixture, and return the pan to low heat. Bring the milk mixture to a boil, whisking constantly, but not too vigorously. Let the mixture boil gently for about 2 minutes, whisking constantly.

4   Remove the pan from the heat and place the yogurt in a large bowl. Whisk the yogurt smooth and whisk in the milk mixture in a stream. Cool the mixture to room temperature, then cover the bowl with plastic wrap and refrigerate it until cold.

5 Freeze the mixture in an ice cream maker according to the manufacturer's directions. For most machines, you'll probably need to divide the mixture and freeze half at a time.

6 While the sherbet is churning, place a bowl or other container in the freezer. Empty the churned sherbet into the bowl as you remove it from the ice cream maker. Press plastic wrap against the surface and freeze the sherbet. Remove the bowl from the freezer to add the remaining sherbet when it is ready.

SERVING: Serve the sherbet in chilled dessert bowls or glasses. A garnish of fresh berries or other sliced fruit makes a good accompaniment. Or use it when an ice is suggested for serving in the cake and fruit desserts chapters.

STORAGE: Keep the sherbet in the freezer. It certainly won't spoil if you keep it frozen for a long time, but its texture will be best if you serve it within 24 hours of churning it.

Per serving: 131 calories, 0 g total fat, 0 g saturated fat, 5 g protein, 30 g carbohydrates, 0 g fiber, 0 mg cholesterol, 80 mg sodium

VARIATION: *Vanilla Yogurt Sherbet* Add a plump vanilla bean, split lengthwise, to the milk mixture when you begin to heat it. Remove the vanilla bean before whisking the milk mixture into the yogurt.

Italian Coffee Granita

Makes about 6 servings

This is the best frozen espresso you can get. It's just sweetened coffee that's frozen in a pan and stirred around while it's freezing to give it a slushy, crystalline texture. The best news is that you can make this dessert and the variations that follow without using an ice cream maker. It couldn't be simpler.

4 cups water

1 cup (3 to 3½ ounces) ground espresso-roast coffee

1 cup sugar

One stainless steel or glass roasting pan, at least 9 x 13 x 2 inches, placed in the freezer before preparing the mixture

1 Bring the water to a boil in a medium saucepan. Remove from the heat and whisk in the coffee.

2 Cover the pan and allow it to steep for 10 minutes.

3 Strain the coffee into a bowl, then strain it again through a strainer lined with a coffee filter.

4 Stir in the sugar until it is dissolved.

5 Cool the mixture to room temperature.

6 Pour the mixture into the prepared pan and freeze it for about 20 minutes. When the mixture begins to become slushy, scrape it away from the bottom and sides of the pan with a wide, flat spatula, such as a pancake turner. Continue scraping and stirring the granita every 10 or 15 minutes until it is very thick and grainy textured.

7 Scrape the granita into a bowl or other container and cover it with plastic wrap or a tight-fitting cover. Store in the freezer.

8 If the granita becomes hard, pop it out of the container or bowl and chop it with a stainless steel knife until it is quite finely textured again. Or chop it into chunks, then pulse it in a food processor until slushy but not smooth. Scrape back into a chilled bowl or container and store, covered, in the freezer.

SERVING: Serve the granita in chilled dessert glasses. Top it with a small spoonful of cold cream.

STORAGE: See steps 7 and 8.

Per serving: 129 calories, 0 g total fat, 0 g saturated fat, 0 g protein, 33 g carbohydrates, 0 g fiber, 0 mg cholesterol, 2 mg sodium

VARIATIONS

Lemon Granita Bring 2 cups water and 1 cup sugar to a boil. Cool. Stir in 1 cup strained lemon juice. Freeze and store as above.

Strawberry Granita Bring 1½ cups water and ¾ cup sugar to a boil. Cool. Rinse, hull, and puree 2 pints strawberries in a blender. Measure 2½ cups strawberry puree and stir into the cooled syrup. Freeze and store as above.

Italian Orange Gelato

Makes about 12 servings

This sprightly flavored ice has just a hint of orange liqueur and is perfect as the finale for an elegant meal. Don't be surprised at the nonfat dry milk in the recipe. It boosts the formula's total volume of solids, making the resulting gelato creamier.

¼ cup sugar

1 teaspoon unflavored gelatin

3 tablespoons (about ½ ounce) nonfat dry milk

3 cups 1% low-fat milk

⅓ cup half-and-half

¼ cup light corn syrup

⅓ cup freshly squeezed orange juice, strained

2 tablespoons orange liqueur, such as Cointreau or Grand Marnier

2 teaspoons finely grated orange zest

1 Combine the sugar, gelatin, and dry milk in a medium saucepan. Stir well to mix.

2 Stir in the low-fat milk gradually to avoid forming lumps. Stir in the half-and-half and the corn syrup.

3 Place the pan over low heat and bring to a simmer, about 160 degrees, stirring occasionally. Pour the mixture into a heatproof bowl and cool it to room temperature.

4 Cover the bowl and chill the milk mixture.

5 When you are ready to churn the gelato, stir in the orange juice, liqueur, and zest.

6 Freeze the mixture in an ice cream maker according to the manufacturer's directions.

7 While the gelato is churning, place a bowl or other container in the freezer. Empty the churned gelato into the bowl as you remove it from the ice cream maker. Press plastic wrap against the surface and freeze the gelato. Remove the bowl from the freezer to add the remaining gelato when it is ready.

SERVING: Serve the gelato in chilled dessert bowls or glasses. A garnish of fresh raspberries or blueberries or other sliced fruit such as peaches makes a good accompaniment. Or use it when an ice is suggested for serving in the cake and fruit desserts chapters.

STORAGE: Keep the gelato in the freezer. It certainly won't spoil if you keep it frozen for a long time, but its texture will be best if you serve it within 24 hours of churning it.

Per serving: 81 calories, 2 g total fat (9% of calories), 1 g saturated fat, 3 g protein, 15 g carbohydrates, 0 g fiber, 6 mg cholesterol, 45 mg sodium

The Gelato Variations

Makes about 8 servings

Here's a basic recipe for milk-based Italian-style gelato that you can vary with any of the flavors suggested below. It's a little more lean than a typical gelato mix, but the real thing is fairly low in fat to begin with, so this recipe doesn't represent a great departure from the original.

⅔ cup sugar

⅓ cup nonfat dry milk

½ teaspoon unflavored gelatin

2½ cups 1% low-fat milk

½ cup half-and-half

3 tablespoons light corn syrup

1 Combine the sugar, dry milk, and gelatin in a medium saucepan. Stir well to mix.

2 Whisk in the low-fat milk, followed by the half-and-half and the corn syrup.

3 Place over low heat and bring to a simmer (about 160 degrees), whisking occasionally.

4 Pour the mixture into a glass or stainless steel bowl and cool it to room temperature.

5 Cover the bowl with plastic wrap and chill the mixture until it is very cold.

6 Freeze the mixture in an ice cream maker according to the manufacturer's directions.

7 While the gelato is churning, place a bowl or other container in the freezer. Empty the churned gelato into the bowl as you remove it from the ice cream maker. Press plastic wrap against the surface and freeze the gelato.

SERVING: Serve the gelato in chilled dessert bowls or glasses. Or use it when an ice is suggested for serving in the cake and fruit desserts chapters.

STORAGE: Keep the gelato in the freezer. It certainly won't spoil if you keep it frozen for a long time, but its texture will be best if you serve it within 24 hours of churning it.

Per serving: 149 calories, 2 g total fat (12% of calories), 2 g saturated fat, 4 g protein, 29 g carbohydrates, 0 g fiber, 10 mg cholesterol, 65 mg sodium

VARIATIONS

Vanilla Gelato Split a plump vanilla bean lengthwise and add it to the gelato mixture, before heating it. Remove the pan from the heat and let the mixture stand for 10 minutes to infuse the vanilla flavor. Remove the vanilla bean before cooling and chilling the mixture.

Chocolate Gelato Cut 6 ounces 70% bittersweet chocolate into ¼-inch pieces and whisk into the gelato mixture as it comes off the heat. After the mixture has chilled, whisk in 2 teaspoons vanilla extract.

Cinnamon Gelato Add 1 tablespoon ground cinnamon to the sugar mixture in step 1.

Coffee Gelato Whisk ½ cup ground espresso-roast coffee into the gelato mixture as it comes off the heat. Let the mixture stand for 10 minutes to infuse the coffee flavor. Strain the mixture through a fine strainer to eliminate most of the coffee grounds, then pass it through a coffee filter or paper towel set in a strainer to eliminate the rest.

Strawberry Gelato Reduce the amount of low-fat milk in the recipe to 1¾ cups. Rinse, hull, and puree 1 pint strawberries in a blender. Measure 1½ cups puree and stir into the chilled gelato mixture before freezing it.

Tangerine Gelato Reduce the amount of low-fat milk to 1¾ cups. Stir 1½ cups strained tangerine juice into the chilled gelato mixture before freezing it. The sweet little clementines that appear in the supermarket in late fall make a good choice for the tangerines.

Frozen Banana Yogurt

Makes about 6 servings

Whenever I make this banana-flecked frozen yogurt I think a monument should be erected to this humble fruit. Bananas impart a wealth of flavor, smoothness, and natural sweetness in exchange for only a modest amount of calories. Just be sure to use bananas that are really ripe. The skin should be flecked with spots. If you use less ripe bananas, the yogurt won't have very much flavor.

2 medium bananas (about ½ pound)

2 tablespoons water

2½ tablespoons sugar

2 tablespoons light corn syrup

2½ cups low-fat or fat-free plain yogurt, preferably Greek yogurt (see Sources, page 291)

1 teaspoon vanilla extract

⅛ teaspoon ground cinnamon

1   Peel and mash the bananas with a fork or potato masher in a shallow bowl. Measure ¾ cups of the mashed bananas. Set aside.

2   Combine the water, sugar, and corn syrup in a medium saucepan and stir several times to mix. Place over low heat and bring the syrup to a boil, stirring occasionally to make sure that all the sugar dissolves. At the boil, remove the pan from the heat and stir in the mashed bananas.

3   Place the yogurt in a large bowl and whisk it smooth. Whisk in the banana mixture, followed by the vanilla and cinnamon.

4   Cover the bowl with plastic wrap and refrigerate it until cold.

5   Freeze the mixture in an ice cream maker according to the manufacturer's directions. For most machines, you'll probably need to divide the mixture and freeze half at a time.

6   While the yogurt is churning, place a bowl or other container in the freezer. Empty the churned yogurt into the bowl as you remove it from the ice cream maker. Press plastic wrap against the surface and freeze the yogurt. Remove the bowl from the freezer to add the remaining yogurt when it is ready.

SERVING: Serve the yogurt in chilled dessert bowls or glasses. A garnish of Cool Chocolate Sauce (page 276), makes a good accompaniment. Or use it when an ice is suggested for serving in the cake and fruit desserts chapters.

Per serving: 118 calories, 0 g total fat, 0 g saturated fat, 4 g protein, 28 g carbohydrates, 1 g fiber, 2 mg cholesterol, 65 mg sodium

VARIATIONS

Banana Chocolate Chip Frozen Yogurt Melt 1 ounce bittersweet chocolate with ½ teaspoon of neutral-tasting vegetable oil, such as corn or canola. Cool to about 100 degrees, but no less or the chocolate will solidify again. When the yogurt is firm and ready to be removed from the ice cream maker, use a teaspoon to drizzle the chocolate mixture into the yogurt while it is turning in the machine; the chocolate will solidify into little flecks throughout the yogurt. Diluting the chocolate with oil makes flecks that are more tender than plain chopped chocolate, which would freeze solid and become very hard.

Strawberry Frozen Yogurt Substitute 1 cup strawberries, rinsed, hulled, and mashed, for the bananas (about ¾ cup strawberry puree). Omit the vanilla and cinnamon.

Ginger Ice Milk

Makes about 10 servings

The lively flavor of this ice is a perfect accompaniment to fruit salad (page 181). The key to its smooth texture is making a ginger "tea," then combining it with the remaining ingredients, rather than simply incorporating pieces of ginger into the custard mixture.

1½ cups water

½ cup coarsely chopped peeled ginger
   (2½ ounces)

Zest of 1 lemon, stripped off with
   a vegetable peeler

2 cups whole milk

½ cup sugar

2 large eggs

1 Bring the water to a boil in a medium saucepan. Remove from the heat and stir in the ginger and lemon zest. Cover the pan and allow the mixture to steep for 10 minutes. Strain the mixture into a large bowl and cool it to room temperature.

2 Combine the milk and sugar in a large saucepan and whisk to mix. Place over medium heat, stirring occasionally to make sure the sugar dissolves.

3 Meanwhile, whisk the eggs in a bowl to break them up.

4 When the milk boils, whisk a third of it into the eggs. Return the remaining milk to a boil over low heat and whisk in the egg mixture in a stream. Cook the custard, whisking constantly, for about 20 seconds. Strain the custard into a bowl and refrigerate it, stirring occasionally, until it is very cold.

5 Whisk the ginger tea into the custard mixture.

6 Freeze the mixture in an ice cream maker according to the manufacturer's directions.

7 While the ice is churning, place a bowl or other container in the freezer. Empty the churned ice into the bowl as you remove it from the ice cream maker. Press plastic wrap against the surface and freeze the ice. Remove the bowl from the freezer to add the remaining ice when it is ready.

SERVING: Serve the ice in chilled dessert bowls or glasses. A garnish of fresh raspberries, cherries, or other sliced fruit makes a good accompaniment. Or use it when an ice is suggested for serving in the cake and fruit desserts chapters.

STORAGE: Keep the ice in the freezer. It certainly won't spoil if you keep it frozen for a long time, but its texture will be best if you serve it within 24 hours of churning it.

Per serving: 86 calories, 3 g total fat (31% of calories), 1 g saturated fat, 3 g protein, 13 g carbohydrates, 0 g fiber, 45 mg cholesterol, 34 mg sodium

VARIATION: *Coconut Ice Milk* Use 2½ cups canned Thai coconut milk and 1 cup milk instead of the quantities of water and milk above. Reduce the ginger to 2 teaspoons. Omit the lemon zest.

Maida's Milk Chocolate Ice Milk

No one will ever believe that this incredibly rich and satisfying ice has only two ingredients. Thanks to my friend and mentor Maida Heatter for sharing this excellent recipe.

3 cups fat-free milk, divided

1 pound best-quality milk chocolate, cut into ¼-inch pieces

1   Bring 1½ cups of the milk to a boil in a medium saucepan.

2   Remove from the heat, whisk in the chocolate, and allow to stand for a couple of minutes to melt the chocolate. Whisk in the remaining 1½ cups milk.

3   Pour the mixture into a bowl and cool it to room temperature.

4   Cover the bowl with plastic wrap and refrigerate it until it is very cold, stirring occasionally to prevent the chocolate from separating out, rising to the top, and solidifying as it chills.

5   Freeze the mixture in an ice cream maker according to the manufacturer's directions.

6   While the ice is churning, place a bowl or other container in the freezer. Empty the churned ice into the bowl as you remove it from the ice cream maker. Press plastic wrap against the surface and freeze the ice. Remove the bowl from the freezer to add the remaining ice when it is ready.

SERVING: Serve the ice in chilled dessert bowls or glasses. A garnish of fresh strawberries or raspberries makes a good accompaniment. Or use it when an ice is suggested for serving in the cake and fruit desserts chapters.

STORAGE: Keep the ice in the freezer. It certainly won't spoil if you keep it frozen for a long time, but its texture will be best if you serve it within 24 hours of churning it.

Per serving: 267 calories, 15 g total fat (51% of calories), 9 g saturated fat, 6 g protein, 31 g carbohydrates, 0 g fiber, 1 mg cholesterol, 61 mg sodium

Rum Raisin Semifreddo

Makes 10 servings

A popular type of Italian dessert, a semifreddo is frozen after mixing but is usually served slightly thawed, so it's only partially frozen, as the name implies. This mixture of ricotta and rum-soaked raisins lightened with a honey-sweetened cooked meringue is a classic example of a semifreddo. I like to freeze this dessert in large ramekins or even coffee cups to eliminate the need to unmold it for serving. Plus, if the semifreddo softens a little too much after you take it out of the freezer, it will still be perfectly creamy in the ramekins and won't ooze all over a plate.

⅓ cup dark raisins or Zante currants

¼ cup dark rum

3 cups (about 1½ fifteen-ounce containers) part–skim milk ricotta

2 large egg whites

Pinch of salt

1 cup dark, flavorful honey

Eight 6-ounce ramekins or large coffee cups placed on a jelly-roll pan

1   Place the raisins in a small saucepan and cover them with water. Bring to a boil over low heat, then drain the raisins. Put the raisins in a small bowl and add the rum. Stir once or twice to mix and let the raisins macerate (absorb the flavor) while you prepare the rest of the recipe.

2   Put the ricotta in the bowl of a food processor fitted with the metal blade. Process the ricotta for about a minute, or until it is very smooth. Remove the blade and scrape the ricotta into a medium mixing bowl. Stir in the raisins and rum.

3   For the meringue, half fill a medium saucepan with water and bring it to a boil over medium heat. Combine the egg whites, salt, and honey in the heatproof bowl of an electric mixer and whisk to mix. Place the bowl over the pan of simmering water and whisk gently but constantly until the mixture is hot, about 140 degrees.

4   Whip the meringue on medium speed with the whisk attachment until it has cooled to room temperature. Be careful not to overwhip the meringue or it might become grainy.

5   Use a large rubber spatula to fold the meringue into the ricotta mixture.

6   Spoon the mixture into the prepared ramekins and cover the pan with a sheet of plastic wrap. Freeze the semifreddo for at least 8 hours or overnight.

SERVING: Remove the ramekins from the freezer for about 30 minutes before serving. Or, if it is warm in the room, let them soften in the refrigerator for 3 or 4 hours. If using coffee cups, place the cups on saucers for serving.

STORAGE: You may keep the semifreddo frozen for several days, but if you keep it too long before serving, it might develop large ice crystals.

Per serving: 223 calories, 5 g total fat (20% of calories), 4 g saturated fat, 8 g protein, 35 g carbohydrates, 0 g fiber, 30 mg cholesterol, 115 mg sodium

Ices and Frozen Desserts

7

COOKIES

Someone once said that "a balanced diet is a cookie in each hand." This quip isn't too far off the mark, considering that most nutritionists recommend occasional indulgences as part of a healthy diet. And, to be fair, two cookies is the typical serving size.

Satisfying, portable, and individually portioned, cookies are the quintessential snack food. They're also easy to make and incredibly versatile, including styles such as drop, bar, and rolled cookies, as well as endless flavor varieties. In this chapter, you'll find a cookie to satisfy every need. Moist and chewy Old-fashioned Hermits (page 270) are perfect for midday cravings or enjoying with a cup of coffee or tea. Crisp, sweet Almond Tuiles (page 250) beautifully complement ices and frozen desserts and make a pretty presentation. There's only one glaring omission in the recipes here: chocolate cookies. But don't worry. Chocolate cookies are featured in the Chocolate Desserts chapter, beginning on page 3.

Like the other recipes in this book, the cookies here have not been surgically altered to remove excess fat. Instead, the recipes have been carefully selected to be naturally low in fat and calories. Swiss Cinnamon Stars (page 244), for instance, are made with no butter at all. Instead, they rely on the natural, good-for-you fat of ground almonds. Most of the ingredients used are very common in baking. A few of the bar cookies do include applesauce for extra moistness and chewiness. The Chewy Oatmeal Raisin Cookies (page 258) also benefit from a smidgen of applesauce for extra chewiness. Otherwise, the ingredients are the very same ones found in most baked goods: butter, sugar, flour, and eggs. They are just used in moderate amounts along with other key flavors, such as grated citrus zest, ground spices, chopped nuts, and peanut butter. In some cases, an egg white stands in for a whole egg, but I find that at least one whole egg is necessary in cookie doughs to provide body and richness.

Technique Tips

While cookies are easy to make, it's the details of technique that create perfect cookies. Try not to overmix these doughs. They may not be *artificially* reduced in fat, but these cookies are still low to moderate in fat content. Use a gentle hand when combining ingredients because overmixing can toughen low-fat doughs and make even the crispest cookies taste rubbery when baked. Also, follow the baking times religiously. Some low-calorie cookies benefit from slight underbaking to help retain moisture. Doneness tests are given in every recipe so that you will know exactly when to remove the cookies from the oven.

Equal portioning is important, too. When cutting or dropping cookie dough, portion each cookie accurately and uniformly to ensure even baking and a faithful calorie count.

Now we get to the heart of perfect cookies: even heating. A smooth and consistent flow of heat is the key to well-browned cookies that aren't burned on the bottom or underdone in the center. Your baking pans and your oven are the deciding factors here. Whether you use flat cookie sheets or rimmed baking sheets, heavy-gauge aluminum provides the most even heating and least chance of burning. Look for the heaviest pans you can find.

Save yourself some trouble by always lining your baking sheets. A lining keeps cookies from sticking, minimizes hot spots, and makes cleanup easy. Line pans with parchment paper or foil, both of which are widely available. The new nonstick foil works especially well to prevent sticking. Since lower-fat cookies are still more likely to stick than other cookies, I recommend a quick spritz of cooking spray on the foil or paper to be absolutely sure those little treats come off the pans without breaking. If you bake often, silicone baking mats, such as Silpat, make a good investment. These liners are dependably nonstick and reusable.

Adjusting your oven racks is the next step toward even heating. It's easiest to adjust the racks before you turn on the oven. However, if you forget, you can put on good oven mitts to adjust hot oven racks. For a single pan of cookies, set an oven rack to the middle level and bake the cookies there. When baking more than one pan of cookies, set oven racks in the upper and lower thirds of the oven to distribute the heat evenly. Most ovens have hot spots, so it's also a good idea to alternate the pans, top to bottom and back to front, at least once during baking.

Most ovens deliver strong bottom heat. When baking more than one pan of cookies, double the pans on the bottom rack of the oven. Stacking two pans together creates an insulating layer of air that helps to keep cookies from burning on the bottom. Some manufacturers make insulated cookie sheets that perform the same function and can be used interchangeably with the stacking technique.

Once they are baked, take care to cool the cookies completely before storing. Otherwise, crisp cookies may become soggy from the trapped steam in the storage container. Of course, it is perfectly acceptable—and encouraged—to sample cookies while they are still warm.

Keep in mind that the nutritional figures in this chapter are given per cookie. But most people eat more than just one. Two is about right—or three if you're splurging.

Swiss Cinnamon Stars

Makes about 36 cookies, depending on the size they are cut

These typical Swiss cookies are often associated with Chur, the capital of the Grisons canton, where St. Moritz is located. I love them because they are naturally low in fat, though they don't taste like it. The ground almonds make them tender and delicious, and besides, almonds are really nutritious.

1½ cups (about 6 ounces) whole unblanched almonds

1½ teaspoons ground cinnamon

1 teaspoon finely grated lemon zest

2 large egg whites

1½ cups confectioners' sugar

1 teaspoon water

2 cookie sheets or jelly-roll pans lined with parchment or foil

1   Finely grind the almonds in a food processor, pulsing it on and off. Add the cinnamon and lemon zest and pulse several times to mix.

2   Whip the egg whites by machine with the whisk attachment on medium speed until they are very white, opaque, and beginning to hold their shape. Increase the speed to medium-high and whip in the confectioners' sugar, about a tablespoon at a time, continuing to whip until the egg whites hold a firm peak, but not until they are dry and grainy.

3   Remove ⅓ cup of the meringue and set aside, covered, in a small bowl.

4   Add the remaining meringue to the bowl of the food processor and pulse to make a firm dough.

5   Invert the dough to a work surface dusted with confectioners' sugar, carefully removing the food processor blade. Use the palm of your hand to press the dough out about ¼ inch thick (it's not necessary to use a rolling pin). Have a metal spatula handy to detach the dough if it sticks to the surface. Cut the dough with a star-shaped cutter frequently dipped in water so the dough doesn't stick; arrange the cookies on the prepared pans about an inch apart in all directions. Press the scraps together and continue cutting cookies until you have used all the dough.

6   Stir the water into the reserved meringue and brush or spread it over the surface of each cookie. Allow the meringue topping to dry for an hour or two, uncovered, at room temperature.

7   About 20 minutes before you are ready to bake the cookies, set racks in the upper and lower thirds of the oven and preheat to 300 degrees.

8   Bake the cookies for 10 to 15 minutes, or until they are firm but still moist. Don't let them become dry in the oven or they will become very hard.

9   Slide the papers from the pans to racks to cool the cookies.

STORAGE: Keep the cookies between sheets of wax paper in a tin or plastic container with a tight-fitting cover.

NOTE: You may use any shape cutter you wish—the stars are probably more appropriate for the year-end holidays, but other shapes may be used at other times of the year.

Per cookie: 53 calories, 2 g total fat (34% of calories), 0 g saturated fat, 1 g protein, 7 g carbohydrates, 1 g fiber, 0 mg cholesterol, 3 mg sodium

Ginger Meringue Kisses

Makes about 40 cookies

Meringue cookies are always popular. They have great crunch and don't skimp on sweetness. The latter is due to the fact that if the meringue lacks a sufficient amount of sugar, it may collapse during baking. I especially like this combination of sweet meringue and peppery crystallized ginger. The two flavors complement each other perfectly.

4 large egg whites

Pinch of salt

1 cup sugar, divided

1 cup (about 6 ounces) crystallized ginger, cut into ¼-inch dice (see Note)

2 cookie sheets or jelly-roll pans lined with parchment or foil

1   Set racks in the upper and lower thirds of the oven and preheat to 250 degrees.

2   Combine the egg whites and salt in the bowl of an electric mixer and whip them with the whisk attachment on medium speed until they are very white, opaque, and just beginning to hold their shape.

3   Whip in ½ cup of the sugar, 1 tablespoon at a time, continuing to whip the whites until they are stiff but not dry.

4   Remove the bowl from the mixer and use a large rubber spatula to fold in the remaining ½ cup sugar and the chopped ginger.

5   Use a teaspoon to form irregular mounds about an inch apart in all directions on the prepared pans.

6   Bake the cookies for about 45 minutes until they are crisp but still slightly moist within.

7   Cool the cookies on the pans on a rack.

NOTE: Crystallized ginger can be very sticky, especially if it's fresh. To prevent sticking and make dicing easier, coat your knife blade with cooking spray.

STORAGE: Keep the cookies between sheets of wax paper in a tin or plastic container with a tight-fitting cover.

Per cookie: 35 calories, 0 g total fat (0% of calories), 0 g saturated fat, 0 g protein, 9 g carbohydrates, 0 g fiber, 0 mg cholesterol, 7 mg sodium

VARIATIONS

Add ½ cup lightly toasted slivered almonds, coarsely chopped, along with the ginger.

Substitute a 6-ounce bag of chocolate chips for the ginger, or add the chips along with the ginger.

Lemonade Cookies

Makes 36 cookies

Like a refreshing glass of lemonade, these simple cookies have a bright and sweet flavor.

1¼ cups all-purpose flour (spoon flour
  into dry-measure cup and level off)

½ teaspoon baking powder

¼ teaspoon salt

4 tablespoons (½ stick) unsalted butter,
  softened

¾ cup sugar

1 large egg white

1 teaspoon finely grated lemon zest

2 tablespoons lemon juice

2 cookie sheets or jelly-roll pans lined
  with parchment or foil

1   Set racks in the upper and lower thirds of the oven and preheat to 350 degrees.

2   Stir the flour, baking powder, and salt together and set aside.

3   Beat the butter and sugar together by machine with the paddle attachment on medium
    speed for about a minute, or until well mixed. Beat in the egg white and lemon zest.

4   Change the speed to low and beat in half the flour mixture, then the lemon juice. Beat
    in the remaining flour mixture.

5   Use a large rubber spatula to give the batter a final mixing.

6   Drop the batter with a teaspoon or small ice cream scoop about an inch apart in all
    directions on the prepared pans.

7   Bake the cookies for 8 to 10 minutes, or until they are light golden on the bottom but
    still very pale on top. Change the position of the pans, from top to bottom and back to
    front, about halfway through the baking.

8   Slide the papers from the pans to racks to cool the cookies.

STORAGE: Keep the cookies between sheets of wax paper in a tin or plastic container
with a tight-fitting cover.

Per cookie: 43 calories, 1 g total fat (21% of calories), 1 g saturated fat, 1 g protein, 7 g carbohydrates,
0 g fiber, 3 mg cholesterol, 24 mg sodium

Almond Tuiles

Makes about 45 cookies

Here's another great cookie that doesn't need to have anything removed from it to be low in calories, as the traditional recipe is light anyway. This variation is made with ground almonds instead of the sliced almonds used in classic tuiles. Using ground almonds gives the cookies a crunchier texture and more delicate flavor. By the way, *tuiles* means roofing tiles in French, and these cookies are meant to be curved on a rolling pin after they are baked so that they resemble their namesake. Don't worry if you don't have time to do the curving. Flat tuiles taste just as good.

¾ cup (about 3 ounces) whole unblanched almonds

½ cup sugar

1 large egg

1 large egg white

Pinch of salt

1 teaspoon dark rum

¼ cup all-purpose flour (spoon flour into dry-measure cup and level off)

2 or 3 cookie sheets or jelly-roll pans (preferably nonstick), sprayed with vegetable cooking spray or lined with foil and then sprayed, plus a pan with a rolling pin or a cardboard roll from a box of foil or a paper-towel roll.

1   Set a rack in the middle level of the oven and preheat to 350 degrees.

2   Combine the almonds and sugar in the bowl of a food processor and pulse repeatedly until the almonds are finely ground.

3   Use a large rubber spatula to stir the egg, egg white, and salt together in a mixing bowl. Do not beat air into the mixture. Stir in the almond mixture.

4   Stir in the rum, followed by the flour.

5   Drop measuring teaspoonfuls of the batter 3 inches apart all around on one of the prepared pans. Flatten the mounds of batter with a fork.

6   Bake the cookies for 6 or 7 minutes, or until they are golden. If you are going to curve the cookies, only bake one pan at a time.

7   Remove the pan from the oven and quickly use a thin, wide spatula to remove the cookies from the pan, one at a time, and drape them over the rolling pin to curve them. If you're not bothering to curve them, place them on a piece of parchment paper or foil set on a cooling rack.

8   When the cookies are cool, arrange them overlapping on a platter for up to 8 hours. Avoid storing these cookies; they are too fragile.

SERVING: Tuiles make a good match with custards and frozen desserts.

Per cookie: 25 calories, 1 g total fat (36% of calories), 0 g saturated fat, 1 g protein, 3 g carbohydrates, 0 g fiber, 5 mg cholesterol, 3 mg sodium

Gingersnaps

Makes about 40 cookies

Classic gingersnap drop cookies have lots of butter in them to help them spread during baking. These gingersnaps are a little different. They are rolled cookies that bake up snappy and crisp with a wonderful ginger aroma. One thing I learned about using ginger surprised me. If you open a fresh package or jar of ground ginger, you may use the amount specified in the recipe. However, if you are using ground ginger that has been open for a few months, its flavor may have diminished so much that you can use up to double the amount specified, especially if you like a strong ginger flavor.

1⅔ cups all-purpose flour

1 tablespoon ground ginger

1 teaspoon ground cinnamon

½ teaspoon ground cloves

½ teaspoon salt

4 tablespoons (½ stick) unsalted butter, softened

½ cup granulated sugar

½ cup dark brown sugar

2 large egg whites

2 cookie sheets or jelly-roll pans lined with parchment or foil

1   Stir the flour, spices, and salt together in a bowl.

2   Beat the butter and sugars together by machine with the paddle attachment on medium speed until well mixed and smooth, about 3 minutes.

3   Beat in the egg whites, one at a time, beating until smooth after each addition.

4   Scrape the bowl and beater with a rubber spatula and beat in the dry ingredients on the lowest speed.

5   Scrape the dough out onto a piece of plastic wrap and cover it with more wrap. Press the dough out between the sheets of plastic to about ¼-inch thickness and slide the package onto a cookie sheet or the back of a jelly-roll pan. Refrigerate for about 1 hour, or until firm. The dough can stay refrigerated for several days before continuing.

6 When you are ready to bake the cookies, set racks in the upper and lower thirds of the oven and preheat to 350 degrees.

7 Divide the dough into 3 pieces and roll one of the pieces on a lightly floured work surface to a 6-inch square. Use a plain or fluted round cutter to cut the dough into nine 2-inch cookies. As they are cut, arrange the cookies on the prepared pans about an inch apart in all directions. Repeat with the remaining pieces of dough. Press together and reroll the scraps to make about another dozen cookies.

8 Pierce each cookie several times with the tines of a fork to prevent them from ballooning up during baking.

9 Bake the cookies for 15 to 20 minutes, or until they are slightly puffed and firm. Cool the cookies on the pans on racks.

SERVING: These crisp, gingery cookies pair well with any kind of plain fruit dessert or ice.

STORAGE: Keep the cookies between sheets of wax paper in a tin or plastic container that has a tight-fitting cover.

Per cookie: 39 calories, 1 g total fat (23% of calories), 1 g saturated fat, 1 g protein, 6 g carbohydrates, 0 g fiber, 3 mg cholesterol, 33 mg sodium

Petit Beurre Cookies

Makes about 50 cookies

Commercially made butter cookies are wildly popular. Here's an excellent homemade and lower-fat version. I'll admit that these cookies are not as exciting as those with gobs of chocolate on them, but I find that a couple of them satisfy my craving for something sweet. They also make a great partner for any creamy or fruity dessert.

3 cups all-purpose flour

½ cup cornstarch

¼ teaspoon salt

½ teaspoon baking powder

½ teaspoon baking soda

8 tablespoons (1 stick) unsalted butter, softened

1 cup sugar

1 large egg

⅔ cup fat-free milk

2 cookie sheets or jelly-roll pans lined with parchment or foil

1   Combine the flour, cornstarch, salt, baking powder, and baking soda in a bowl; stir well to mix.

2   Beat the butter and sugar by machine with the paddle attachment on medium speed for about a minute. Beat in the egg.

3   Scrape down the bowl and beater and reduce the speed to low. Beat in half the flour mixture. As soon as it's absorbed, beat in the milk, followed by the remaining flour mixture.

4   Scrape the dough out onto a floured work surface and form it into a rectangle about ½ inch thick. Wrap the dough in plastic and refrigerate it until firm, about an hour or up to 3 days.

5   When you are ready to bake the cookies, set racks in the upper and lower thirds of the oven and preheat to 325 degrees.

6 Place the dough on a floured work surface and lightly flour the dough. Press and pound the dough gently with a rolling pin to soften it, then roll the dough to a 12-inch square. Cut the square into 3 equal pieces. Roll one of the pieces of dough to a 9-inch square and pierce it all over with the tines of a fork.

7 Use a pizza wheel to cut the square of dough into three 3-inch strips. Then cut across the strips at 1½-inch intervals to make eighteen 1½ x 3-inch cookies. Use a narrow metal spatula to transfer the cookies to the prepared pans, spacing them about an inch apart in all directions. Repeat with the remaining pieces of dough.

8 Bake the cookies for about 15 to 20 minutes, or until they are an even golden color all over. Cool the cookies on the pans on a rack. If the cookies are not crisp after they cool, return them to the oven for another 10 to 15 minutes.

STORAGE: Keep the cookies between sheets of wax paper in a tin or plastic container with a tight-fitting cover.

Per cookie: 65 calories, 2 g total fat (28% of calories), 1 g saturated fat, 1 g protein, 11 g carbohydrates, 0 g fiber, 9 mg cholesterol, 31 mg sodium

David's Skinny Chocolate Chip Cookies

Makes 30 cookies

My co-author David Joachim eats tons of these moist cookies but still stays very thin. What I love about them is the fact that they are reduced in fat and sugar, yet every bit as good as traditional chocolate chip cookies.

1¼ cups all-purpose flour (spoon flour into dry-measure cup and level off)

1 teaspoon baking soda

½ teaspoon salt

4 tablespoons (½ stick) unsalted butter, softened

½ cup light brown sugar, firmly packed

6 tablespoons granulated sugar

1 large egg

2 tablespoons whole milk

1 teaspoon vanilla extract

1½ cups (about ¾ of a 12-ounce bag) chocolate chips

2 cookie sheets or jelly-roll pans lined with parchment or foil

1 Set racks in the upper and lower thirds of the oven and preheat to 350 degrees.

2 Mix the flour, baking soda, and salt together and set aside.

3 Beat the butter and sugars together by machine with the paddle attachment on medium speed until well mixed, about a minute. Beat in the egg and milk until they are absorbed, and then the vanilla. Don't worry if the mixture looks curdled, the flour mixture will smooth it out.

4 Scrape down the bowl and beater and beat in the flour mixture on low speed.

5 Use a large rubber spatula to fold in the chocolate chips.

6 Chill the dough in the bowl for 15 minutes to keep the cookies from spreading too much while they're baking.

7 Form the dough into 1½-inch balls or use a small ice cream scoop to form the cookies. Arrange the balls of dough 2 inches apart all around on the prepared pans.

8   Bake the cookies for 8 to 12 minutes, or until they look dull on the surface, have spread, and are still quite moist. Cool the cookies on the pans on racks for 5 minutes.

9   Slide the papers to racks to cool the cookies completely.

STORAGE: Keep the cookies between sheets of wax paper in a tin or plastic container with a tight-fitting cover.

Per cookie: 114 calories, 5 g total fat (39% of calories), 3 g saturated fat, 2 g protein, 17 g carbohydrates, 1 g fiber, 11 mg cholesterol, 85 mg sodium

Chewy Oatmeal Raisin Cookies

Makes about 36 cookies

Try to resist the temptation to bake these cookies for longer than 10 to 12 minutes. They'll still look pretty underdone at the end of that time, but if you bake them longer, they won't be chewy, they'll be crisp, which is also fine if that's how you want your oatmeal cookies.

1 cup all-purpose flour (spoon flour into dry-measure cup and level off)

1 teaspoon baking powder

½ teaspoon baking soda

½ teaspoon salt

2 tablespoons unsalted butter, softened

½ cup granulated sugar

½ cup light brown sugar

1 large egg

¼ cup unsweetened applesauce (see Note, page 87)

1 teaspoon vanilla extract

1⅓ cups rolled oats (regular oatmeal)

½ cup dark raisins

2 cookie sheets or jelly-roll pans lined with parchment or foil

1   Set racks in the upper and lower thirds of the oven and preheat to 375 degrees.

2   Stir together the flour, baking powder, baking soda, and salt.

3   In a medium mixing bowl, beat the butter and granulated sugar together with a large rubber spatula. Beat in the brown sugar, then the egg.

4   Beat in the applesauce, followed by the vanilla.

5   Gently stir in the flour mixture, the oats, and the raisins, one at a time.

6   Drop the dough by teaspoonfuls 2 inches apart all around on the prepared pans. Use a fork to gently flatten the mounds of dough.

7   Bake the cookies for 10 to 12 minutes, or until they look dull on the surface but are still moist and soft. Change the position of the pans, top to bottom and back to front, halfway through the baking.

8   Slide the papers from the pans to racks to cool the cookies.

STORAGE: Keep the cookies between sheets of wax paper in a tin or plastic container with a tight-fitting cover.

Per cookie: 54 calories, 1 g total fat (17% of calories), 1 g saturated fat, 1 g protein, 10 g carbohydrates, 1 g fiber, 7 mg cholesterol, 65 mg sodium

Mincemeat Cookies

Makes about 40 cookies

These are perfect Christmas cookies. They have a festive holiday flavor and are really easy to make. Use the mincemeat on page 114 or prepared commercial mincemeat.

5 tablespoons unsalted butter, softened

1 cup dark brown sugar

1 large egg

1 large egg yolk

2 cups all-purpose flour

½ cup mincemeat (page 114) or prepared mincemeat

½ teaspoon baking soda

⅛ teaspoon ground ginger

½ teaspoon ground cloves

½ teaspoon freshly grated nutmeg

¼ teaspoon salt

½ cup chopped walnuts or pecans

2 cookie sheets or jelly-roll pans lined with parchment or foil

1   Set racks in the upper and lower thirds of the oven and preheat to 375 degrees.

2   Beat the butter and sugar until soft and light, then beat in the egg and egg yolk, continuing to beat until smooth.

3   Beat in a ½ cup of the flour, then the mincemeat.

4   Combine the remaining flour with the remaining ingredients and incorporate into the mincemeat mixture by hand, using a large rubber spatula.

5   Drop teaspoons of the batter on the prepared pans, keeping them a couple of inches apart.

6   Bake for 10 to 12 minutes, or until they are well risen, golden, and still a bit moist.

7   Slide the papers from the pans to racks to cool the cookies.

STORAGE: Store the cookies between sheets of wax paper in a tin or plastic container with a tight-fitting cover.

Per cookie: 65 calories, 3 g total fat (42% of calories), 1 g saturated fat, 1 g protein, 9 g carbohydrates, 0 g fiber, 15 mg cholesterol, 34 mg sodium

Cantuccini

Makes about 90 small biscotti

Classic Tuscan biscotti, these cookies are tasty, crunchy, and everything you could want biscotti to be. Slice the biscotti as thinly as the recipe states or else they will be very hard after they are baked. Of course, you could make them thicker if you intend to always dunk them in your caffè latte.

2¼ cups all-purpose flour (spoon flour into dry-measure cup and level off)

¾ cup sugar

2 teaspoons baking powder

1 teaspoon ground cinnamon

1 cup (about 4 ounces) unblanched almonds, coarsely chopped

2 large eggs

2 large egg whites

2 teaspoons vanilla extract

2 cookie sheets or jelly-roll pans lined with parchment or foil

1 Set a rack in the middle level of the oven and preheat to 350 degrees.

2 Combine the flour, sugar, baking powder, and cinnamon in a medium mixing bowl and stir well to mix. Stir in the almonds.

3 In a separate bowl, whisk the eggs, egg whites, and vanilla together.

4 Use a large rubber spatula to stir the egg mixture into the dry ingredients. Continue stirring until a firm dough forms.

5 Scrape the dough out on a floured surface and press it together well. Divide the dough into 3 equal pieces. Roll each piece of dough into a cylinder approximately the length of the pan. Arrange the cylinders of dough, equidistant from each other and the edges of the pan, on one of the pans (the other pan is used later for toasting the biscotti). Use the palm of your hand to flatten the logs.

6 Bake the logs for about 30 minutes, or until they are well risen and firm when pressed with a fingertip.

7   Cool the logs on the pan on a rack. Leave the oven on and set racks in the upper and lower thirds.

8   When the logs are completely cool, place them on a cutting board and use a sharp serrated knife to cut them into straight or diagonal slices ⅓ inch thick. Arrange the slices, cut side down, on the prepared pan and return them to the oven to toast for about 20 minutes—they should be light golden and the almonds should also appear toasted.

9   Cool the biscotti on the pan on racks.

SERVING: In Tuscany, it is traditional to dunk these cookies in a glass of sweet wine called Vin Santo (holy wine). Coffee and tea are also perfectly acceptable for dunking.

STORAGE: These cookies keep indefinitely. Store the biscotti between sheets of wax paper in a tin or plastic container with a tight-fitting cover.

Per biscotto: 28 calories, 1 g total fat (32% of calories), 0 g saturated fat, 1 g protein, 4 g carbohydrates, 0 g fiber, 5 mg cholesterol, 11 mg sodium

Honey and Hazelnut Biscotti

Makes about 90 thin biscotti

The only fat in these Italian-style cookies comes from hazelnuts, so they make a good snack at any time of the day. Take care to cut the biscotti thinly to prevent them from becoming too hard when baked.

2 cups all-purpose flour (spoon flour into dry-measure cup and level off)

¾ cup sugar

¾ cup (about 3 ounces) whole hazelnuts, with or without skin, finely ground in the food processor

2 teaspoons baking powder

1 teaspoon ground cinnamon (optional)

1 cup (about 4 ounces) whole hazelnuts, with or without the skin, coarsely chopped

⅓ cup dark, flavorful honey

⅓ cup water

2 cookie sheets or jelly-roll pans lined with parchment or foil

1. Set a rack in the middle level of the oven and preheat to 350 degrees.

2. Stir together all the ingredients except the honey and water in a mixing bowl.

3. Mix the honey and water together and use a large rubber spatula to stir them into the flour mixture. The dough may seem dry at first, but don't add any water to it—just continue stirring up the dry bits of dough from the bottom of the bowl and pressing them together with the spatula.

4. Scrape the dough out onto a lightly floured surface and press it together. Divide the dough into 2 equal pieces and roll each to a cylinder the approximate length of the pan you are using. Arrange the 2 pieces of dough, equidistant from each other and the edges of the pan, on one pan (the other pan will be used later for toasting the biscotti). Use the palm of your hand to flatten the logs.

5. Bake the logs for about 30 minutes, or until they are well risen and firm when pressed with a fingertip.

6. Cool the logs on the pan on a rack. Leave the oven on and set racks in the upper and lower thirds.

7   When the logs are completely cool, place them on a cutting board and use a sharp serrated knife to cut them into straight or diagonal slices ⅓ inch thick. Arrange the slices, cut side down, on the prepared pan and return them to the oven to toast for about 15 minutes.

8   Cool the toasted biscotti on the pan on racks.

SERVING: While quite good on their own, these biscotti also dress up a plain sherbet or ice milk.

STORAGE: Keep the biscotti between sheets of wax paper in a tin or plastic container with a tight-fitting cover.

Per biscotto: 34 calories, 1 g total fat (26% of calories), 0 g saturated fat, 1 g protein, 5 g carbohydrates, 0 g fiber, 0 mg cholesterol, 9 mg sodium

Granola Bars

Makes about twenty-four 2-inch squares

These snacks resemble an energy bar but taste a lot better. Peanut butter makes them rich and satisfying, yet they are still low in calories.

¾ cup rolled oats (regular oatmeal)

¾ cup (about 3 ounces) sliced almonds or chopped walnuts

¾ cup dark or golden raisins, or a combination

2 large egg whites

⅓ cup vegetable oil, such as corn or canola

¾ cup light brown sugar

¾ cup peanut butter

1 teaspoon ground cinnamon

½ teaspoon salt

One 9 x 13 x 2-inch pan, sprayed with vegetable cooking spray and lined, bottom and sides, with parchment or foil, lightly sprayed

1   Set a rack in the middle level of the oven and preheat to 325 degrees.

2   Stir the oats, almonds, and raisins together in a bowl.

3   Combine the remaining ingredients in a heatproof mixing bowl and stir well with a rubber spatula. Place the bowl over a pan of simmering water and gently stir until the sugar has melted.

4   Stir in the oatmeal mixture.

5   Evenly spread the batter in the prepared pan.

6   Bake for about 30 minutes, or until firm when pressed with a fingertip.

7   Cool in the pan on a rack.

8   Invert to a cutting board and peel off the paper.

9   Use a ruler to cut into 2-inch bars.

STORAGE: Keep the bars between sheets of wax paper in a tin or plastic container with a tight-fitting cover.

Per bar: 126 calories, 9 g total fat (64% of calories), 2 g saturated fat, 4 g protein, 9 g carbohydrates, 2 g fiber, 0 mg cholesterol, 95 mg sodium

Egg Alternatives

Most desserts, except for some fruit desserts and sauces, include eggs. In cookies and cakes, the egg yolks and whites contribute tenderness, structure, leavening, and flavor. Eggs also form the very basis of binding and coagulation in desserts like custards and puddings.

One large egg (about 3 tablespoons in volume) contains approximately 75 calories and 5 grams of fat. These numbers are not as high as those in butter, which has 306 calories and 35 grams of fat in every 3 tablespoons. If you're looking to make a dessert with less fat, reducing butter might be a better place to start. But replacing an egg or two will reduce the cholesterol count by about 213 milligrams for each egg and that's good for your health. Use the following methods to cut back safely on eggs in your favorite higher-calorie recipes outside of this book. The recipes in this book have already applied these techniques.

REPLACE SOME OF THE WHOLE EGGS WITH EGG WHITES. Almost all of the binding and leavening properties of eggs are contained in the whites. To make use of these properties without the fat and cholesterol, you can sometimes omit the yolks. For precise measurement, especially in baking recipes, replace 1 large whole egg with 3 tablespoons egg white for binding and leavening. If the precise volume of the eggs isn't critical, you can simply replace 1 egg with 2 egg whites. Keep in mind that you will lose some moisture, tenderness, and flavor by omitting egg yolks, so you may want to add a bit more liquid or enhance the flavor by adding spices or other aromatics. Generally, it's best to keep at least 1 whole egg in dessert recipes to retain the dessert's integrity. This method works well in cookies and cakes.

LOOK FOR PASTEURIZED LIQUID EGGS. Here's an option if you need real eggs for uncooked or partially cooked desserts but are concerned about salmonella. Makers of this product mix the yolks and whites, then pasteurize the blend at low heat to avoid scrambling the eggs. Look for pasteurized liquid eggs in the refrigerated section of supermarkets and use about 3 tablespoons to replace 1 large egg. For salmonella-safe meringues, pasteurized liquid egg whites are also available. Use a scant 3 tablespoons to replace 1 large egg white.

Cranberry Oatmeal Bars

Makes twenty-four 2-inch bars

Turn to these moist, chewy bars when you want the perfect snack. The dried cranberries add a tangy note that makes them really satisfying on their own or with a cup of tea or coffee.

3 cups rolled oats (regular oatmeal)

1 cup all-purpose flour (spoon flour into dry-measure cup and level off)

1 cup (about 4 ounces) pecan pieces, cut into ¼-inch pieces

1 cup dried cranberries

1 teaspoon baking soda

4 tablespoons (½ stick) unsalted butter, melted

¾ cup dark brown sugar, firmly packed

1 large egg

1 cup unsweetened applesauce (see Note on page 87)

1 teaspoon ground cinnamon

1 teaspoon ground ginger

One 9 x 13 x 2-inch pan, sprayed with vegetable cooking spray and lined, bottom and sides, with parchment or foil, lightly sprayed

1 Set a rack in the middle level of the oven and preheat to 350 degrees.

2 Stir the oats, flour, pecans, cranberries, and baking soda together in a bowl.

3 In a large mixing bowl, beat together the butter and brown sugar with a large rubber spatula. Beat in the egg, then the applesauce, cinnamon, and ginger.

4 Stir in the dry ingredients and scrape the batter into the prepared pan. Smooth the top.

5 Bake the bars for about 25 minutes, or until they are firm when pressed with a fingertip.

6 Cool in the pan on a rack.

7 Invert to a cutting board and peel off the paper.

8 Use a ruler to cut into 2-inch bars.

STORAGE: Keep the bars between sheets of wax paper in a tin or plastic container with a tight-fitting cover.

Per bar: 163 calories, 7 g total fat (39% of calories), 2 g saturated fat, 3 g protein, 24 g carbohydrates, 2 g fiber, 14 mg cholesterol, 60 mg sodium

Old-fashioned Hermits

Makes about thirty-six 2-inch squares

Betty Shaw was a talented cook and baker born in New England and transplanted to Fort Worth, Texas. She always came to my classes in Dallas and was very generous with the recipes in her large collection. Here is a lower-fat version of Betty Shaw's Hermits that originally appeared in *How to Bake*. If Betty were here to taste them, I'm sure she would approve.

2 cups all-purpose flour (spoon flour into dry-measure cup and level off)

1 teaspoon baking soda

1 teaspoon ground cinnamon

¼ teaspoon ground cloves

¼ teaspoon freshly grated nutmeg

4 tablespoons (½ stick) unsalted butter, softened

¾ cup dark brown sugar

2 large eggs

½ cup unsweetened applesauce (see Note on page 87)

¼ cup unsulfured molasses

½ cup buttermilk

½ cup dark raisins

½ cup pecan pieces, coarsely chopped

One 10 x 15-inch jelly-roll pan, sprayed with vegetable cooking spray and lined, bottom and sides, with parchment or foil, lightly sprayed

1 Set a rack in the middle level of the oven and preheat to 350 degrees.

2 Stir together the flour, baking soda, and spices.

3 Beat together the butter and brown sugar by machine with the paddle attachment on medium speed for 2 to 3 minutes. Beat in the eggs, one at a time, until smooth after each addition.

4 Mix the applesauce, molasses, and buttermilk in a bowl.

5 Beat a third of the flour mixture into the butter mixture, followed by half the applesauce mixture. Stop and scrape the bowl and beater.

6   Beat in another third of the flour mixture, followed by the remaining applesauce mixture. Stop and scrape again.

7   Finally beat in the last of the flour mixture.

8   Use a large rubber spatula to stir in the raisins and pecans.

9   Evenly spread the batter on the prepared pan. Bake the hermits for about 15 to 20 minutes, or until they are firm but not hard.

10   Slide the paper from the pan to a rack to cool the cake.

11   When the cake is completely cool, use a ruler to cut it into 2-inch bars.

STORAGE: Keep the hermits between sheets of wax paper in a tin or plastic container that has a tight-fitting cover.

Per hermit: 85 calories, 3 g total fat (32% of calories), 1 g saturated fat, 1 g protein, 14 g carbohydrates, 1 g fiber, 15 mg cholesterol, 46 mg sodium

Nothing enhances a simple dessert more than whipped cream, a spoonful of sauce, or a lively decoration. Especially when serving lean desserts, a little extra flourish can transform a good-looking dessert into a gorgeous one—without adding a lot of calories. Serve any of the sauces or creams in this chapter with the dessert recipes throughout the rest of the book. I have also included two essential garnishes: Chocolate Shavings (page 286) and Caramel Lace (page 289). Either of these will instantly dress up a mousse, ice, or fruit preparation and turn it into a fancy-looking plated dessert.

Remember when decorating desserts that the watchwords are neatness and restraint. A few chocolate shavings go a long way and will ultimately make a much better-looking dessert than a whole cup of them dumped over the top. Here are a few other hints for serving beautiful desserts.

1   Use a light hand with sauce. Some of the desserts in this book come close to the recommended 300-calorie limit for a single serving. Add only the quantity of sauce necessary to accompany the dessert. In most cases, that means about 2 tablespoons.

2   Swirled sauces may make for pretty presentations, but the real place of a dessert sauce is on the dessert itself, where you can taste it. Passing some sauce at the table may be more practical than making artistic designs on a plate with it.

3   If you do sauce a dessert before serving, use a light hand to tastefully nap the dessert with sauce rather than drenching it. Think of sauces as the supporting players; the dessert itself is the real star of the plate.

4   A very small amount of real whipped cream can make all the difference between an ordinary and a special dessert. If you can spare the calories, each tablespoon of lightly sweetened real whipped cream only adds about 32 calories and 3 grams of fat to your dessert.

5   Whenever possible, make sauces and/or creams ahead of time so that they are ready to serve when your dessert is ready. Most of the recipes in this chapter keep well and may be prepared several days in advance.

Cool Chocolate Sauce

Makes about 1¼ cups sauce, 10 servings, 2 tablespoons each

This recipe makes a great alternative to a hot, fudgy sauce. It is meant to be served after it has cooled completely to room temperature, so don't be surprised if it is thin when warm. It will thicken upon cooling.

½ cup milk

3 tablespoons sugar

3 tablespoons light corn syrup

6 ounces 70% bittersweet chocolate, cut into ¼-inch pieces

Pinch of salt

2 teaspoons vanilla extract or dark rum

1   Combine the milk, sugar, and corn syrup in a small saucepan. Stir well to mix, then place the pan over low heat and bring to a boil, stirring occasionally.

2   Remove from the heat, stir in the chocolate, and whisk smooth. Whisk in the salt and vanilla.

3   Pour the sauce into a bowl and cool it to room temperature, stirring occasionally. Cover the bowl with plastic wrap and keep the sauce at room temperature if you are serving it on the day it is made.

SERVING: Pass the sauce in a sauceboat or bowl.

STORAGE: Refrigerate any leftover sauce covered with plastic wrap. Bring the sauce to room temperature before serving again. For advance preparation, store the sauce the same way. Reheat the bowl of sauce over a pan of simmering water, stirring occasionally, then cool it to room temperature before serving.

Per serving: 109 calories, 8 g total fat (66% of calories), 4 g saturated fat, 2 g protein, 13 g carbohydrates, 2 g fiber, 2 mg cholesterol, 5 mg sodium

Warm Chocolate Sauce

Makes about 1¾ cups sauce, 10 servings, 2 tablespoons each

This is a pared-down version of Lean Mean Hot Fudge Sauce from my book *Chocolate*. For a chocolate sauce that will be served cold, see the recipe on page 276.

¼ cup water

½ cup light corn syrup

¾ cup sugar

⅛ teaspoon salt

½ cup (about 1½ ounces) alkalized (Dutch-process) cocoa powder

1 tablespoon unsalted butter

2 teaspoons vanilla extract

1 Combine the water, corn syrup, and sugar in a medium saucepan. Place over low heat and bring to a boil, stirring often to make sure all the sugar dissolves.

2 Remove the pan from the heat and add the salt. Sift the cocoa over the hot syrup and whisk it in. If there are a few lumps, they will cook out.

3 Place the pan over low heat and cook, whisking constantly, until the sauce is smooth.

4 Remove from the heat and whisk in the butter and vanilla.

SERVING: Serve the sauce hot or warm in a sauceboat or bowl.

STORAGE: For advance preparation, pour the sauce into a shallow bowl and cool it to room temperature. Cover the bowl with plastic wrap and refrigerate the sauce until needed. Reheat it directly in the bowl set over a pan of simmering water, stirring occasionally.

Per serving: 129 calories, 2 g total fat (14% of calories), 1 g saturated fat, 1 g protein, 30 g carbohydrates, 2 g fiber, 3 mg cholesterol, 58 mg sodium

Caramel Sauce

Makes about 1 cup sauce, 8 servings, 2 tablespoons each

You may prepare this amber-colored sauce with either cream or water added to the caramelized sugar near the end of cooking. I recommend the cream-based version if the sauce will be served with a very lean dessert, such as a fruit dessert.

⅓ cup water	1 cup sugar
2 tablespoons light corn syrup	½ cup water or heavy whipping cream

1   Combine the water, corn syrup, and sugar in a medium saucepan and stir well to mix.

2   Bring the syrup to a boil over low heat, stirring occasionally. At the boil, use a clean pastry brush dipped in cold water to wipe the inside of the pan at the level of the syrup to keep any undissolved sugar crystals from remaining stuck to the inside of the pan.

3   Continue cooking the syrup until the color begins to turn to a light amber.

4   Remove the pan from the heat and let it stand on the stovetop. The caramel will continue to darken as the heat in the pan continues to cook it. Check the color by lifting a spoonful of the caramel and letting it fall back into the pan; this will give you a more accurate idea of the color than looking into the pan, where the caramel always appears darker than it is. You're looking for a deep golden-amber color. If the caramel is too light, return it to the heat briefly, then remove and test the color again.

5   While the syrup is cooking, pour the water or cream into a small saucepan and heat to a simmer.

6   When the caramel is deep amber in color, add the hot water or cream to it, a little at a time, at arm's length, averting your face in case the caramel splatters.

7   After all the liquid has been added, return the pan to the heat and bring it to the boil again. If any of the sugar hardened while the liquid was being added, decrease the heat to very low and cook, stirring, until all the sugar is melted again.

SERVING: Pass the sauce in a sauceboat or a bowl. Serve it warm or at room temperature.

STORAGE: Cover the sauce and keep it at a cool room temperature. If the sauce hardens too much upon standing, gently reheat it over low heat, adding a tablespoon or two of water or cream as necessary.

Per serving: 146 calories, 4 g total fat (25% of calories), 2 g saturated fat, 0 g protein, 29 g carbohydrates, 0 g fiber, 13 mg cholesterol, 10 mg sodium

Custard Sauce

Makes about 2 cups sauce, 10 servings, about 3 tablespoons each

A lightened variation of the famous French crème anglaise, this is a good accompaniment to fruit desserts. Or try a couple of spoonfuls of the sauce with a simple angel food cake or chiffon cake.

1½ cups milk

¼ cup sugar

1 vanilla bean, split lengthwise

3 large eggs

1 Combine the milk, sugar, and vanilla bean in a medium saucepan and whisk a couple of times to mix. Place over low heat and bring to a boil.

2 Meanwhile, whisk the eggs in a medium mixing bowl to break them up. When the milk boils, whisk about a third of it into the eggs. Return the remaining milk to a boil and whisk the egg mixture in a stream, whisking constantly. Cook the custard, whisking constantly, for about 20 seconds, or until it thickens slightly and reaches a temperature of about 180 degrees. It won't thicken a lot; most of the thickening takes place as the custard is cooling. If you cook the custard until the temperature gets too close to the boiling point, the eggs will scramble, since there is no starch in the custard to bind them with the milk.

3 Immediately strain the custard into a glass or stainless steel bowl. Cool the custard to room temperature, stirring occasionally to prevent a skin from forming on it. Cover the bowl with plastic wrap and chill the custard. You may prepare the custard the day before to save time.

SERVING: Pass the sauce in a sauceboat or a bowl.

STORAGE: Keep the sauce refrigerated for no more than 48 hours after it is made.

Per serving: 63 calories, 3 g total fat (43% of calories), 1 g saturated fat, 3 g protein, 7 g carbohydrates, 0 g fiber, 67 mg cholesterol, 36 mg sodium

VARIATIONS

Lemon or Orange Custard Sauce For a custard subtly scented with lemon or orange, replace the vanilla bean with the zest of a large lemon or a medium orange, stripped off with a vegetable peeler. Add the zest to the milk along with the sugar and bring to a simmer. Remove from the heat, cover the pan, and let the zest steep in the milk for 10 minutes. Remove the zest with a slotted spoon and return the milk to a boil. Proceed with the recipe.

Coffee Custard Sauce Whisk ¼ cup ground espresso coffee into the boiled milk and vanilla bean. Cover and allow to steep for 10 minutes. Strain out the coffee and vanilla bean and strain the mixture through a coffee filter. Reheat the milk and proceed with the recipe.

Chocolate Custard Sauce Heat ¼ cup water to a boil in a small saucepan, then remove from the heat and stir in 3 ounces 70% bittersweet chocolate, cut into ¼-inch pieces. Whisk smooth and whisk into the cooked custard sauce as it comes off the heat.

Fresh Raspberry Sauce

About 1 cup sauce, 8 servings, 2 tablespoons each

This bright-colored sauce is best with fresh berries. A few of the whole berries are folded into the sauce for visual contrast. If you are working with frozen berries, see the recipe for cooked berry sauce on the opposite page.

2 half-pint baskets fresh raspberries, divided

3 tablespoons sugar

1 teaspoon strained lemon juice

1 teaspoon Kirsch or framboise (raspberry eau-de-vie)

1   Reserve a quarter of the total raspberries for adding to the sauce whole.

2   Combine the remaining raspberries with the sugar, lemon juice, and Kirsch, and puree in a blender until just smooth. Don't overdo the pureeing or the seeds will become too small to strain out.

3   Strain the sauce into a bowl, then fold in the reserved berries.

4   Cover the bowl and chill the sauce until it is needed.

SERVING: Bring the sauce to the table in a sauceboat or decorative bowl. Spoon the sauce over or next to the dessert.

STORAGE: This is best on the day it's made, but leftovers will keep, covered, in the refrigerator for a couple of days.

Per serving: 33 calories, 0 g total fat (0% of calories), 0 g saturated fat, 0 g protein, 9 g carbohydrates, 2 g fiber, 0 mg cholesterol, 0 mg sodium

VARIATION: *Fresh Strawberry Sauce* Use 1 pint strawberries, rinsed and hulled. Reserve a quarter of the berries to add either sliced or diced to the sauce.

Cooked Raspberry Sauce

About 1 cup sauce, 8 servings, 2 tablespoons each

Here's a good base recipe for using frozen berries to prepare a flavorful sauce. I find that frozen berries need to cook a little to make them less watery and to concentrate their flavor. Look for raspberries that come frozen in a bag. Feel the bag to make sure all of the individual berries are loose and not clumped together. Bags of frozen berries tend to taste better than those frozen in a block.

12 ounces individually quick-frozen raspberries, thawed

3 tablespoons sugar

1 teaspoon strained lemon juice

1 teaspoon Kirsch or Framboise (raspberry eau-de-vie)

1 Combine the berries and sugar in a medium saucepan over low heat. Bring to a boil, stirring occasionally.

2 Cook the berries and sugar for about 5 minutes, allowing them to boil very gently, or until they are slightly thickened.

3 Cool the mixture and puree it in a blender. Strain the sauce into a bowl to remove the seeds.

4 Stir in the lemon juice and Kirsch.

SERVING: Pass the sauce in a sauceboat or bowl.

STORAGE: Keep the sauce covered and refrigerated before and after use.

Per serving: 38 calories, 0 g total fat (0% of calories), 0 g saturated fat, 0 g protein, 9 g carbohydrates, 1 g fiber, 0 mg cholesterol, 0 mg sodium

VARIATION: Substitute a 12-ounce bag of strawberries or blueberries for the raspberries. Don't use Kirsch or Framboise with blueberries, though a dash of white rum works nicely.

Cooked Fruit Sauce

About 1½ cups sauce, 12 servings, 2 tablespoons each

Use this as a base recipe for any type of stone fruit, although the sauce tastes best with peaches or apricots.

1 pound ripe peaches, peeled (see page 220 for instructions)

⅓ cup sugar

2 teaspoons lemon juice

Pinch of freshly grated nutmeg

1 Halve and pit the peaches, then dice them coarsely.

2 Combine the peaches and sugar in a medium saucepan and place over low heat. Bring to a boil, stirring occasionally. Cook at a gentle simmer for about 5 minutes, or until slightly thickened.

3 Cool the sauce and pour it into the bowl of a food processor fitted with the metal blade. Pulse a couple of times to make the sauce a little smoother, but not until it is entirely liquid.

4 Pour the sauce into a bowl and stir in the lemon juice and nutmeg.

5 Chill the sauce before serving.

SERVING: Pass the sauce in a sauceboat or bowl.

STORAGE: Keep the sauce covered and refrigerated before and after use.

Per serving: 36 calories, 0 g total fat (0% of calories), 0 g saturated fat, 1 g protein, 11 g carbohydrates, 1 g fiber, 0 mg cholesterol, 0 mg sodium

VARIATION: Substitute a pound of apricots or plums for the peaches. Don't attempt to peel the apricots. For plums, peel half of them. Both of these might need a bit more sugar, depending upon the ripeness of the fruit. Taste a little of the sauce before removing the pan from the heat and add small amounts of sugar as necessary. Omit the nutmeg.

Maida's Skinny Whipped Cream

Makes about 3 cups cream, 16 servings, 3 tablespoons each

When I was just starting to put some ideas together for recipes that I wanted to be included in this book, I had a conversation about lightened whipped cream with my friend and mentor Maida Heatter. She suggested that I try a recipe of hers called Cream Ooh-La-La, which she uses to top strawberries macerated with sugar and Grand Marnier, in *Maida Heatter's Best Dessert Book Ever* (Random House, 1990). It's basically sweetened whipped cream with the addition of some sour cream and whipped egg whites. I've transformed it a little by substituting reduced-fat sour cream and a cooked meringue. This results in a whipped cream with overtones of crème fraîche and an exquisite lightness.

¼ cup reduced-fat sour cream

½ cup heavy whipping cream

2 large egg whites

¼ cup sugar

1 Whisk the sour cream in a small bowl until smooth. Set aside.

2 Whip the heavy cream until it holds soft peaks, either by hand or by machine.

3 For the meringue, half fill a saucepan with water and bring it to a boil over medium heat. Reduce the heat so that the water boils gently.

4 Combine the egg whites and sugar in the heatproof bowl of an electric mixer and place over the pan of simmering water. Whisk gently until the egg whites are hot and the sugar is dissolved. Whip by machine with the whisk attachment on medium speed until the meringue is risen in volume and cooled. Be careful not to overwhip or the meringue may become grainy.

5 Test the meringue with a fingertip to see if it is still warm. If the meringue is well risen in volume before it has cooled to room temperature, remove the bowl from the mixer and set it in a bowl of cold tap water. Use a large rubber spatula to stir the meringue over the cold water until it is cool when you test it with a fingertip.

6   Quickly whisk the cream again if it has become separated and whisk in the sour cream. Use a large rubber spatula to fold in the meringue.

SERVING: Use this with any dessert that's crying out for a spoonful of whipped cream.

STORAGE: If you prepare the cream in advance, scrape it into a shallow bowl and cover it with plastic wrap. Keep the cream refrigerated for no more than a couple of hours or it will separate.

Per serving: 46 calories, 3 g total fat (59% of calories), 2 g saturated fat, 1 g protein, 4 g carbohydrates, 0 g fiber, 12 mg cholesterol, 12 mg sodium

Chocolate Shavings

Makes 1¼ cups, 20 servings, 1 tablespoon each

The best and easiest way to make chocolate shavings is to use room-temperature milk chocolate. It's a little softer than dark chocolate and will produce large, thick, appetizing-looking shavings. If you can purchase a thick block of chocolate cut from a large bar, you'll have an easier time, but the procedures below will also work well with a thin bar of chocolate.

4 ounces milk chocolate in 1 piece (you may use a larger piece of chocolate to make the shavings), at room temperature

One jelly-roll pan lined with parchment or foil

1   Vegetable peeler method: Stand the bar of chocolate on its side on a parchment- or wax paper–lined jelly-roll pan. Use a swivel-bladed vegetable peeler to make curled shavings from the top of one of the long, narrow sides, downward. Try to keep the pressure even from top to bottom or the middle of the bar of chocolate will become bowed and will break, especially if you are using a thin bar.

2   Melon-ball scoop method: Place the bar of chocolate, widest side down, on a parchment- or wax paper–lined jelly-roll pan. Use a melon-ball scoop to make large, wide curls, holding the end of the scoop at a 45-degree angle to the chocolate and scraping from the far end toward you.

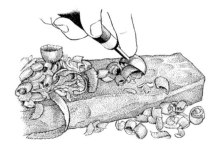

3   Tartlet pan method: Use an individual 2- to 3-inch sloping-sided tartlet pan instead of the melon-ball scoop in method 2.

4   After you have finished making the shavings, gently bend the paper and slide the shavings into a shallow bowl or plastic container. Cover and refrigerate the shavings.

SERVING: Use a tablespoon of shavings on any chocolate dessert that needs a little decoration.

STORAGE: The shavings will keep indefinitely in the refrigerator.

Per serving: 30 calories, 2 g total fat (60% of calories), 1 g saturated fat, 0 g protein, 3 g carbohydrates, 0 g fiber, 0 mg cholesterol, 0 mg sodium

Milk and Honey Yogurt Cream

About 1½ cups yogurt cream, 8 servings, 3 tablespoons each

This is a variation of a wonderful recipe that appears in *Maida Heatter's New Book of Great Desserts* (Knopf, 1982). It is simply drained yogurt thinned out with a little milk and sweetened with honey. It goes perfectly with any dessert that would benefit from a sweet, slightly tangy accompaniment. To give the yogurt enough time to drain, start this about 24 hours in advance.

3 cups low-fat or fat-free yogurt, preferably Greek yogurt (see Sources, page 291)

¼ cup fat-free milk

¼ cup dark, flavorful honey

1   Line a large strainer with dampened cheesecloth or paper towels. Scrape the yogurt into the lined strainer and set it over a bowl. Cover the strainer with plastic wrap and refrigerate it for about 24 hours.

2   Check the yogurt after about 12 hours have elapsed and stir it around a little to help it release more whey.

3   Once the yogurt has drained for 24 hours, you should have about a cup of firm yogurt "cheese" in the strainer.

4   Invert the yogurt from the strainer to a small bowl and stir in the milk and honey.

5   Cover the bowl with plastic wrap and refrigerate it until serving time.

SERVING: Pass the yogurt cream in a sauceboat or serving bowl.

STORAGE: Keep the yogurt cream refrigerated. For advance preparation, drain the yogurt and keep it tightly covered in the refrigerator for up to 5 days. Stir in the milk and honey when you wish to serve it.

Per serving: 72 calories, 0 g total fat (0% of calories), 0 g saturated fat, 4 g protein, 16 g carbohydrates, 0 g fiber, 2 mg cholesterol, 54 mg sodium

Caramel Lace

Makes 20 to 24 pieces

Spinning strands of caramel onto greased parchment or wax paper yields beautiful, lacy pieces of brittle golden sugar that can be speared into the top of a dessert or placed alongside it. One note of caution: If you're not experienced in handling hot sugar, wear a pair of rubber dishwashing gloves to protect your hands from drips or splatters of caramel, which could cause painful burns.

⅓ cup water

1 tablespoon light corn syrup

1 cup sugar

One jelly-roll pan lined with parchment or foil and sprayed with vegetable cooking spray

1   Combine the water, corn syrup, and sugar in a medium saucepan and stir well to mix.

2   Bring the syrup to a boil over low heat, stirring occasionally. At the boil, use a clean pastry brush dipped in cold water to wipe the inside of the pan at the level of the syrup to keep any undissolved sugar crystals from remaining stuck to the inside of the pan.

3   While the syrup is cooking, place a heatproof bowl in the sink and fill it with cold water. Add a few ice cubes.

4   Continue cooking the syrup until the color begins to turn to a light amber.

5   Remove the pan from the heat and let it stand on the stovetop. The caramel will continue to darken as the heat in the pan continues to cook it. Check the color by lifting a spoonful of the caramel and letting it fall back into the pan; this will give you a more accurate idea of the color than looking into the pan, where the caramel always appears darker than it is. You're looking for a deep golden-amber color. If the caramel is too light, return it to the heat briefly, then remove and test the color again.

6   Once the caramel is the right color, briefly immerse the bottom of the pan in the ice water. Don't leave it in more than a few seconds or the caramel will harden and become unusable.

7 Position the pan of caramel on a potholder or trivet on the work surface next to the prepared jelly-roll pan. Lift a spoonful of the caramel with an oval tablespoon and turn the spoon perpendicular to the work surface. Quickly let the caramel on the spoon drizzle onto the paper. Make a series of parallel lines about ½ inch apart all over the width of the pan. After you have enough lines on the width of the pan, continue by making a series of lines perpendicular to the first ones. Then make a series of lines that are diagonal to the first ones, continuing until you have used up most of the sugar. See the illustration below.

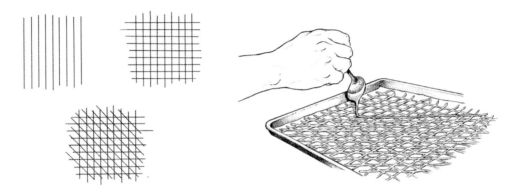

8 If the caramel becomes too thick to make thin lines, reheat it briefly over low heat, stirring occasionally, until the caramel is liquid but not too thin. Continue making lines of caramel on the pan in all three directions until you have used up the sugar.

9 Let the caramel harden, then break it up into 2- to 3-inch irregular pieces.

10 To clean the pan and spoon with the hardened caramel on it, just place them in the sink and fill the pan with hot water. It will take a few hours for the caramel in the pan and on the spoon to melt.

SERVING: Use a piece of caramel lace to decorate any fruit, cream, or frozen dessert.

STORAGE: Keep the pieces of caramel lace on the pan until you need to use them. They'll hold up well for the entire day on which they are made. If the weather is cool and dry, they might hold up well until a second day, but they'll always look best on the day they are made.

Per piece: 38 calories, 0 g total fat (0% of calories), 0 g saturated fat, 0 g protein, 10 g carbohydrates, 0 g fiber, 1 mg cholesterol, 0 mg sodium

SOURCES

The Baker's Catalogue
P.O. Box 876
Norwich, VT 05055-0876
Telephone: (800) 827-6836
Website: www.bakerscatalogue.com

General baking ingredients and equipment. Also candied fruit.

La Gondola
Viale della Vittoria, 255—31029 Vittorio Veneto (TV)—Italy
Telephone: +39-0438-949936 or
+39-0438-57603
Website: www.bella-italia.com/gondola

Gaggia, Simac, and Musso home and commercial ice cream machines.

Bridge Kitchenware
214 East 52nd Street
New York, NY 10022
Telephone: (212) 688-4220
Website: www.bridgekitchenware.com

Cookware, bakeware, including tart pans.

Bonnie Slotnick Cookbooks
163 West 10th Street
New York, NY 10014
Telephone: (212) 989-8962
Website: www.bonnieslotnickbooks.com

Out-of-print and antiquarian cookbooks.

Calphalon Corporation
P.O. Box 583
Toledo, OH 43697
Telephone: (800) 809-7267
Website: www.calphalon.com

Cookware, bakeware, and other baking tools.

Fage USA
25–26 50th Street
Woodside, NY 11377
Telephone: (718) 204-5323
Website: www.fageusa.com

Greek yogurts and dairy products.

Guittard Chocolate Company
10 Guittard Road
Burlingame, CA 94010
Telephone: (650) 697-4424
Website: www.guittard.com

A range of interesting chocolate products.

Kaiser Bakeware
3512 Faith Church Road
Indian Trail, NC 28079
Telephone: (800) 966-3009
Website: www.kaiserbakeware.com

Bakeware, including excellent springform pans.

Kalustyan's
123 Lexington Avenue
New York, NY 10016
Telephone: (212) 685-3451
Website: www.kalustyan.com

Herbs, spices, nuts, and seeds.

KitchenAid
KitchenAid Customer Satisfaction Center
P.O. Box 218
St. Joseph, MI 49085
Telephone: (800) 541-6390
Website: www.kitchenaid.com

Stand mixers, food processors, blenders, automatic ice cream machines, bakeware, and major appliances such as stoves and refrigerators.

New York Cake and Baking Distributors
56 West 22nd Street
New York, NY 10010
Telephone: (212) 675-2253; (800) 942-2539
Website: nycake.com

A full line of pans, decorating equipment, and chocolate. Also, molds and offset spatulas.

Nordicware
Highway 7 at Highway 100
Minneapolis, MN 55416
Telephone: (952) 920-2888; (800) 328-4310
Website: www.nordicware.com

Bakeware, including a variety of Bundt pans.

Penzey's Spices
P.O. Box 933
Muskego, WI 53150
Telephone: (262) 785-7678; (800) 741-7787
Website: www.penzeys.com

Herbs, spices (such as Nielsen-Massey vanilla), and extracts.

Rival
Rival Consumer Services
c/o The Holmes Group
13052 Jurupa Avenue
Fontana, CA 92337
Telephone: (800) 323-9519
Website: www.rivalproducts.com

White Mountain hand-cranked and electric ice cream makers. These are the large-volume, old-fashioned makers that require rock salt and ice.

Sur La Table
Pike Place Farmers Market
84 Pine Street
Seattle, WA 98101
Telephone: (206) 448-2245; (800) 243-0852
Website: www.surlatable.com

Pans, molds, and assorted baking equipment and cookware, including tart and tartlet pans.

Sweet Celebrations
(formerly Maid of Scandinavia)
P.O. Box 39426
Edina, MN 55439
Telephone: (952) 943-1508; (800) 328-6722
Website: www.sweetc.com

Wide variety of decorating supplies.

Valrhona
Website: www.valrhona.com

Chocolate blocks and bars for baking, as well as cocoa.

Williams-Sonoma
100 North Point Street
San Francisco, CA 94133
Telephone: (877) 812-6235
Website: www.williams-sonoma.com

Pans, molds, and assorted baking equipment and cookware.

ACKNOWLEDGMENTS

Writing this book has been full of little pleasures . . . eating sushi between writing sessions, discovering old recipes, and developing new friendships. Among these pleasures has been the joy of working with such a talented group of people. First of all, we would like to thank Phyllis Wender, Nick's agent, and her associate Sonia Pabley, as well as Lisa Ekus, David's agent. Thank you to Kathleen Hanuschak, R.D., for calculating the nutritional analyses, and recalculating them after some recipe retests. At HarperCollins, thanks to Hugh Van Dusen and his associate editor, Marie Estrada, copy editor Sonia Greenbaum, production editor Christine Tanigawa, and publicists Carrie Bachman and Milena Perez.

Thank you to Joel Avirom and his associates Jason Snyder and Meghan Day Healey for the clean design; to Tom Eckerle and Ceci Gallini for the beautiful photography and props; and to Laura Hartman Maestro for her precise line drawings.

Enormous thanks to Cara Tannenbaum, who tested most of the recipes and styled food in the photography studio; to her husband Bruce Beiland who made sure all the recipe testing notes made it back to us; to Andrea Tutunjian who tested recipes, styled food, and kept everything organized in her usual impeccable way; and to Rebecca Millican, who tested the remainder of the recipes. Thanks also to Jeff Yoskowitz for food preparation and styling in the studio.

Rick Smilow, president of the Institute of Culinary Education (ICE), again generously provided space for recipe testing. ICE's director of purchasing, Josh Pappas, was also helpful and patient with last-minute requests for specialty food and equipment.

Finally, a special thank-you to the many friends and colleagues who contributed recipes or inspired our own, including Ellen Baumwoll, Flo Braker, Kyra Effren, Dorie Greenspan, Claudia Fleming Hayden, Maida Heatter, Pierre Hermé, Sam Mason, Maureen McKeon, Ana Rambaldi, Mary Risley, Denis Ruffel, Bonnie Slotnick, Cara Tannenbaum, Andrea Tutunjian, and Joseph Viggiani.

295

INDEX

297

cooking pans, xxiii
cool chocolate sauce, 276
cornmeal, xiii
    in baked Indian pudding, 144–45
cornstarch, xiii
    in butterscotch pie, 98–99
    in lemon meringue tartlets, 128–31
    in petit beurre cookies, 254–55
corn syrup, xiv
    in bittersweet chocolate sorbet, 222–23
    in chocolate rum cake, 22–23
    in devil's food cake with fluffy white icing,
        24–25
    in Earl Grey sherbet, 218
    in fruit fondue, 183–84
    in Italian orange gelato, 228–29
    in warm chocolate sauce, 278
    in yogurt sherbet, 224
cranberry(ies):
    in holiday fruitcake, 75–76
    in holiday mincemeat tart, 115
    oatmeal bars, 268–69
    walnut tart, 112–13
cream(y):
    apricot sherbet, 221
    Maida's skinny whipped, 285–86
    milk and honey yogurt, 288
    peach sherbet, 220–21
    plum sherbet, 221
    see also sour cream
cream, heavy, xix
cream, whipping, xix, 275
    in best and easiest chocolate roll, 26–27
    in blancmange with yogurt and honey, 139–40
    in caramel sauce, 279–80
    in coconut tapioca with lime and mint-
        scented pineapple, 141–43
    in individual Pavlovas with berries, 45–47
    in Maida's skinny whipped cream, 285–86
    in real chocolate truffles, 38–39
    in white chocolate raspberry tartlets, 32–33

cream cheese, xix
    in lemon cheese tart with strawberries,
        124–25
    in Thanksgiving Day pumpkin mousse, 166–67
crisp chocolate biscotti, 12–13
crumb cake, blueberry, 82–83
crumb crusts, 95
cupcake pans, xxiii
cupcakes:
    chocolate, with brown sugar icing, 18–19
    lemon, with milk chocolate frosting, 65–66
currants, Zante:
    in holiday mince meat tart, 114–15
    in individual apple strudels, 126–27
custard(s), 135, 153
    coffee caramel, 152
    Earl Grey panna cotta, 149
    espresso panna cotta, 149
    lemon, with raspberry sauce, 154–56
    Mary's cappuccino brûlé, 160–61
    orange, 156
    panna cotta, 148–49
    rum caramel, 152
    sauce, in snow eggs, 157–59
    sauces, 280–81
    tart, apricot, 119–20
    tart, chocolate banana, 30–31
    tips for creamy, 135–36
    vanilla caramel, 152
    Viennese caramel, 150–52

dairy products, xvii–xix
dates, 209
    in holiday fruitcake, 75–76
David's skinny chocolate chip cookies, 256–58
devil's food cake with fluffy white icing, 24–25
Dorie's blueberry sherbet, 219
dough, 92
    cocoa, 28–29, 30, 32
    flaky pastry, 94
    sweet pastry, 92

Index

INDEX

raspberry, in Flo's spectacular jelly roll, 56–59

raspberry, in Kyra's hot milk sponge layer cake, 63–66

raspberry, in updated Linzertorte, 110–11

in strawberry meringue tart, 116–18

see also marmalade

fudgy brownies, 16–17

galettes, plum and ginger, 104–5

garnishes, 275

    caramel lace, 289–90

    chocolate shavings, 275, 286–87

gelatin, xiii, 162–63

    in blancmange with yogurt and honey, 139–40

    in easy chocolate mousse, 34–36

    in lemon yogurt mousse, 164–65

    in panna cotta, 148–49

    in raspberry mousse cake, 60–62

    in Thanksgiving Day pumpkin mousse, 166–67

    tips for, 138

gelato, 213

    Italian orange, 228–29

    strawberry, 230

    variations of, 229–30

German chocolate, 7

ginger, xv, 153

    ice milk, 233–34

    ice milk, grilled curried mangoes with, 186–87

    lovers' pound cake, 67–68

    marmalade, in Kyra's hot milk sponge layer cake, 63–64

    and plum galettes, 104–5

gingersnaps, 252–53

gooseberries, in gratin of summer berries, 200–201

Gramercy Tavern, 178

Grand Marnier, 228

granita, 214

    Italian coffee, 226–27

    lemon, 227

    strawberry, 227

granola bars, 266

granulated sugar, xiv

grapefruit and Campari sherbet, 216

grapes, 209

    in not just any fruit salad, 181–82

graters, xxiv, 68

gratin dishes, xxii

gratin of summer berries, 200–201

Greek yogurt:

    in blancmange with yogurt and honey, 139–40

    in coconut poppy seed coffee cake, 84–85

    in frozen banana yogurt, 231–32

    in lemon yogurt mousse, 164–65

    in milk and honey yogurt cream, 288

    in yogurt sherbet, 224–25

Greenspan, Dorie, 219

grilled curried mangoes with ginger ice milk, 186–87

hand tools, xxiii–xxvi

Hayden, Claudia Fleming, 178

hazelnut(s), xvi, 48

    and honey biscotti, 264–65

    in updated Linzertorte, 110–11

Heatter, Maida, 214, 235, 285, 288

heavy cream, xix

height of summer blueberry pie, 96–98

herbs and spices, xvi, 241

    tips on, 153

Hermé, Pierre, 135, 141, 196

holiday fruitcake, 75–76

holiday mincemeat tart, 114–15

honey, xiv

    blancmange with yogurt and, 139–40

    and hazelnut biscotti, 264–65

    and milk yogurt cream, 288

    in rum raisin semifreddo, 236–37

    spice cookies, Italian cocoa, 14–15

honeydew, 209

    in not just any fruit salad, 181–82

How to Bake (Malgieri), 100, 114, 270

ice cream, 213
ice cream machines, 215
ice milk, 213
ices and frozen desserts, 213–37
    banana chocolate chip frozen yogurt, 232
    bittersweet chocolate sherbet, 222–23
    coconut ice milk, 234
    creamy apricot sherbet, 221
    creamy peach sherbet, 220–21
    creamy plum sherbet, 221
    Dorie's blueberry sherbet, 219
    Earl Grey sherbet, 218
    frozen banana yogurt, 231–32
    gelato variations, 229–30
    ginger ice milk, 233–34
    grapefruit and Campari sherbet, 216
    Italian coffee granita, 226–27
    Italian orange gelato, 228–29
    lemon granita, 227
    Maida's milk chocolate ice milk, 235
    rum raisin semifreddo, 236–37
    strawberry frozen yogurt, 232
    strawberry granita, 227
    technique tips for, 214–15
    vanilla yogurt sherbet, 225
    yogurt sherbet, 224–25
icing:
    chocolate cupcakes with brown sugar, 18–19
    devil's food cake with fluffy white, 24–25
    see also frosting
Indian pudding, baked, 144–45
ingredients, xiii–xx
    dairy products, xvii–xix
    eggs, xvii
    flavorings, xv–xvi
    flours, starches, gelatin and filo dough,
        xiii–xiv
    leaveners, xv
    nuts and nut products, xvi–xvii
    sugars and sweeteners, xiv–xv
instant-read thermometers, xxiv

Institute of Culinary Education, 141, 196
Italian:
    -American ricotta pie, 102–3
    cocoa honey spice cookies, 14–15
    coffee granita, 226–27
    orange gelato, 228–29
    poached whole oranges, 188–89

jam, xvi
    see also fruit spread
jelly roll, Flo's spectacular, 56–59

Kirsch, xv, 162, 168, 181, 282, 283
    poached pineapple with, 190–92
kisses, ginger meringue, 246–48
knives, xxiii
Kump, Peter, 95
Kyra's hot milk sponge layer cake, 63–64

labels, definitions of, xvii–xviii
Last Course, The (Hayden), 178
layer pans, xxi
leavenings, xv
lemon(s), 153, 209
    angel food cake, 52
    cheese tart with strawberries, 124–25
    chiffon cake, 55
    cupcakes with milk chocolate frosting,
        65–66
    custard sauce, 281
    custard with raspberry sauce, 154–56
    granita, 227
    in holiday mincemeat tart, 114–15
    juice, in Dorie's blueberry sherbet, 219
    meringue tartlets, 128–31
    in orange custard, 156
    in strawberry rhubarb compote with sugared
        pecans, 193–95
    yogurt mousse, 164–65
    zest, in ginger ice milk, 233–34
    zest, in panna cotta, 148–49

Pesche alla Piemontese, 198–99
petit beurre cookies, 254–55
pies, 91
    black bottom, 99
    butterscotch, 98–99
    cherry, 98
    crumb, 98
    crumb crust for, 95
    flaky pastry dough for, 94
    height of summer blueberry, 96–98
    Italian-American ricotta, 102–3
    pans for, xxii
    sweet crumb crust for, 95
    sweet pastry dough for, 93
    technique tips for, 92
    see also tartlets; tarts
pineapple(s), 209
    coconut tapioca with lime and mint-scented,
        141–43
    in crumb cake, 82–83
    poached, with Kirsch, 190–92
pine nuts, in roasted pear compote, 196–97
pistachios, xvi–xvii
pizza wheel, xxiv
plum(s), 175
    in cooked fruit sauce, 284
    in crumb cake, 82–83
    in fruit fondue, 183–84
    and ginger galettes, 104–5
    in not just any fruit salad, 181–82
    sherbet, creamy, 221
poppy seed coffee cake, coconut, 84–85
pound cake, ginger lovers', 67–68
puddings, 135
    baked Indian, 144–45
    blancmange with yogurt and honey,
        139–40
    Coach House bread, 146–47
    coconut tapioca with lime and mint-scented
        pineapple, 141–43
    old-fashioned chocolate, 37

pumpkin:
    loaf cake, 80–81
    mousse, Thanksgiving Day, 166–67
    pie, perfect, 100–101
    spice muffins, 81

Quiche and Pâté (Kump), 95

raisin(s), 209
    cookies, chewy oatmeal, 258–59
    in granola bars, 266
    in holiday fruitcake, 75–76
    in holiday mincemeat tart, 114–15
    in old-fashioned carrot cake, 70–71
    in old-fashioned hermits, 270–71
    rum, semifreddo, 236–37
    in shredded apple cake, 72–73
ramekins, xxiii
raspberry(ies):
    fruit spread, in Flo's spectacular jelly roll,
        56–59
    fruit spread, in Kyra's hot milk sponge layer
        cake, 63–64
    fruit spread, in updated Linzertorte, 110–11
    in gratin of summer berries, 200–201
    in individual Pavlovas with berries, 45–47
    in lemon cheese tart with strawberries,
        124–25
    mousse, 163
    mousse cake, 60–62
    in not just any fruit salad, 181–82
    sauce, cooked, 283
    sauce, fresh, 282
    sauce, lemon custard with, 154–56
    soufflé, 169
    tart, old-fashioned, 121–22
    tartlets, white chocolate, 32–33
real chocolate truffles, 38–39
rectangular pans, xxi
red currants, in gratin of summer berries, 200–201
red wine, peaches in, 176–77

307

in lemon cupcakes with milk chocolate
frosting, 65–66
in Maida's skinny whipped cream, 285–86
spatulas, xxiii
spice cake, easy, 86–87
spice cookies:
chocolate, 10
Italian cocoa honey, 14–15
spiced angel food cake, 52
spice muffins, pumpkin, 81
spices, see herbs and spices
spices, tips on, 153
sponge layer cake, Kyra's hot milk, 63–64
spoons:
measuring, xxv
wooden, xxiv
springforms, xxii
springtime rhubarb crisp, 207–8
square pans, xxi
stand mixers, xxvi
strawberry(ies), 153, 209
with balsamic vinegar and tarragon, 178–80
in cooked sauce, 283
frozen yogurt, 232
in fruit fondue, 183–84
gelato, 230
granita, 227
in gratin of summer berries, 200–201
lemon cheese tart with, 124–25
meringue tart, 116–18
mousse, 162–63
in not just any fruit salad, 181–82
in old-fashioned raspberry tart, 121–22
rhubarb compote with sugared pecans,
193–95
sauce, fresh, 282
soufflé, fresh, 168–69
soufflés, individual, 169
strudels, individual apple, 126–27
sugars and sweeteners, xiv–xv
reducing of, 79

sweet chocolate, 7
sweet crumb crust, 95
sweetened condensed milk, xix
sweet pastry dough, 92
syrup, for not just any fruit salad, 181–82

tangerine(s), 209
in fruit fondue, 183–84
gelato, 230
Tannenbaum, Cara, 67
Tante Marie's Cooking School, 160–61
Tante Marie's Cooking School Cookbook (Risley),
160
tapioca, xiv
coconut, with lime and mint-scented
pineapple, 141–43
tarragon, strawberries with balsamic vinegar and,
178–80
tartlets:
lemon meringue, 128–31
pans for, xxii
white chocolate raspberry, 32–33
see also pies
tarts, 91
apricot custard, 119–20
banana walnut, 108–9
chocolate banana custard, 30–31
chocolate buttermilk, 28–29
cranberry mincemeat, 115
cranberry walnut, 112–13
crumb crust for, 95
flaky pastry dough for, 94
holiday mincemeat, 114–15
individual apple strudels, 126–27
lemon cheese, with strawberries, 124–25
old-fashioned raspberry, 121–22
pans for, xxii
plum and ginger galettes, 104–5
roasted pear, 197
rustic apple, 106–7
strawberry meringue, 116–18

THE IMPORTANCE OF

Norman Rockwell

These and other titles are included in The Importance
Of biography series:

Alexander the Great	Adolf Hitler
Muhammad Ali	Harry Houdini
Louis Armstrong	Thomas Jefferson
James Baldwin	Mother Jones
Clara Barton	Chief Joseph
Napoleon Bonaparte	Malcolm X
Julius Caesar	Margaret Mead
Rachel Carson	Michelangelo
Charlie Chaplin	Wolfgang Amadeus Mozart
Cesar Chavez	John Muir
Winston Churchill	Sir Isaac Newton
Cleopatra	Richard Nixon
Christopher Columbus	Georgia O'Keeffe
Hernando Cortes	Louis Pasteur
Marie Curie	Pablo Picasso
Amelia Earhart	Elvis Presley
Thomas Edison	Jackie Robinson
Albert Einstein	Norman Rockwell
Duke Ellington	Anwar Sadat
Dian Fossey	Margaret Sanger
Benjamin Franklin	Oskar Schindler
Galileo Galilei	John Steinbeck
Emma Goldman	Jim Thorpe
Jane Goodall	Mark Twain
Martha Graham	Queen Victoria
Stephen Hawking	Pancho Villa
Jim Henson	H. G. Wells

Norman Rockwell

by
Deanne Durrett

Lucent Books, P.O. Box 289011, San Diego, CA 92198-9011

Library of Congress Cataloging-in-Publication Data

Durrett, Deanne, 1940–
    Norman Rockwell / by Deanne Durrett.
        p. cm.—(The Importance of)
    Includes bibliographical references and index.
    Summary: A biography of the artist best known for his
portrayals of "common people caught in ordinary
situations."
    ISBN 1-56006-080-8 (alk. paper)
    1. Rockwell, Norman, 1894–1978—Juvenile literature.
2. Illustrators—United States—Biography—Juvenile
literature. [1. Rockwell, Norman, 1894–1978.
2. Illustrators.]   I. Title. II. Series.
ND237.R68D87   1997
759.13—dc20   96-3956
    [B]   CIP
                                                     AC

Copyright 1997 by Lucent Books, Inc., P.O. Box 289011,
San Diego, California, 92198-9011

Printed in the U.S.A.

*In memory of Booger, who taught me to enjoy artistic
beauty, and dedicated to Martin Corcorran,
a talented young artist who may one day
record world events on canvas.*

Contents

Foreword

THE IMPORTANCE OF biography series deals with individuals who have made a unique contribution to history. The editors of the series have deliberately chosen to cast a wide net and include people from all fields of endeavor. Individuals from politics, music, art, literature, philosophy, science, sports, and religion are all represented. In addition, the editors did not restrict the series to individuals whose accomplishments have helped change the course of history. Of necessity, this criterion would have eliminated many whose contribution was great, though limited. Charles Darwin, for example, was responsible for radically altering the scientific view of the natural history of the world. His achievements continue to impact the study of science today. Others, such as Chief Joseph of the Nez Percé, played a pivotal role in the history of their own people. While Joseph's influence does not extend much beyond the Nez Percé, his nonviolent resistance to white expansion and his continuing role in protecting his tribe and his homeland remain an inspiration to all.

These biographies are more than factual chronicles. Each volume attempts to emphasize an individual's contributions both in his or her own time and for posterity. For example, the voyages of Christopher Columbus opened the way to European colonization of the New World. Unquestionably, his encounter with the New World brought monumental changes to both Europe and the Americas in his day. Today, however, the broader impact of Columbus's voyages is being critically scrutinized. *Christopher Columbus,* as well as every biography in The Importance Of series, includes and evaluates the most recent scholarship available on each subject.

Each author includes a wide variety of primary and secondary source quotations to document and substantiate his or her work. All quotes are footnoted to show readers exactly how and where biographers derive their information, as well as provide stepping stones to further research. These quotations enliven the text by giving readers eyewitness views of the life and times of each individual covered in The Importance Of series.

Finally, each volume is enhanced by photographs, bibliographies, chronologies, and comprehensive indexes. For both the casual reader and the student engaged in research, The Importance Of biographies will be a fascinating adventure into the lives of people who have helped shape humanity's past and present, and who will continue to shape its future.

IMPORTANT DATES IN THE LIFE OF NORMAN ROCKWELL

1894
Norman Percevel Rockwell is born in New York City on February 3.

1899
Begins sketching.

1908
Studies at Chase School of Fine and Applied Art.

1910
Enrolls at National Academy of Design; transfers to Art Students League.

1911
Illustrates first book, *Tell Me Why.*

1913
Becomes art director at *Boys' Life* at age nineteen.

1916
First *Saturday Evening Post* cover at age twenty-two; marries Irene O'Connor.

1917
United States enters World War I; Rockwell enlists in the navy.

1918
Rockwell is discharged from the navy.

1929
Divorces Irene.

1930
Marries Mary Rhodes Barstow.

1932
Son Jarvis is born.

1933
Son Tom is born.

1936
Son Peter is born.

1937
Begins using photography in addition to live models.

1939
Moves to Arlington, Vermont.

1943
Four Freedoms printed in the *Post*; studio burns to the ground.

1951
Paints *Saying Grace.*

1952
Paints President Dwight D. Eisenhower.

1953
Moves to Stockbridge, Massachusetts.

1959
Mary Rockwell dies.

1961
Receives Interfaith Award of the National Conference of Christians and Jews; marries Mary L. Punderson.

1963
Rockwell's last *Post* cover is published.

1976
Stockbridge celebrates Norman Rockwell Day.

1978
Rockwell dies in Stockbridge on November 8.

America's Best-Loved Illustrator

With a gentle touch of wit and humor, artist Norman Rockwell's *Saturday Evening Post* covers portrayed common people caught in ordinary situations. Rockwell painted pictures that invited the viewer into the scene to enjoy these moments and share the feelings.

As Rockwell's work made its way into the American home on the covers of the *Saturday Evening Post*, one of the most

Norman Rockwell stands before one of his many paintings, this one in honor of Mother's Day 1951. Rockwell's realistic and humorous paintings of life in America have made him the nation's best-loved illustrator.

Rockwell Painted Life

Lynda Pflueger, a friend of the author's, shared this memory of Norman Rockwell and the Saturday Evening Post.

"I was a latchkey kid in the fourth through sixth grades. I was not a good reader (I spent all of the second grade in a hospital in Los Angeles) but loved to look at magazines. My favorite magazine was the *Post,* and one of my weekly treats was to run home on Wednesdays to see what the artist had put on the cover. My favorite is the one called *The Runaway.* My father was a policeman; . . . his uniform looked like the officer's in the picture. Dad patrolled Ocean Beach [San Diego] and coached more than one runaway back home."

popular magazines of all time, he became as familiar to the public as the flag and apple pie. Each of his 317 *Post* covers is said to have been seen by an average of four million people.

From the beginning of his career, Rockwell wanted to be an illustrator. He began paying his own way to art school at the age of fourteen and worked hard to learn his craft. This included learning anatomy and being able not only to draw the human body in any position, but to draw it from the skeleton out. Although Rockwell became a master of his craft, his desire to continually improve his skills offered him challenge throughout his career. He wrote in his autobiography: "I am not satisfied with my work. . . . But that keeps me working. If I thought I was perfect or even close to it I'd probably pawn my brushes and quit."[1]

As he became famous, some tried to label him a folk artist. Others referred to him as the Lawrence Welk of art. These people viewed him as old-fashioned and out of touch with modern society. However, Rockwell had his own way of looking at life, and many Americans liked his view. He portrayed strength, courage, friendship, character, and all that was good in America. Rockwell viewed life the way everyone would like it to be all the time, the way it was for average Americans—at least some of the time.

1 Young Norman Rockwell

Norman Rockwell was born on February 3, 1894, in a fifth-floor apartment located just west of Central Park in New York City. He was the second son of Jarvis Waring Rockwell and Nancy Hill Rockwell.

His father, Waring Rockwell, worked his way up from office boy to office manager of the New York branch of George Woods, Sons, and Company, a Philadelphia textile mill. Norman remembered his father as a dignified, handsome man—a Victorian gentleman who observed the courtesies of the time:

There was something aristocratic about him, the way he carried himself or the set of his fine dark eyes. His substantial mustache was always neatly trimmed. He wore dark, well-tailored suits and never removed his coat in the presence

A young Norman Rockwell (second from left) poses for a portrait with his parents and older brother.

of ladies. He did not drink but was a gentlemanly smoker. Dignified, holding to the proprieties [customs and manners of polite society], gentle and at the same time stern; but distant, aware of Jarvis [Norman's older brother] and me, but always, even when we were children, treating us as sons who have grown up and been away for a long time—that's how I remember my father. I was never close to him.[2]

Rockwell's memories of his mother, Nancy Hill Rockwell, revolved around her poor health. Thought by some to be a hypochondriac, she became ill long before Norman was born and continued in poor health until she died at the age of eighty-five.

Norman inherited his love of art from his father and his grandfather on his mother's side. Howard Hill, Nancy's father, came to America from England shortly after the Civil War. An aspiring artist, he dreamed of opening a portrait studio and becoming famous. Instead, in order to feed his twelve children, he went door to door offering to paint pets and

Norman inherited his love of art from both his father, Jarvis Rockwell, and his grandfather, Howard Hill. This intricate oil painting by Hill is quite similar to Norman's early works.

Rockwell's Father

In his autobiography Rockwell wrote about the evenings he and his brother sat at the dining room table listening to his father read:

"On weekday evenings, after Jarvis and I had finished our homework, we would sit around the dining-room table and my father would read Dickens out loud to us. I would . . . draw pictures of the different characters, Mr. Pickwick, Oliver Twist, Uriah Heep. They were pretty crude pictures, but I was very deeply impressed and moved by Dickens. I remember how I suffered with Little Dorrit in the Marshalsea Prison, had nightmares over Bill Sikes and Fagin, felt ennobled by Sydney Carton. . . . The variety, sadness, horror, happiness, treachery, the twists and turns of life; the sharp impressions of dirt, food, inns, horses, streets; the people—Micawber, Pickwick, Dombey (and son), Joe Gragery—in Dickens shocked and delighted me. So that, I thought, is what the world is really like. I began to look around me; I became insatiably curious."

farm animals for a price. When this activity failed to bring in enough money to support his family, he worked as a housepainter. Because of this apparent failure, Nancy Hill had little respect for her father. However she took great pride in her English heritage from her mother's family. She even claimed to be descended from nobility, citing a distant relative, Sir Norman Percevel.

Mercy Percy!

Norman's mother named him after Sir Norman, her family hero. She insisted that Norman always sign his full name and often called him Norman Percevel. Nor-

man intensely disliked this middle name. He wrote:

I had the queer notion that Percevel (and especially the form Percy) was a sissy name, almost effeminate. . . . I darn near died when a boy called me "Mercy Percy"; to my relief it didn't stick. When I left home I dropped the Percevel immediately, despite my mother's earnest protestations.[3]

As a concession to his mother, he signed his early magazine covers and illustrations for *Boys' Life* and *St. Nicholas* as Norman P. Rockwell. However, so many people wanted to know what the P stood for that by the time he did his first *Post* cover in 1916, he had dropped the initial.

From that time on he signed his artwork and legal papers simply Norman Rockwell.

Discovery at the Dining Table

Although Norman did not consider his family close-knit, they shared some good times together. He had fond memories of sitting at the dining room table with Jarvis, his older brother, while his father read from Dickens. As his father read, Norman drew pictures of Dickens's characters, Mr. Pickwick, Oliver Twist, and Uriah Heep. Rockwell biographer Donald Walton wrote of this experience:

> He took the big jump which made him . . . a true artist. He had gone beyond mere copying and was creating images in his own mind's eye. By listening to stories and then drawing, he was in a sense teaching himself to be an illustrator of books.[4]

Norman also adopted a Dickensian view of his surroundings. He wrote, "I began to look at things the way I imagined Dickens would have looked at them."[5] He applied this perspective to his uncle, Gil Waughlum. Although Waughlum had been a scientist and inventor, in his later years he lost some of his mental ability. As a result he mixed up the holidays, bringing Christmas gifts on Easter and Fourth of July fireworks at Christmas. Norman compared his uncle to Mr. Dick in Dickens's *David Copperfield:* "I guessed it was all a matter of how you looked at something. Mr. Dick was a simpleton, yet Dickens saw that he was something more: kindly, generous, loving, and endowed with a measure of uncommon common sense."[6] That is how Norman chose to see his uncle Gil. This forgiving and optimistic attitude would carry over into his idealized illustrations.

In addition to sharing a love of Dickens, Norman and his father enjoyed sketching the illustrations they found in magazines such as *Leslie's Illustrated Weekly Newspaper* or *Harper's Weekly.* As a result Norman Rockwell began to discover his inborn talent and soon began to realize a great deal of pleasure from drawing.

Summers in the Country

Throughout his childhood Norman's family moved from one apartment to another, each time attempting to better themselves. Then as Nancy Rockwell's health grew worse and she could no longer do housework, the family moved from one boardinghouse to another.

To escape the city, the Rockwell family spent every summer in the country until Norman was about nine years old. They stayed at working farms with large houses that advertised in the New York papers as resorts. The farmers rented rooms to city people, like the Rockwells, who wanted to enjoy the rural setting. Norman relished the country. He helped with the chores, fished, swam in muddy ponds, and hunted. For three glorious months he left the city behind and basked in the fresh air of the country.

It seemed to him that everything in the country was beautiful and everything in the city was ugly. He wrote:

> A country cur [dog] has just as many fleas as any city mongrel. But I didn't see them or, if I did, they were crowded out by the first sleepy cries of

the whippoorwills at dawn . . . and long lazy afternoons spent fishing for bullheads, the emerald dragonflies darting around our heads. . . . That's the way I thought of the country then and still do in spite of myself. . . . Later on I came to realize (reluctantly) that ugly things happen in the country as well as in the city. Still that didn't change my ideas.[7]

Norman filled his mind with memories of the details of rural life: the way a horse's long, shaggy mane hung almost to the water as it drank from a farm pond, how it would raise its head and snort, then drink again. He remembered wrestling and tumbling in a barn with his brother until they collapsed, giggling in the fragrant hay at first, then silently watching dust motes, or specks, swirl in the shafts of sunlight. He never forgot the feel of wiggling his toes in the cool, green grass on his first day in the country each year. These memories of his childhood summers greatly impacted the way Norman Rockwell would paint in years to come. He wrote:

> Maybe as I grew up and found that the world wasn't the perfectly pleasant place I had thought it to be I unconsciously decided that, even if it wasn't an ideal world, it should be and so painted only the ideal aspects of it. . . . The summers I spent in the country as a child became part of this idealized view of life. . . . I wasn't a country boy. I didn't really live that kind of life. Except . . . later on in my paintings.[8]

In 1903 when Norman was nine years old, the Rockwells moved to Mamaroneck, a small town about twenty miles outside New York City. After the move to Mamaroneck, a more or less rural setting, the Rockwell family no longer went to the country for the summer.

Rockwell the Choirboy

In contrast to the relaxed summers in the country, Norman's boyhood included rigorous religious discipline. His parents were very religious, and the family went to church several times a week. Norman sang in the boys choir until his voice changed. He sang at Saint Luke's Episcopal Church and then later at the Cathedral of Saint John the Divine. He attended choir rehearsal four times a week and sang at four services every Sunday. Rockwell remembered it as hard work that he did not enjoy much.

Although Norman and his brother kept busy with church activities and homework, they still found time to get into mischief with their friends. Sometimes the boys would sneak up the narrow stairs that led to the roof of the apartment building. From there they would lean over the wall and spit on people passing by. Other times they would toss stones at children playing in the street.

At less mischievous times Norman sometimes became the center of attention as the other boys watched him draw pictures on the sidewalk. He drew horses, soldiers, dogs, or whatever they wanted. Inspired by reports of sea battles in the Spanish-American War, Norman drew ships on cardboard that he and his friends cut out to wage pretend sea battles. However, as the boys grew older, they lost interest in sidewalk art and sea battles with cardboard ships. How hard one could swing a bat and how far one could throw a

football ranked far above Norman's ability to use a piece of chalk or lead pencil.

The Young Artist

Norman described himself as a skinny, pigeon-toed, narrow-shouldered kid with a big Adam's apple and glasses. When the neighborhood kids chose sides to play tag, baseball, or touch football, Norman, the slowest runner on the block, was chosen last, if at all. By the time he reached twelve, Norman could see he had no future on the athletic field and decided to make the most of his artistic ability. He explained it this way:

At that age boys who are athletes are expressing themselves fully. They have an identity, a recognized place among others boys. I didn't have that. All I

The Hard Life of a Choirboy

Norman Rockwell wrote in his autobiography about being in the choir at Saint Luke's in New York City and then in Mamaroneck:

"At rehearsals we had to sit on high stools around a grand piano, our heads just on a level with the broad, shiny top. When one of us hit a false note or dozed off, the choirmaster would slide a hymnbook sharply across the smooth surface of the top of the piano so that it cracked the culprit on the head. . . . He'd rage about on his piano bench, calling us all sorts of names, reaching out to cuff the boys nearest him, while we perched there, silent, white-faced, on our stools. . . . I dare say he could not have got us to sing as beautifully as we did except by treating us harshly. We were only kids, most of us not more than seven or eight years old, and we would have skipped rehearsals or sung lackadaisically if we had not been so fearful of provoking his wrath. Jarvis and I had a reason for not wanting to attend rehearsals. A slum lay between our house and the church. We'd walk hurriedly through the dim, gaslighted streets. Gangs of ragged children taunted us. Drunken men lurched against us. We clutched rocks in our fists, expecting every minute to be set upon.

In Mamaroneck, the choir boys were treated with more leniency. And so we had good times and enjoyed ourselves more. And, of course, sang jarringly at times, never matching the excellence of the St. Luke's choir."

Norman began to hone his artistic talent at an early age. Over the years, his warmhearted memories of childhood served as an endless source of inspiration for his illustrations.

had was the ability to draw, which as far as I could see didn't count for much. But because it was all I had I began to make it my whole life. I drew all the time. Gradually my narrow shoulders, long neck, and pigeon toes became less important to me. My feelings no longer paralyzed me. I drew and drew and drew.[9]

Norman became a loner. He withdrew into himself with paper and pencil to practice his art. In this area he excelled.

In spite of Norman Rockwell's natural talent, he had to work hard to cultivate his inborn ability. Although still very young, once Rockwell decided to be an artist, he sought formal training and dedicated himself to being the best he could be.

2 Education and Early Work

Norman's eighth-grade teacher, Miss Julia Smith, helped him recognize the value of his artistic ability. She looked beyond his low grades and saw a boy with talent. She asked him to decorate the blackboards for Christmas and draw pictures to illustrate history and science lessons. The compliments Norman received from other students and teachers gave him confidence in his work and helped him find his niche in the world. Years later he remembered Miss Smith in his autobiography: "I *know* she saw where I was headed and, because she was a fine teacher, helped me along. God bless her."[10]

Art School

While in Miss Smith's class, Norman Rockwell decided he would go to art school. As soon as he made this decision, he began looking for a part-time job. He later recalled, "My brother and I never got an allowance. . . . We'd go out and earn our spending money at odd jobs. I had to scrape up the tuition for art schools, or I couldn't have gone."[11]

Besides being unable to give him financial support, Norman's parents did not want him to become an artist. His mother feared that Norman would be a failure like his grandfather, Howard Hill. Rockwell later recalled, "My mother thought I would end up dying of starvation in an attic, but it didn't work out that way."[12]

Determined to go to art school, Norman let it be known that he needed work. As a result the minister at his church put him in contact with a wealthy young lady named Ethel Barrymore, who later became a famous stage and movie actress. She paid Norman to escort her and a friend to the country to sketch on Saturdays that summer.

Norman also delivered mail to wealthy people who lived outside the Mamaroneck postal delivery routes. The mail delivery led to other jobs, including tutoring art and his first art commission: Mrs. Arnold Constable, one of his postal customers, hired him to design a set of four custom Christmas cards for her.

Chase School of Fine and Applied Art

Through these part-time jobs Norman earned enough money to attend the Chase School of Fine and Applied Art in New York City during his freshman year at

While trying to raise his tuition for art school, Norman held many odd jobs. Ethel Barrymore (pictured) hired the aspiring artist to accompany her and a friend to the country to sketch during the summer.

Mamaroneck High School. At first he went only on Saturdays. Shortly after Thanksgiving the principal excused him from school on Wednesdays to study at Chase. Norman began making the four-hour trolley and subway trip to New York twice a week. His earnings barely stretched to cover tuition and the round-trip fares that year. He had to budget carefully, taking a sandwich from home for lunch and allowing himself only a nickel for pocket change each day.

The following summer, 1909, Norman accepted an offer to teach French, English, and athletics at Pennington's Academy for Boys. Although Norman, a poor student and even worse athlete, had few qualifications, the headmaster, Dr. J. J. Pennington, promised to pay him twenty-five dollars a week plus one meal a day. Rockwell later wrote, "So off I went to begin my career as a teacher of French, my one advantage over my students being that I had a textbook and they didn't."[13]

Norman counted on the money from this summer job to pay his tuition to art school. Every payday Dr. Pennington promised Norman that he would be paid the next week. When the summer ended, Norman had received no money. Still Dr. Pennington offered excuses instead of payment. In the end Norman worked the summer for free. He wrote of the loss:

> The last day of school he vowed . . . to send me my money by mail. . . . Of course Dr. Pennington never sent it. So the whole summer was shot—a long, hard summer, too—and I went off to art school with barely enough money to get me through the first term.[14]

Regular school and art classes left Norman with little time for odd jobs. As a result he soon had to make a choice between high school and art school.

The National Academy of Design

Midway through his sophomore year Norman dropped out of high school and enrolled at the National Academy of Design to study art full-time. The National Academy offered a better selection of classes and instructors than Chase and charged no tuition.

In the first weeks at the academy, Norman spent eight hours a day, six days a week sketching plaster reproductions of statues of the ancient Greek gods. He found this class, called the antique class, boring. He could not wait to move to the life class in the next room, where they painted from live models. He wrote:

As I toiled away at my drawing of Mercury or Venus . . . I'd sneak a look through one of the peepholes carved in the wall. . . . I'd make a little sketch of the part of the model I could see and turn back to my drawing of Mercury or Venus with determination and a new hope.[15]

Norman, only sixteen and much younger than the other students, worked hard. He missed out on the fun and social activities other teenagers enjoyed as he dedicated himself to art. He sketched almost every part of every statue in class. As a result he mastered the ability to draw the human body and advanced to life class after only two months at the academy.

Life Class

Although the aspiring artist had been stealing peeks at the live models, young Rockwell found facing flesh-and-blood

---

Norman Rockwell Meets Ethel Barrymore Again

More than thirty years later while preparing to do a Post *cover, Rockwell met Miss Barrymore again. He related the experience to biographer Donald Walton:*

" 'It was many years later—sometime in the 1940s I think—when I met Miss Barrymore again, to start that *Post* cover with her and the other movie stars. When we went out to take the photographs of her on the studio lot,' Norman recalled, 'the photographer and I had to wait for awhile in a small room where he had the camera set up. People kept coming in. There was some kind of agent, her maid, and another woman who arranged her makeup. Then Ethel Barrymore swept into the room, like the grand lady she was. And she walked right over to me and said "Why, it's Norman Rockwell. I remember you used to give me sketching lessons." In that marvelous voice of hers, so deep and dramatic. There was no one else like her and still so beautiful. Golly, I was so thrilled to think that she still knew me after all those years. We talked about those days out on the [Long Island] Sound. It was great.' "

---

nude females a bit unsettling. Then, too, as a newcomer his turn to choose a spot for his easel came last, and of course he had the least desirable view. He later described the experience:

> The model was posed lying on her side, her head propped on one elbow. All I could see were the soles of her feet and her rather large rear end. So that's what I drew during my first two weeks in life class. But I didn't care; at least I was working from a live model.[16]

Although the fundamental lessons offered at the National Academy were valuable, Norman wanted more freedom and less of the academy's formal academic style.

The Art Students League

Norman heard about the Art Students League from other students. In addition to boasting Norman's idol, Howard Pyle, as one of its founders, the school had a reputation as the most liberal and exciting art school in the country. This was the place young Rockwell wanted to go.

Norman transferred to the Art Students League in 1910. He then faced a decision that would have major impact on his life: which drawing teacher should he choose, George Bridgman or Kenneth Hayes Miller? Without knowing anything about either teacher, he chose Bridgman. The other choice, as it turned out, would have been completely wrong for Norman Rockwell. He later wrote:

> If I had signed up with Mr. Miller, I might be a modernist now. I guess it's a good thing I didn't because my ability evidently lies in telling stories and

modern art doesn't go in much for that sort of thing. I probably would have been lost in modern art with my temperament and experience, my Dickensian view of people.[17]

George Bridgman proved to be the perfect choice for Norman. Bridgman taught his students to draw the human body from the skeleton out: bones, ligaments, muscle, and skin. He said:

> You can't draw a leg if you don't know what makes it move backward from the knee instead of forward. The body isn't a . . . hollow drum covered with skin. The bones, muscles give the body its shape, determine how it moves.[18]

As a result of Bridgman's teaching, Norman learned the difference between drawing a living body pulled into position by muscle and bone as opposed to a hollow tube with no inner structure. This allowed him to accurately shade body contours with his pencil, giving his figures depth and life.

Bridgman's Tough Evaluation

Bridgman evaluated the students' work regularly and often suggested changes with a heavy black charcoal line. After Norman received one of Bridgman's evaluations, he would work for hours to erase the mark before showing his week's work to his parents. He explained his experience this way:

> He'd study my meticulous drawing, on which I'd been working very carefully with a finely pointed piece of charcoal all week. After a minute he'd burst

A young couple pose as Norman Rockwell makes a sketch of their portrait.
Dedicated to becoming a masterful illustrator, Norman devoted himself to
continually improving his skills.

out, "You haven't got the main line of the action. Look here. Down *through the hip.*" And he'd demonstrate, char-coaling a heavy black line down the center of my drawing.[19]

Bridgman used this method only for evaluating drawings he thought showed promise. He treated drawings he did not like more harshly. Rockwell later recalled this unfortunate event, although he never received this treatment himself:

> If he really hated your drawing, he'd sit there in your chair for awhile glar-ing at your sketch and chewing on . . . [his] cigar harder and harder, until he couldn't contain himself any longer. Then he'd sort of lurch forward and *spit tobacco juice right on it.* . . . Usually up near the top of the paper, so it would run down to hide your horrible drawing.[20]

Other times a more gentle Bridgman demonstrated the correct way to draw a head or a hand on a promising student's paper. Norman appreciated Bridgman's skill and treasured these small sketches at the side of his work.

Each week Bridgman graded the best work number one, with the others follow-ing in order. Although Norman tried hard, he sometimes placed second, but seldom first. The individuality, or ten-dency to draw his own way, that would one day make him a top illustrator kept him from earning the best grade in Bridg-man's class. In fact, when no one else was around to hear, Bridgman encouraged Norman to "be individual."

Hard Work and Dedication

Norman dedicated himself to becoming a great illustrator. Some students who shared Norman's ambition pushed themselves to exhaustion, working day after day without sleeping, but Norman kept a sensible routine.

Because Norman worked hard and used common sense, Bridgman chose him to be class monitor during his second year at the Art Students League. The monitor helped select and pose the models, acted as Bridgman's assistant, called the models' rest periods, and kept order in the class when the teacher was out. In return for monitoring he received free tuition.

Norman Rockwell later credited Bridgman with teaching him most of what he knew about drawing: "I worshiped George Bridgman, absorbing his every word, not to the suffocation of my own ideas and abilities, but to the development of them. I entered Mr. Bridgman's class raw; I came out browned to a turn."[21]

Paying Tribute to a Sensitive Teacher

Rockwell wrote in his autobiography about receiving a letter about Miss Julia Smith, his eighth-grade teacher:

"Forty-odd years later I received a letter from a woman who was taking care of Miss Smith (she had married and her name was now Mrs. Ottley; but I've never been able to think of her as anyone but Miss Smith) somewhere in upstate New York. Miss Smith, the woman wrote, was going blind but every time one of my covers appeared on the *Post* she would ask her friend to describe it to her. Then she'd tell about how I used to be her pupil, how I used to draw on the blackboard at Christmastime. And she'd asked her friend to write the note to me just to see if I remembered those old times. I wrote back, asking the woman to tell Miss Smith that she had been my favorite teacher and that I remembered her very well because she'd done me so much good.

That letter and others which followed brought back my school days. I recalled how devoted and kind Miss Smith had been. Then I thought of how hardworking and underpaid schoolteachers were. And after I'd mulled all this over for a while I decided to do a *Post* cover of a schoolteacher—sort of a tribute to Miss Smith and all the other schoolteachers."

In addition, Thomas S. Buechner, director of the Brooklyn Museum, made this observation: "George Bridgman was Rockwell's great teacher. If Pyle showed him where he wanted to go, Bridgman gave him the basic equipment for getting there."[22]

Thomas Fogarty

At the Art Students League Norman studied drawing under Bridgman in the afternoon and illustration under Thomas Fogarty in the morning. Illustration class included studying the outlines of stories, deciding which scenes to illustrate, and examining the work of other illustrators. Mr. Fogarty helped his students discover how these artists captured the tone of a story, why they chose light or dark backgrounds, and how the technique, such as line drawing or oil painting, suited the mood of the story. Rockwell later wrote about the benefits of studying the works of other artists:

> I guess an artist just stores up in his mind what he learns from looking at the work of other artists. And after a while all the different things he has learned become mixed with each other and with his own ideas and abilities to form his technique, his way of painting. You start by following other artists—a spaniel. Then, if you've got it, you become yourself—a lion.[23]

The assignments in Mr. Fogarty's class were much like job assignments the students could expect from magazines and book publishers in the future. These assignments included reading the story, studying the details, choosing a scene to illustrate, and finding authentic costumes and props. For example, if the chosen scene described a character sitting on a three-legged milk stool, the students were expected to find an authentic model of a three-legged milk stool. The illustrations had to match the story in every detail. Rockwell quoted Fogarty as saying, "An Illustration is an illustration. Quite simply that. Nothing less, nothing more. An author's words in paint, gentlemen and ladies, an author's words in paint."[24]

Fogarty also insisted that in order to paint a good illustration, the artist had to feel it. He encouraged his students to learn to draw so well that they could focus on the feelings they wanted to convey rather than drawing techniques. Rockwell remembered him saying, "Step over the frame, Norman. . . . Over the frame and live in the picture."[25]

Norman learned this lesson well. For example, after he became a professional illustrator, he often acted out the situation for his models, including body language and facial expression. The scene existed in such reality within Rockwell that he knew the exact expression and body position he wanted. He did not ask models to look happy or pretend to make a mad dash through the rain; he showed them how. As Mr. Fogarty told Norman, "Painting a picture's like throwing a ball against a wall. Throw it hard, ball comes back hard. Feel a picture hard, public feels it the same way."[26]

Mr. Fogarty, who worked as an illustrator as well as a teacher, used his contacts to get illustrating assignments for his students. He knew that Norman needed money to stay in school and passed an assignment on to him now and then. As a re-

sult Norman illustrated medical textbooks, a Christmas booklet for a Catholic church, and a catalog for a tombstone company.

Before long he began getting jobs on his own, including making a sign for a store near the Art Students League and a few posters for church suppers. As Norman gained more experience, Mr. Fogarty sent him to a book publisher, McBride, Nast, and Company, where Norman received an assignment in 1911 to illustrate a children's book, *Tell Me Why*. They paid him $150 for ten or twelve illustrations for the book.

At the end of the term, Rockwell's charcoal drawing of a little boy in bed with the mumps, longing to join the Fourth of July celebration he could see from his window, was honored as the best illustration made in class that year. In addition he received a scholarship to Fogarty's class for 1911, which he did not use. By this time Rockwell was getting assignments from children's magazines. A professional after one year at the Art Students League, he continued to attend Bridgman's class but dropped Fogarty's.

The Golden Age of Illustration

During Rockwell's early career, illustrators had only begun to scratch the surface of commercialism and still shared a certain amount of idealism with the fine arts community. Rockwell explains:

In those days there wasn't the cleavage [division] between fine arts and illustration that there is now. In art school the

With the help of his beloved teacher Thomas Fogarty, Norman Rockwell (pictured) learned to step beyond his ideas and "into" his paintings. He would often act out the exact expression or body position he wished his models to imitate.

illustration class was just as highly respected as the portrait or landscape classes. . . . It was the end of what you might call the golden age of illustration. We thought of an illustrator then as a recorder of history and the contemporary scene, as an interpreter of the classics—Shakespeare, Dante, Milton.[27]

As advances in printing made mass production of artwork possible, the golden age of illustration arrived. During this era, from 1880 to 1918, popular magazines competed on the newsstand with attractive covers and images of characters from the classics such as *Robin Hood* and *Rip Van Winkle*, encouraging children to read.

Illustrators like Howard Pyle, Rockwell's idol, captured life in historical

The renowned illustrator Howard Pyle was Norman Rockwell's inspiration and idol.

Three of the great illustrators—Howard Pyle, Edwin Austin Abbey, and Frederic Remington—died while Norman was in art school, and the golden age of illustration came to a close. The market for illustration narrowed as the technology of photography improved and the photograph became more desirable in publishing than the artist's illustration. Moments in history could be caught in an instant with the snap of the shutter, and the public became a witness through the camera lens rather than viewing the observation of the illustrator. As the golden age of illustration came to an end, a new era opened.

In Rockwell's long career he bridged the best of both worlds. Unlike a photographer, Rockwell gave us a scene from American life as he saw it, touched with humor and edited with a tender heart. Yet his images were true to life, and his details exact.

First Studio

Once Rockwell became a full-fledged professional artist, he and a fellow student rented an attic room in a brownstone on the Upper West Side of New York. To reach the studio, the two young artists climbed rickety stairs to a trap door in the third-floor ceiling. There they crawled through to a room with a skylight, barely large enough to hold two easels. Pleased to have a studio and busy with their work, they paid little attention to the other tenants. After about three months Waring Rockwell came to visit his son's studio. Mr. Rockwell climbed into the small room, carefully closed the trap door, and said, "Do you realize that you have a studio in a house of prostitution?"[29]

times—colonial days, the Revolutionary War, and pirates on the high seas. Pyle's authentic re-creations, based on years of research, made a contribution to the recorded history of our nation. Author Verlyn Klinkenborg wrote about Pyle:

> In Pyle's paintings, history means a sweep of time against a landscape. [For example] he seizes a moment in the Battle of Bunker Hill, but he does not still [stop] the battle. Instead, he incorporates the viewer's perspective, making us feel as though we are walking downhill toward the British flank, calf-deep in early summer grass. Pyle's paintings include us without disrupting the action: no one detects our presence.[28]

The young artists moved out the next morning. Norman later remembered his embarrassment: "We went off down the street carrying our easels and paintboxes, rather shamefaced, because the girls had come out on the stoop in a crowd and were waving and calling good-by to us."[30]

Norman next rented space in another studio already occupied by artists. Two of these artists lived there, sleeping in hammocks strung from the ceiling, but Norman still lived with his parents. Nancy Rockwell's health, however, continued to fail, and she no longer had the strength to do housework. Norman's father sold the house in Mamaroneck and moved the family to a boardinghouse in New York City.

Norman's career continued to progress. After he completed the *Tell Me*

The Death of the Golden Age of Illustration

In his autobiography Norman Rockwell speculated on the cause of the death of the golden age of illustration:

"I don't know, really, what killed the golden age of illustration. I think it can be traced to a change in audience. The people who bought the mass magazines, the best-selling books, didn't particularly care about fine illustration. They were as well satisfied with a good illustration as a great one. Or with none at all.

But then it might have been something altogether different. All I know for certain is that the golden age of illustration existed and that it ended. And that end has always been typified for me by one experience. When I first left art school and was making the rounds of the various magazines looking for work, the office of the very aristocratic and dignified art director of the *Century* magazine was dimly lit, quiet and furnished like the living room in a wealthy home. . . . We rarely, if ever mentioned money. A few years later the *Century* moved uptown. The new art director's office was functional and efficient. Light blared through the curtainless windows. The furnishings consisted of a desk, two plain chairs, and three gunmetal-blue filing cabinets. . . . Everything was done on a strict business basis—MONEY: PROFIT, LOSS. The golden age of illustration was as dead as poor Yorick [from *Hamlet*]. You can't conduct a golden age with a heart of copper."

Read "Fighting Fire", by Ex-Chief Croker.

BOYS' LIFE

PRICE 10 CENTS   THE BOY SCOUTS' MAGAZINE.

Famous Writers
in this number

JANUARY
1914

PUBLISHED BY
THE BOY SCOUTS
OF AMERICA

In 1913, Norman Rockwell became the art director of the Boy Scout magazine Boys' Life. *During his employ, Rockwell illustrated many of the magazine's articles as well as covers, like this one from January 1914.*

Why book, Edward Cabe, the editor of *Boys' Life*, asked him to illustrate a handbook on camping. Cabe liked Norman's work and began to give him stories to illustrate for the magazine. In 1913, at the age of nineteen, Norman Rockwell became art director for *Boys' Life*, the magazine for Boy Scouts. In this position he received seventy-five dollars a month to do the cover and illustrate one story for each issue. He also interviewed artists, assigned story illustrations, and approved the finished art. This put him in charge of choosing his own assignments and approving his own work, a dream job for an illustrator of any age. Thus began Rockwell's relationship with the Boy Scouts, which would continue for more than sixty years.

3 Rockwell Arrives

Becoming art director at *Boys' Life* whetted Rockwell's appetite for success. With a portfolio of sample illustrations selected from the Boy Scout handbooks, *Boys' Life* magazine, and the *Tell Me Why* book, Rock-

well competed with other artists for assignments. Each artist's portfolio contained work for sale that represented hours of labor and unique ideas. The artists jealously guarded their work, extremely fearful

With each painting Rockwell's collection of work increased in size and value. Intense competition for assignments meant that Rockwell had to carefully guard his ideas from other artists.

because another artist could steal an idea with no more than a glance.

This threat made life difficult for Norman and stirred his insecurities. While waiting in reception rooms to show his portfolio, he stewed over the order in which he should present his work to the editors. Every time he changed his mind, he had to switch the order of the work in his portfolio. He soon learned to shuffle his pictures within the case without exposing any of them to the other artists' view. He wrote:

> I didn't trust anyone (the feeling was mutual); the others might snitch my best ideas. I'd open my portfolio a crack and, reaching in, rearrange the drawings by bending them over each other or pulling one on its end and shuffling the others around it. All the other artists were doing the same. . . . We must have looked like a side show at a circus, all of us sitting in a line along that bench, struggling with our drawings and glancing suspiciously at each other.[31]

Getting Ahead of the Competition

To give himself an edge over his artistic competitors, Rockwell once coaxed a building janitor to let him into the waiting room of an art director's office at seven each morning for three weeks. He greeted the art director and introduced himself with an open portfolio daily. Finally one morning the art director paused and uttered an exclamation. Norman continued his vigil, and this persistence finally re-sulted in an assignment. When he later recounted the incident, he wrote: "Two days later when I introduced myself he asked, 'If I give you a job will you permit me to digest my breakfast in peace?' I said yes, and he assigned me a book on American history."[32]

At the time Rockwell seemed caught in a hectic scramble for assignments, but he later wrote: "A good many of my forays into the offices of art directors were successful. I really didn't have much trouble getting started: the kind of work I did seemed to be what the magazines wanted."[33] Rockwell had talent, imagination, and the ability to understand and convey feelings. This proved to be what magazines wanted for many years to come.

Doubts Arose

As he began to realize success, Rockwell also began to experience doubt and lack of confidence in his work. He wrote:

> I'd lie in bed at night . . . and exult over my mounting prosperity. But then, all of a sudden, I'd begin to doubt my ability. Maybe I'd stumble, blunder, lose everything. I'd think about the painting I was working on and be all in a sweat to look at it, see if it was good, reassure myself that I wasn't slipping.[34]

At that time his studio was blocks away. He could not sneak out of bed for a few minutes to view his work in the middle of the night. This problem was solved when Norman and his artist friends were evicted from the studio they shared for sweeping trash down the hall to the door of another

Norman Rockwell took great care when selecting models for his illustrations. Because he primarily freelanced for children's magazines, the majority of these models were spirited children and dogs.

tenant. He then moved his studio to the second floor of a deserted brownstone building beside the boardinghouse where his family lived. It was so close that he could, and sometimes did, climb out his bedroom window, crawl down a narrow ledge, and slip in the window of his studio. Although now a professional illustrator and art director, Norman, no more than twenty, was still more boy than man, and some called him the boy illustrator.

Models

Most of his illustrations for children's magazines in the early days were black and white or brown and white. At this time Rockwell always painted from a live model. He looked for models everywhere: next door, on the street, and in the park. Since his early work consisted of illustrations for children's magazines, most of his models were children and dogs.

Because of the influence of Thomas Fogarty, his illustration instructor at the Art Students League, Norman always sought out exactly the right model. He wrote:

Say I was doing a picture of a boy and a dog running. First off I had to locate the right boy. For days I'd hang about the grade schools at recess, peer over fences into back yards, haunt the vacant lots, and stop little boys on the

street, turning them around sideways to see if they were the type I wanted.[35]

Since most boys would rather play ball than pose, an offer of fifty cents an hour was not enough to get an agreement from a boy. However, if Rockwell could talk to the boy's mother, *she* would thrill at the thought of her child's picture in a magazine. That would clinch the deal.

Getting a dog as a model proved far more difficult. With no leash laws in those days, small-town dogs roamed as freely as neighborhood boys. Once Rockwell found his dog, however, the job had just begun. He remembered the trouble he had once when he spotted a perfect dog:

> Once I chased a dog all afternoon through vacant lots, over fences, down and up gullies, through briars, burrs, and nettles. He was a perfect mutt, the best I've ever seen—black patch of fur around one eye, woebegone, lanky, and rough. But he was tricky and escaped through a back yard crisscrossed by clotheslines hung with clammy sheets and shirts.[36]

After Norman had been seen chasing dogs all over town, rumors flew through the neighborhood. Some thought he wanted the dogs for animal research, and a few thought he liked dog meat. Others accused him of being the dogcatcher.

After all this work to find his models, Norman had to get the boy and the dog to pose and hold still while he painted. To make posing easier, Rockwell drew one part of a model at a time. He would pose one arm and draw, then pose the other arm and draw.

Facial expression proved even more difficult. Real smiles are hard to fake and even harder to hold. When asked to smile, a boy would clench his teeth while turning up the corners of his mouth—showing more pain than joy. Rockwell soon learned that the words "Here's an extra nickel" almost always brought the exact smile he wanted, along with a twinkle to the child's eye.[37]

The models posed twenty-five minutes then took a five-minute rest. Child models often wanted to leave when the first rest period came. Norman solved this problem by placing a stack of nickels in the child's view. At each rest period Norman shifted five nickels from his stack to the child's pile. In this way Norman motivated the child to stay longer to get more nickels.

Norman used girl models as well as boys. However, girls required a chaperon, which made the sitting more expensive. In those days people thought of artists as dangerous, wild, and not someone to trust with a young girl alone in a studio.

Best Models in the Early Days

Once Rockwell stopped chasing children and dogs around the neighborhood, he ceased to be a suspected villain. Instead he acquired a reputation as a moral gentleman, and mothers began allowing their daughters to pose without a chaperon. Rockwell soon had a number of willing models on his list. He used a good model again and again. Sometimes the same model posed for more than one character in a picture.

Rockwell discovered three of his favorite models after moving to New Rochelle, not far from Mamaroneck: two

boys and a dog—Billy Paine, Eddie Carson, and Lambert. The boys, only eight when they began to pose, could give Rockwell any expression he requested and hold it as long as needed. Norman could count on Lambert the dog to hold his position hour after hour unless a cat strayed into the studio to lure the dog into a chase.

Eddie Carson, one of Norman Rockwell's favorite models, poses for a playful photograph with the artist.

With the help of these models, Norman established an impressive list of credits for a young artist just past twenty. His illustrations appeared regularly in all the children's magazines of the time, including *Boys' Life, American Boy, Youth's Companion, St. Nicholas, Harper's Young People,* and *Everyland.* However, Rockwell soon became dissatisfied.

Unknown Forever

Many other artists lived in New Rochelle, including Coles Phillips, known for painting beautiful girls; Clare Briggs, a famous cartoonist; and J. C. Leyendecker, a famous *Saturday Evening Post* illustrator. Surrounded by these great artists, Rockwell longed for better assignments. His work consisted of small-paying jobs, all in black and white, all of the same subjects, and all in children's magazines and books. Rockwell saw himself going nowhere, trapped forever as an unknown illustrator of children's magazines. He wanted to do illustrations for adult magazines.

By this time Rockwell had become close friends with Clyde Forsythe, a well-known cartoonist who drew a daily comic strip about a Swedish prizefighter. Norman and Clyde decided to rent a studio that had once belonged to the late Frederic Remington. Remington was famous for historical sketches, paintings, and bronze statues of the old West such as the *Bronco Buster* in Fairmont Park in San Francisco.

Norman and Clyde worked in the studio together, encouraging each other as they tried to improve. Norman painted "100%" in gold letters at the top of his

easel. This reminded him to paint every picture 100 percent as good as he could make it.

Secret Ambition

As Clyde watched Norman work, he encouraged him to take his portfolio to the adult magazine and book publishers. This was just the push Norman needed. He nurtured a secret ambition to paint a cover for *Saturday Evening Post.* He later wrote:

> In those days the cover of the *Post* was the greatest show window in America for an illustrator. If you did a cover for the *Post* you had arrived. . . . I used to sit in the studio with a copy of the *Post* laid across my knees. . . . And then I'd conjure up a picture of myself as a famous illustrator and gloat over it, putting myself in various happy situations; surrounded by admiring females, deferred to by office

flunkies at the magazines, wined and dined by the editor of the *Post*, Mr. George Horace Lorimer.[38]

At the thought of "THE GREAT MR. LORIMER, the Baron of publishing," Norman lost his dream to an overwhelming fear.[39] Under George Horace Lorimer's guidance, the *Post* had grown from a small family-run journal to an influential mass-marketed magazine. The *Post*, the most widely read magazine in the world, counted its readership in the millions. Norman, caught up in a tangle of fear and ambition, became torn between his desire to be a cover artist and fear of rejection, especially from George Horace Lorimer.

When he shared this dilemma with Clyde Forsythe, Clyde insisted that Norman work out two ideas for *Post* covers and have one finished in two weeks. Norman went to work painting what he had seen on the cover of the *Post*—handsome men and beautiful women. When Clyde saw the paintings, he exploded with an instant critique:

Rockwell and the *Post*

The editors of the Saturday Evening Post *wrote in the* Norman Rockwell Memory Album *about the beginning of Rockwell's relationship with the* Post:

"His linkup with the *Post* was significant. Many magazines were exploring photography and abstract ideas as cover art. But the *Post* nurtured a kind of sincerity in its contributors and readers that only representational art could make concrete. Serious entertainment, i.e., humor, was the business of the magazine, and Rockwell, hardened by city life and freshened by visits to the country, was a young man of perfect paradox, anecdotal, moral."

Fear of rejection from George Horace Lorimer, publishing baron of the Saturday Evening Post, *hindered Rockwell from submitting cover illustrations to the illustrious magazine.*

C-R-U-D, crud. Terrible. Awful. Hopeless. You can't do a beautiful seductive woman. She looks like a tomboy who's been scrubbed with a rough washcloth and pinned into a new dress by her mother. Give it up.

He held up an illustration Rockwell had recently completed for *Boys' Life*.

"Do that," he said. "Do what you're best at. Kids. Just adapt it to the *Post.* . . . They don't want warmed-over Gibson [painter]. If they take your stuff it'll havta be good. And you're a terrible Gibson, But a pretty good Rockwell."[40]

Norman took Clyde's advice. He called in one of his best models, Billy Paine, and went to work. He chose five ideas, painted two, and sketched the other three. He painted the pictures in black and white with a touch of red. Billy Paine posed for all three characters in a painting of two boys in baseball uniforms scoffing at the third boy in his Sunday suit pushing a baby carriage. The other picture featured kids in makeshift costumes performing in a backyard circus.

Off to Philadelphia

Norman bought a new suit, a black hat, and had a special case made for presenting his work to the editors at the *Saturday Evening Post.* The custom-made case measured forty by thirty by twelve inches.

In March 1916 Norman headed for Philadelphia to present the two finished paintings and three sketches to Mr. Lorimer. Rockwell related the struggles of the trip in his autobiography:

The trip didn't begin auspiciously [favorably]. When I tried to board the subway at Grand Central to go to Penn[sylvania] Station, "Here," said a guard, pointing to my suitcase, "You can't go on the subway with that thing in the rush.". . . So I tried the el[evated train], but a guard stopped me, saying: "not until after rush hour, young man. You'd be takin' a place from three men or five children with that black box of yours." So I walked to Penn Station.[41]

Norman Rockwell's insecurities heightened at the prospect of illustrating a Saturday Evening Post cover. These fears were quelled when two of Rockwell's finished paintings and three of his sketches were accepted as Post covers. The final version of this sketch appeared as a cover in late 1925.

Once he arrived at the Curtis Publishing Company building, where the *Post*'s offices were located, Rockwell lost his courage and almost went home without presenting his work to the *Post*. He wrote: "I could feel my Adam's apple sink beneath my collar. Maybe I'd better work on the paintings some more. Then I thought of Clyde—'you mean you didn't even go into the office?'"[42] When Rockwell realized he would have to face Clyde, he regained his courage. Once he made it to the receptionist, he discovered that no one ever saw Mr. Lorimer without an appointment. Rockwell told biographer Donald Walton:

Boy was that a shock. Here I had come all that way dragging that heavy, stupid case, and it was all a big waste of time, it seemed. I just stood there in that fancy room—you know how impressive those Curtis offices were—and I would have cried if people weren't watching me.[43]

Fortunately Mr. Dower, the art director, liked Rockwell's paintings and presented them to Mr. Lorimer. Norman later wrote about the upside of that day: "Mr. Dower . . . brought back word that Mr. Lorimer was pleased, would accept the two finished paintings, and had okayed the three sketches for future *Post* covers."[44]

Rockwell could not believe it. Mr. Lorimer had accepted all he had offered and promised to pay seventy-five dollars for each painting. At age twenty-two Norman Rockwell was a *Post* cover artist! He later wrote:

> I was elated. A cover on the *Post*! Two covers on the *Post*. Seventy-five dollars for one painting. An audience of two million! I had arrived. . . . As I crossed a grating in the sidewalk, blissfully contemplating my success, I happened to look down and for a moment I thought I was walking on air.[45]

As soon as he returned to New Rochelle, Rockwell, overcome with joy and sure of his future, proposed to Irene O'Connor, a young schoolteacher he had met at the boardinghouse. She accepted, after a brief hesitation, and they made plans for a fall wedding.

Norman Rockwell's first *Saturday Evening Post* cover appeared on May 20, 1916. It is the painting of a young man pushing a baby carriage and is titled *Mother's Day Out.* The other painting accepted that day appeared in the June 3 issue.

Before the first cover had been published, Rockwell went to work on the third, a picture of an old man playing baseball with some kids. When he presented this painting, Mr. Dower brought back word that Mr. Lorimer thought the

Mother's Day Out *was Norman Rockwell's first* Saturday Evening Post *cover, appearing on the May 20, 1916, edition.*

old man looked like a tramp. Norman painted it over on a new canvas. In the second version Mr. Lorimer thought the old man was too old, and in the third, the boy was too small. Norman painted his third *Post* cover five times before it finally appeared in August 1916.

Norman had not faced these difficulties with other magazines and was not sure he liked working for such a demanding editor. He later found out that Mr. Lorimer had been testing him by asking him to repaint the picture again and again to see if he could accept direction. Rockwell later wrote: "I wonder if he ever knew how near I came to flunking his test."[46] Rockwell's career for the *Post* could have ended within months, but it was destined to last decades.

With the *Post* covers added to his portfolio, Rockwell began getting assignments from other adult magazines, including *Life*, *Leslie's*, and *Judge*. Norman Rockwell had indeed arrived!

4 Rockwell the Illustrator

Rockwell sold his first *Post* cover in March 1916, and his last illustration for *Boys' Life* appeared that same month. He resigned his position as art director for *Boys' Life* and from that time on earned his living as a freelance artist.

In 1925 Brown and Bigelow began publishing Boy Scout calendars with Rockwell's illustrations. For the first calendar they used an illustration he had done earlier for the organization. In following years he donated illustrations for Boy

Norman Rockwell worked as a freelance artist for the majority of his career. This gave his art diversity and allowed him to work for many worthwhile organizations, including the Boy Scouts.

Scout calendars until he realized that the publisher was making money from his effort; from that time on he took payment for the illustrations. Rockwell painted a Boy Scout calendar illustration for every year from 1925 through 1976. That year he painted *The Spirit of '76* in recognition of America's bicentennial and as a salute to scouting. Throughout his life the Boy Scouts remained dear to Rockwell's heart, and he continued to promote the scouting movement and its ideals. In appreciation of his support, the Boy Scouts of America awarded Rockwell their highest honor, the Silver Buffalo, in 1938. This award is presented to those who have rendered distinguished service to the nation's boys.

Although Rockwell had achieved his goal of becoming a *Post* cover artist, he continued to accept freelance story illustration and cover assignments from other publishers. Although cover art and story illustrations differ in composition and style, Rockwell could paint either equally well.

Cover Illustrations

A good magazine cover, for example, attracts attention and silently cries out with its bold type and eye-catching illustration: "Look at me! See what I have to offer!" The artwork must fit the magazine format. The illustration fills a specific space between the logo—the unique design of the magazine title—and space allowed for promoting the features to be found inside.

The Silver Buffalo

In an article in the Saturday Evening Post's *Norman Rockwell Memory Album,* William Hillcourt reports the Boy Scout citation when Rockwell received the Silver Buffalo in 1938.

"Norman Rockwell, artist, distinguished delineator [portrayer] of Boy Scouts and of boyhood.

To the people of America he has brought a deepened understanding of the psychology of boys of Scout age.

At the very outset of his career he became an illustrator for *Boys' Life* in the first year of its publication by the Boy Scouts of America. He gave the joy and inspiration of Scouting ideals to hundreds of thousands of youthful citizens of the nation.

He has assisted the Boy Scout movement through his interpretive paintings of the flesh-and-blood boys and has helped to win the American people to an appreciation of the fundamentals of Scouting."

Each Rockwell *Post* cover illustration told a story within itself. Details in the picture included a hint of what had happened before the scene and what would happen later. The cover drew attention to the magazine, invited the potential reader in, and enticed readers to put their money on the counter. (At that time the *Saturday Evening Post* sold for only five cents a copy.) The *Post* described Rockwell's covers this way:

> Rockwell told the story with an honesty and directness that the *Post* audience of millions could not miss. But the richness of his details, the weight of his moral values, the sheer surprise of beauty in the overlooked, drench the viewer in the warmth of significant human emotions.[47]

Because of these qualities in his work, America soon fell in love with Norman Rockwell. As he gained popularity, a Rockwell on the cover would sell fifty to seventy thousand additional copies of the magazine.

Story illustrations inside also play an important part in the sale of magazines. To draw attention to the written text, the size and shape vary from page to page. Story illustrations are designed to catch the attention of a reader thumbing through the magazine. The illustrator poses a subtle mystery to make the viewer wonder what happens. Reading the story is the only way to find out.

World War I

Rockwell had been illustrating for the *Post* for more than a year when President

Jarvis Rockwell, wearing his World War I naval uniform, is photographed with his younger brother Norman, who had yet to enlist in the navy.

Woodrow Wilson declared war on Germany in April 1917. The war pulled the country together and gave everyone a common purpose. Norman found universal ideas to illustrate in the headlines, from people on the street and children in backyards, everywhere he looked. He later wrote:

Sailoring

In his autobiography Rockwell told of his first assignments in the navy:

"Flu was raging through the camp like a pack of rabid wolves; men were dying every day. Being short of able-bodied men, the authorities assigned the new arrivals in the camp to guard duty and burial squads. I got a piece of both. At dusk twelve of us were issued guns and marched off behind a wagon laden with rough pine coffins. When we reached the cemetery the coffins were unloaded. Then the bugler bugled taps while the coffins were lowered into the graves, the officer said: 'Readyaimfire,' and . . . bang, bang, bang . . . bang, we fired. (The last bang was me; I hardly knew the butt of a rifle from the barrel.)

Guard duty was cold, damp, and frightening, but uneventful. I stood in a mud puddle for four hours, scared silly of snakes, Germans, and my fellow guards, who had a propensity for shooting wildly at anything which made the least sound. As the cold yellow light of morning shimmered in the puddle at my feet I decided that sailoring . . . wasn't for me."

In 1917 I couldn't read a newspaper without finding an idea for a cover. . . . Ideas were dropping from trees, from the lips of babes. . . . All this made my work much easier. I was pretty well satisfied with myself, knocking out covers and illustrations . . . receiving three or four fan letters a week, making quite a bit of money.[48]

Although Rockwell's illustrations helped improve the nation's morale, he did not feel he was doing his part. One day while riding the subway, Rockwell offered his seat to a wounded sailor. As he watched the once strong, now weakened man struggle to seat himself, guilt from not serving in the military overwhelmed Rockwell. He later wrote:

All I could think of as he lowered himself clumsily into the seat was how easily I'd got out of it, of the careless way I rocked on my feet with the motion of the train. By the time I left the train at New Rochelle, I'd made up my mind. I took a taxi to the Pelham Bay Naval Training and Receiving Center.[49]

Rockwell found enlisting more difficult than he imagined. With only 115 pounds on his five foot eleven-inch frame, he weighed in seventeen pounds under

the minimum for his height, and the recruiter rejected him. Determined to serve his country, Rockwell went to another enlistment center. His confidence level rose when he recognized the yeoman at the scale as a fellow student from the Art Students League. Knowing that the artist would get a special assignment, the yeoman agreed to help Rockwell meet the weight requirements with what he called the treatment. The doctor on duty explained: "You eat seven pounds' worth, we waive the other ten pounds, and you're in."[50] Rockwell gorged himself on bananas and doughnuts until he pushed the marker on the scale within range of navy regulations. He later wrote: "I could hardly walk; the seven pounds of doughnuts, bananas, and water sloshing about in my stomach threw me off balance."[51]

Afloat and Ashore

A few days later Rockwell reported to the Brooklyn Naval Yard to board a ship for Queenstown, Ireland, where he could paint insignias on airplanes. Soon after the ship set sail for Queenstown, however, a German submarine was detected in the waters ahead. The captain received orders to change course and head for Charleston, South Carolina. In Charleston Rockwell and the other new recruits were issued uniforms and detailed to guard duty and manual labor—pulling stumps and digging graves.

Neither task appealed to Rockwell. After one night of guard duty he began trying to think of a way out. His problem was solved the next morning after he filled out a questionnaire. A chief petty officer saw

the word *illustrator* on Rockwell's form and asked him to paint his portrait. Word of Rockwell's talent spread through the ranks to the captain. The captain assigned him to the camp newspaper, *Afloat and Ashore*, and gave him ten days' leave to go back to New York for his art supplies. As a navy artist he continued to do what he did best. Whether he painted portraits or drew cartoons, Rockwell had a knack for bringing out the best in a person. The navy called it building morale.

He worked two days a week on the newspaper doing layouts and cartoons. The rest of the week he was allowed to continue his personal work, which included painting portraits of navy personnel and his freelance magazine illustrations and covers. Throughout his enlistment Rockwell continued to work for the *Post*, *Collier's*, *Life*, *Leslie's*, *Judge*, *Country Gentleman*, *Literary Digest*, *People's Popular Monthly*, *Farm and Fireside*, and *Popular Science*. As a result the low-ranking recruit continued to earn a good living—more than he would have made as a high-ranking officer. Rockwell remembered his time in the navy:

> In spite of the fact that I worked hard, it was an easy life. I was getting my room, board, and clothes free and still earning almost as much money as I had as a civilian (an ensign figured out that with the free meals, etc., I was making more than an admiral). I had no military duties and aside from the two days a week at *Afloat and Ashore* could do pretty much as I wished.[52]

Rockwell considered the loss of individuality and identity the worst part of navy life. He ate navy beans along with everyone else in the mess hall, wore navy issues, went to bed in navy quarters, and stuck to

the navy regime along with 150 other men.

In some ways, however, Rockwell enjoyed his time in the navy. This, like all other aspects of his life, proved valuable to him later. He met people and went places he would never have known otherwise. As usual he stored away feelings, sights, and experiences that would later appear in his paintings in one way or another.

Rockwell's reputation spread throughout the navy, and he was transferred to the U.S.S. *Hartford* and assigned to the commander's personal staff. As his first duty he painted the portraits of Captain Mark St. Clair Ellis and his wife. By the time Rockwell finished the portraits, the war was almost over. Peace negotiations were in progress, and in the excitement, rumors spread quickly. In fact Rockwell and his friends went ashore to celebrate a false armistice.

In anticipation of the coming truce, everyone wanted to return to civilian life, especially Rockwell. To prevent chaos, the navy issued an order canceling all leaves and witholding all honorable discharges. Rockwell thought the captain would help him get a discharge if he could make him an offer he could not resist. Rockwell told the captain that he knew where to find the perfect frames for his portraits: "I can pick

Entitled "Detention Days," this cartoon appeared in Afloat and Ashore, *a navy newspaper illustrated by Norman Rockwell.*

The Morale Builder

Rockwell wrote in his autobiography of his painting experience in the navy and the boost he gave to morale:

"Two days a week I drew cartoons and made layouts for *Afloat and Ashore;* the rest of the time I was allowed to do my own work as long as it was in some way related to the Navy. I painted a *Post* cover of one sailor showing another a picture of his girl; a *Life* cover of a group of smiling soldiers, sailors, and marines. (Title: 'Are we Downhearted?' Everywhere you went during the war—in bars, trolleys, meetings—somebody would yell, 'Are we downhearted?' and everyone would chorus [shout], 'No!') I drew countless portraits of officers and ordinary sailors, not because I was ordered to do so, but because I thought it was a good morale builder. Most of the men sent their portraits home to their wives and sweethearts; it seemed to cheer them up considerably, especially if they were about to be shipped overseas. (Promotions were so rapid that I had to paint the officers one rank above their present rank; I expect that cheered them up too.)"

out just the right ones . . . the best frames money can buy or man can make."[53] The captain considered the portraits masterpieces and set out to get Rockwell a discharge so that he could purchase the frames. The only discharges available were less than honorable but not quite dishonorable. On November 12, 1918, after serving about seventeen months, Rockwell received an inaptitude discharge. A description of the discharge in Rockwell's service record reads as follows:

Discharged with Inaptitude Discharge. Rockwell is an artist and unaccustomed to hard manual labor. His patriotic impulse caused him to enlist in a rating for which he has no aptitude. Moreover, he is unsuited to Naval routine and hard work.

I concur in the above statement. (signed) Norman Rockwell[54]

On his way home from the navy, Rockwell stopped by the frame shop in New York City and had three of their most elaborate frames shipped to the captain and his wife. Then he hurried back to New Rochelle, his studio, and civilian life.

Chapter

5 How Rockwell Painted America

After World War I America enjoyed a time of prosperity and so did the Rockwells. As the leading *Post* cover artist, Rockwell averaged ten covers a year during the 1920s. He worked for other magazines and did advertising as well. His rates went up and his income spiraled. By the end of the decade, Rockwell was earning about forty thousand dollars a year. At that time a week's groceries could be bought for a few dollars; a car, for a few hundred; and nice houses, a few thousand.

Social Whirl

Wealthy and living well, Irene and Norman Rockwell joined the social scene. Rockwell worked his painting schedule around their busy party life. This hectic high living, however, conflicted with Rockwell's passion for a peaceful rural setting and ordinary people. As a result he often traveled to escape his heavy workload and social obligations. His old friend Clyde Forsythe said at that time, "When his work calls too heavily upon the artist's energy and knocks him flat, he will all of a sudden leap from his easel to a far-off land—Venezuela, Europe, California. . . ."[55]

Irene loved the party life in New Rochelle. She usually stayed home to so-

Although Norman Rockwell's popularity as an illustrator soared during the 1920s, the breakup of his marriage to Irene left him lonely and downhearted.

cialize while Norman traveled alone, even on long trips. On returning from such a trip, Norman found that Irene had fallen in love with someone else and wanted a divorce. Although it had been a loveless marriage, Norman suffered from the loss and loneliness. In 1929 he moved to a

fancy hotel in New York to live among other artists. Even with a beautiful apartment that included a nice studio, Rockwell continued to be lonely and lost enthusiasm for his work.

Norman Finds Mary

During this time Clyde, who had married and moved to California, came to see Rockwell and invited him to California. The visit with Forsythe and his wife cheered Rockwell and renewed his interest in his work. In the short time he was there, he painted his first *Post* cover of a Hollywood celebrity, Gary Cooper, and met Mary Rhodes Barstow, a young teacher and friend of the Forsythes. Soon after meeting Mary, Norman Rockwell fell in love for the first time in his life. Unlike Irene, Mary loved art and travel and enjoyed a simpler style of life. They were married on April 17, 1930, only a few months after they met.

The new Mr. and Mrs. Rockwell immediately left the social whirl and settled into the quieter side of life back in New Rochelle. Rockwell resigned from the country club and the yacht club. He kept his fancy party clothes, however, as part of his costume collection for use in future paintings.

Mary enjoyed spending time in the studio. They discussed Norman's painting, and she sometimes read to him from Dickens while he worked. When he got the urge to travel, Mary went along.

Rockwell Loses Confidence in His Work

Rockwell wrote in his autobiography about having trouble with his work after attempting to follow advice to modernize his painting:

"During the next few months my self-confidence deteriorated rapidly. I began to go out to the studio at all hours to look at my picture and reassure myself that it wasn't as bad as I'd suddenly remembered it to be. But when I'd get out there I couldn't tell whether it was good or bad. Or if I decided that it was bad I couldn't figure out why. I'd rub a head out and repaint it. . . . I'd change the color of a dress or shirt. . . . I'd redraw a hand or eyes, repaint a face, try a different expression. . . . I'd sit there before the easel in the dead silence of early morning, hopelessly confused. And pretty soon, as the birds began to chirp sleepily in the trees along the street and the electric lights faded in the cold blue light of the dawn, I'd take the canvas off the easel and set it against the wall. I'd have to start over. . . ."

Struggle with Insecurity

Outwardly it appeared that the Rockwells lived the happy life his paintings portrayed. However, Norman Rockwell struggled with professional insecurity. He sought perfection but saw something wrong with every finished painting. As he and Mary traveled, he studied other artists' work, trying to pick up new trends. One artist he met suggested that his work might be old-fashioned. When Rockwell came home, he attempted a more modern style. He later wrote of this crisis:

Norman Rockwell and his bride Mary Rhodes Barstow were married on April 17, 1930, only a few months after they first met.

I don't usually accept other people's advice so recklessly. But when I'm having trouble with my work—real trouble, not just the everyday difficulties and problems—I don't trust my own judgment and follow suggestions thoughtlessly because it's easier to do that than make my own decisions.[56]

The *Post* did not like the changes, and few of these new Rockwells appeared on the cover. In fact the *Post* accepted only three of his covers in 1932. Rockwell considered all the work he did at this time third-rate. However, he stuck to his regular routine, painting a full day, every day. After several months his work began to improve. As he pulled himself out of this dark time, Rockwell concentrated on story illustration rather than magazine covers. He wrote:

> About the time that I was dragging myself up from the depths I began to do a great deal of magazine illustration. And I think it helped me to recover my self-confidence because illustration has never been difficult, as compared with *Post* covers, for me. . . . I romp right through them.[57]

Turning Point

In 1935 George Macy, publisher of Heritage Press and Limited Editions Club books, asked Norman to illustrate *Tom Sawyer* and *Huckleberry Finn*. Rockwell loved Mark Twain's work, and this assignment came at exactly the right time for him. He later remembered: "I was asked to illustrate the classics of Mark Twain. . . . I felt so honored that they had come to

Tom Sawyer and Huckleberry Finn

Rockwell remembered in his autobiography his excitement at the chance to illustrate the classic works of Mark Twain:

"I can remember how really thrilled I was when, in 1935, George Macy, the publisher of the Heritage Press and Limited Editions Club books, asked me to illustrate Mark Twain's *Tom Sawyer* and *Huckleberry Finn*.

Right off I decided I would try to do as good a job as I was able. After all, this was the chance of a lifetime. These were classics. I read through the books, making notes of which scenes would make good pictures. Of course certain scenes—for instance, Tom whitewashing his aunt Polly's fence—were required. And I had to space the illustrations evenly throughout the book. . . .

I made rough little sketches of the scenes I wanted to do. Then I discovered that none of the illustrators—and there had been quite a few—who had done *Tom Sawyer* and *Huckleberry Finn* had taken the trouble to visit Hannibal, Missouri, where Twain had lived as a boy. I'd go to Hannibal to get authentic details."

me to illustrate his books. . . . It was to be *Tom Sawyer* and *Huckleberry Finn* both—eight color paintings for each book."[58]

As Rockwell began analyzing the existing illustrations, he saw clearly that none of the other artists had gone to the location of the stories. Determined to capture the smell of the place, Rockwell set out for Hannibal, Missouri. He found the small town still much the same as Twain had described it in his books. He later wrote in his autobiography:

Twain had used Hannibal as the setting for his two books . . . the actual house, streets, countryside. . . . The 'ell' was there, outside the window, and below that the woodshed. And there had been a widow who lived on the hill above the town. . . . And there was a labyrinthine cave not far from town. Almost every physical detail in the books was an actual fact, remembered by Twain from his boyhood.[59]

A Visit to Hannibal

Rockwell walked the same streets Twain had Tom and Huck walk, visited the stores and houses mentioned in the book, and explored the secret cave. He sketched the town, the countryside, and the people—everything and everyone he saw.

An illustration from Mark Twain's classic work Tom Sawyer. *Rockwell was greatly honored to be commissioned to illustrate the Heritage Press editions of both* Tom Sawyer *and* Huckleberry Finn.

As he planned the illustrations, he saw his characters dressed in well-worn clothing. In his desire for accuracy he stopped people on the street in Hannibal to buy the clothes off their backs. Back in New Rochelle, as he began work on the illustrations, Rockwell realized that the material he had gathered was well worth the effort. He wrote: "The clothes were perfect. With them backing me up and the authentic details I'd gathered, the illustrations glided along like a raft on the Mississippi in flood."[60]

Extremely pleased with the illustrations for *Tom Sawyer* and *Huckleberry Finn*, Rockwell began traveling to the original location when an illustration required a special setting. Furthermore, he spared no expense in obtaining props and costumes. He wrote: "I've made it a rule to never fake anything, always to use, if possible authentic props and costumes."[61] In addition he always used the best canvas, paints, and brushes for the project. He refused to risk the quality of his work because of fakery or inferior art supplies.

The year 1935 proved to be a turning point in Rockwell's career. With renewed confidence he began to create his best work to this time. This included illustrations of the life of Lousia May Alcott for *Woman's Home Companion* and a thirteen-foot-long mural for a tavern in Princeton, New Jersey, depicting the song "Yankee Doodle."

Rockwell's *Post* covers in the late 1930s represent some of his best. Many of the covers he painted during this time reflect his experiences as a father. The Rockwell children were born during the 1930s: Jarvis, or Jerry, in 1932, Tom in 1933, and Peter in 1936.

Models

Rockwell always chose his models carefully. He used ordinary people, usually a neighbor, but sometimes one of his sons or a friend. He often tucked a self-portrait in the background or sidelines and sometimes included an artist friend. Grandma Moses, painter of primitive-style landscapes, can be found in the crowd in one of his paintings. She was over eighty-five years old when Rockwell met her. According to Jim Edgerton, one of Rockwell's neighbors, "She used to come over from Eagle Bridge (New York) to see him. Both

Rockwell Gains Insight in Hannibal

Rockwell told about his discoveries in Hannibal, Missouri, in Norman Rockwell: Illustrator, *by Arthur L. Guptill:*

"I'm the only illustrator of the Tom Sawyer–Huckleberry Finn stories who ever went to Hannibal, Missouri, to see the place. I wondered before I went there if I could absorb the feeling that Mark Twain had put into his writing. I certainly tried! The whole town of Hannibal lives in the memories of Tom and Huck—or, rather, of Mark Twain. He depicted things just as they actually were. The widow who lived on the hill lived on the hill. If the author says it is twenty paces across the street to Becky Thatcher's, it is twenty paces. He tells about sliding down the water pipe, crawling along to the woodshed, and dropping off to the ground. I actually did it myself. When he talks about rolling the rock down the hill, you may be sure he rolled the rock down the hill. In other words, the Tom Sawyer story is truly autobiographical in the sense that even if Mark Twain didn't personally do some of the things attributed to Tom, he understood exactly how Tom would have done them. That made my task as illustrator an exceptionally interesting one."

of them are in one of his paintings. It was on a cover of the *Post* for Christmas (1948)."[62]

Before Rockwell began painting from photographs, his models posed the whole time he painted them. Rockwell had to find not only the right model for his characters, but models who had time to pose three to four days for one character. This situation limited the number of available models. As a result Rockwell used the same models again and again.

One such character was James K. Van Brunt, a tiny man who was barely five feet two inches tall. As soon as Rockwell laid eyes on Van Brunt's mustache, which measured eight inches from tip to tip, he knew he had to paint him. In addition to the mustache, Rockwell was fascinated with the character of his face. He wrote:

> What a face! . . . Knobby nose, thick and square at the end with a bump in the middle; those big, sad, dog eyes which, however, burned with a fierce, warlike sparkle; that mustache. And all crammed together in a small, narrow head so that if you glanced at him quickly that was all you saw—eyes, nose, and mustache.[63]

Rockwell used Van Brunt in several illustrations, changing his character a little each time. He painted him with the mustache, with the mustache concealed, without the mustache, and as a woman. He honored Van Brunt by using him as the model for the first full-color *Post* cover, which appeared February 6, 1926.

In his long career Rockwell had many models he ranked as favorites. His top choices were selected for facial character, ability to create the desired expression, and ability to hold a pose.

Since facial expression was essential to most of Rockwell's paintings, he had a test to determine the flexibility of a model's face. He asked each potential model to raise his or her eyebrows. If the eyebrows went halfway up the forehead, Rockwell had a new model. Once he found a model with a mobile face, Rockwell demonstrated the expression he wanted. Then he fought to capture the image on canvas before the model tired or became restless and lost the pose.

A young model imitates Norman Rockwell's expression as they set the scene of a new illustration.

The use of photography assisted Norman Rockwell in achieving new angles and portraying difficult poses in his illustrations.

From Live Models to Photographs

In 1921, faced with a young model who could not hold a posed yawn, Rockwell decided to experiment with photography for the first time. He used the live model for the bored schoolboy who appeared on the cover of *American* magazine in May. However, the boy's yawn was painted from a photograph of Rockwell yawning.

Although this experience clearly revealed the benefits of photography, Rock-well considered the use of photography "a bit dishonest, like cheating at solitaire."[64] He continued to paint from live models. In the mid-1930s, however, art directors began demanding new angles and poses. In an effort to meet these demands and still use a live model, Rockwell built a platform for his easel so that he could paint a scene from above. After almost falling off the platform when he stepped back to evaluate his work, he decided to take advantage of the camera's mobility. The October 2, 1937, *Post* cover, with an aerial view of a policeman painting a street line,

offers a good example of new angles that could be achieved with photography.

The change in Rockwell's method came slowly. At first he painted from the live model as well as from posed photographs but gradually began to depend more on photographs. Although he eventually used photographs extensively, he never attempted photography himself but always hired a professional photographer.

Everything Rockwell read, witnessed, or experienced either triggered an idea or became lodged in his memory, awaiting future use. However, only universal ideas qualified as covers for the *Post*. Universal meant that the majority of subscribers—more than two million—and their families would understand the idea of the cover and that most of them would relate to it in some way. In other words, on seeing the cover they would recall an incident that happened to them and share familiar feelings with the subjects in Rockwell's picture. Rockwell wrote:

> One of the most difficult problems in painting magazine covers is thinking up ideas which a majority of readers will understand. The farmer worries about the price of milk; the housewife fusses over the drapes for the dining room; the gossip gossips about Mrs. Purdy and her highfalutin airs. You have to think of an idea which will mean something to all of them. And it's darned hard to be universal, to find some situation which will strike the farmer, the housewife, the gossip, *and* Mrs. Purdy.[65]

The universal idea lies in the theme more than in the character in the painting. Whether old or young, male or female, only a portion of Rockwell's viewers

could personally relate to a character. However, they could relate to the theme, which came from the situation, and feelings generated by the situation. Everyone has suffered a small embarrassment, a little discomfort, or slight humiliation and later laughed about it.

For example, Rockwell's cover on the June 4, 1921, *Post* shows three boys and a dog who have obviously left a forbidden swimming hole in a hurry. The boy in the foreground clutches his clothes as he looks over his shoulder. The other two are partially dressed; one holds up his trousers, while the other advances from the rear with his unbuttoned shirt flapping in the breeze. Even those who have never sneaked past a NO SWIMMING sign for a skinny-dip relate to the embarrassment Rockwell captured so well in the facial expressions. Thomas S. Buechner, director of the Brooklyn Museum, wrote: "Capturing just the right expression has long been one of Rockwell's great if not unique strengths."[66]

Themes that worked well for Rockwell include growing up, patriotism, the simple joys of life, and the young relating to the old. These themes involved feelings common to everyone and made the pictures universal.

Flops

Although Rockwell's ideas for the *Post* and other magazines had gained the approval of art directors and editors, a few were flops. One idea that did not sell well was a picture of Mrs. O'Leary's cow for a Brown and Bigelow calendar in 1945. The picture showed Mrs. O'Leary milking her cow by

the light of a lantern near the cow's right hind hoof. Because the placement of the lantern, which started the great Chicago fire of 1871, was an essential part of the picture, the back end of the cow occupied the center of the canvas. Rockwell declared this to be his worst failure: "Not that it was a bad painting. But who wants to look at the rear end of a cow for twelve months? And that's how long a calendar hangs on the wall."[67]

An apparently three-legged grocery boy slipped by the editors and appeared on a *Post* cover for January 18, 1930. He stands with three other people, checking the stock quotes. The grocery boy is leaning forward with his hands on his two bent knees and seems to have a third, straight leg in back of him.

Other Rockwell flops were caught in the editor's office. A sketch of a murder mystery *Post* cover filled with clues and

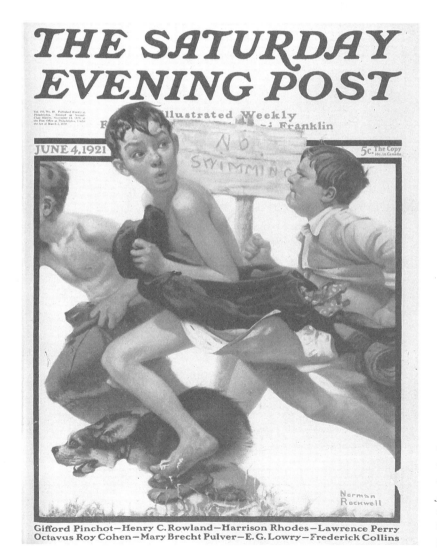

Three young boys make a mad dash from a forbidden swimming hole in Norman Rockwell's Post *cover for the June 4, 1921, edition. Many of Rockwell's illustrations revolve around the universal theme of growing up.*

movie stars failed to gain approval. The editors at the *Post* rejected the sketch because the movie stars overshadowed the theme of the picture. For another *Post* cover Rockwell went to great lengths to pose an umpire dusting home plate. To get the pose, he had the umpire turn his back to the stands, but to be authentic, he should have faced the stands. The authentic picture would have been filled with the umpire's rear.

Few of Rockwell's paintings could be considered flops. He composed most of them in his mind, where he balanced his desire for authenticity with skilled composition and artistic inspiration. He finished most of his paintings a few days after he had the idea and the props and models set. Some required months before he got just what he wanted. He repainted faces, changed hair color, switched models, swapped costumes, and changed backgrounds until he achieved the exact look he wanted. This drive to achieve made him restless at the times in his life when his self-confidence waned. Often these restless periods resulted in a trip abroad.

In 1938 Rockwell took his whole family, including a nurse for the boys, to Europe for an extended stay. The trip proved

Rockwell's Use of Photographs

Rockwell wrote in his autobiography about painting from photographs:

"I don't copy photographs. Lots of people have the idea that when you work from a photograph you just tint it. If that were so, anybody could paint a *Post* cover, which they manifestly [obviously] cannot. I use an average of a hundred photographs for a single *Post* cover. They are guides, nothing more. The essential ingredient in every one of my finished paintings is me—my feelings, ideals, skills. Photographs, I repeat, are only aids.

Working from photographs has many advantages. Take models, for instance. Now, if I want a bank president, why, I call up a bank president and ask him to come over to the studio for an hour or two. Before, I had to fake it, putting Pop Fredericks in a wing collar and business suit, trying to make him look like a bank president, which he didn't. Now I can get the real thing. I no longer have to depend on four or five professional models, painting them over and over again. I can use anybody—the butcher, the baker, the plumber, Mrs. Grundy, Grandma Wilcox."

Norman Rockwell and a friend examine one of Rockwell's latest illustrations in his Arlington, Vermont, studio. The Rockwells were enamored with the beautiful scenery in Vermont and settled in Arlington in 1939.

to be expensive, even for the Rockwells. On return they began to look for a less expensive vacation getaway. A friend had told them about a place in Vermont with beautiful scenery and great fishing. Norman and Mary visited the area in 1939 and immediately decided to buy a small farm on the Batten Kill River near Arlington, Vermont. At first they made short visits to the farm but soon decided to make Vermont their home.

Moving to Arlington rekindled Rockwell's enthusiasm for his work. He wrote: "I'd met one or two hundred people I wanted to paint . . . a whole raft of them. And ideas were jumping in my brain like trout on the Batten Kill at sunset."[68]

Willie Gillis

Shortly after the Rockwells moved to Vermont, America went to war again. Young Vermont men began joining the service and coming home on leave. During the early days of World War II, Rockwell saw these neighborhood boys as children he knew, not fighting men. To tell their story he created Willie Gillis. Rockwell painted Willie in a series of lighthearted scenes that avoided the battlefield but portrayed the young man away from home for the first time, the girls he left behind, and coming home on leave. Rockwell ended the series with a painting of Willie Gillis as

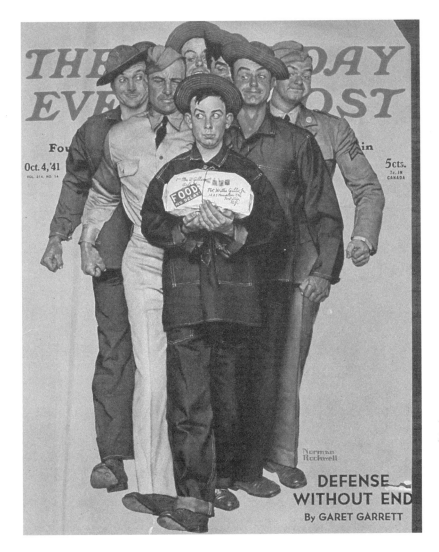

American G.I. Willie Gillis is portrayed in this Post *cover, which appeared on October 4, 1941. Through the Willie Gillis series, Rockwell illustrated the life of the neighborhood boy turned soldier.*

a college student sitting on a window seat reading a book. The painting contains symbols of Willie's past, present, and future: his helmet and bayonet hang at the top of the window, college textbooks clutter the window seat, and a golf bag and clubs rest against the wall. Two thirds of Rockwell's *Post* covers during the war years related to Americans dealing with the war, mostly on the home front.

In war posters Rockwell presented a more serious side of the war effort. One famous poster shows a gallant machine gunner firing his last few shells. The caption at the bottom says, "Let's give him enough and on time." Rockwell, a sincere patriot, wanted to do more for his country. He searched for an idea that would clearly express to the average person what America was fighting for.

6 Losses and Triumphs

An idea began to glimmer in Rockwell's mind when President Franklin D. Roosevelt addressed the joint session of the Seventy-seventh Congress on January 6, 1941. Although the United States was not yet involved in World War II, President Roosevelt felt that support for England, then at war with Germany, would protect U.S. shores. He closed the speech with a proclamation of four freedoms for everyone in the world:

> In the future days, which we seek to make secure, we look forward to a world founded upon four essential human freedoms.

> The first is freedom of speech and expression. . . . The second is freedom of every person to worship God in his own way. . . . The third is freedom from want. . . . The fourth is freedom from fear.[69]

Rockwell, deeply moved by Roosevelt's speech, wanted to illustrate the four freedoms in some grand manner.

Several months later, on December 7, 1941, Japan bombed Pearl Harbor. The United States immediately declared war. With American liberty now at stake, every artist in the nation wanted to be the one to illustrate Roosevelt's concept of freedom. For months Rockwell lay awake at night searching for an idea. During this time he created Willie Gillis and painted war posters, but no grand idea for the four freedoms came to him. He later wrote:

> My worst enemy is the world-shaking idea. Every so often I try to paint the *BIG* picture, something serious and colossal which will change the world, save mankind. . . . And off I go, stretching my neck like a swan and forgetting that I'm a duck. . . . I do ordinary people in everyday situations, and that's about all I can do.[70]

In other words, when Rockwell lost sight of the quality that made his work so popular, he became blind to the ideas around him.

Rockwell's *Four Freedoms*

As the war raged, everyday life went on in Arlington. One evening Rockwell went to a town meeting. Jim Edgerton, who later became Rockwell's neighbor, remembered the evening this way:

> They were having a meeting in town about building a high school. He got there a little late and walked in as someone was saying they wanted to

President Roosevelt's Speech

A portion of President Franklin D. Roosevelt's speech before a joint session of the Seventy-seventh Congress proclaiming four essential freedoms for the people of the world appears in Stuart Murray and James McCabe's Norman Rockwell's Four Freedoms:

"In the future days, which we seek to make secure, we look forward to a world founded upon four essential human freedoms.

The first is freedom of speech and expression—everywhere in the world.

The second is freedom of every person to worship God in his own way—everywhere in the world.

The third is freedom from want—which, translated into world terms, means economic understandings which will secure to every nation a healthy peacetime life for its inhabitants—everywhere in the world.

The fourth is freedom from fear—which, translated into world terms, means a worldwide reduction of armaments to such a point and in such a thorough fashion that no nation will be in a position to commit an act of physical aggression against any neighbor—anywhere in the world.

That is no vision of a distant millennium. It is a definite basis for a kind of world attainable in our own time and generation. That kind of world is the very antithesis [direct opposite] of the so-called new order of tyranny which the dictators seek to create with the crash of a bomb.

To that new order we oppose the great conception—the moral order."

build something for $90,000. This fellow spoke up and asked why they couldn't build something for $80,000.[71]

The fact that townspeople could disagree and yet allow everyone to express their views impressed Rockwell.

This thought whirled around in his head along with the four freedoms from Roosevelt's speech. They finally came together in a grand notion in the wee hours of the morning. At 3:00 A.M. on July 16, 1942, Rockwell sat straight up in bed. He finally knew what he would do—paint the four freedoms in the usual Rockwell style. He later wrote:

My gosh, I thought, that's it. . . . I'll illustrate the Four Freedoms using my Vermont neighbors as models. I'll express the ideas in simple everyday

scenes. Freedom of Speech—a New England town meeting. Freedom from Want—Thanksgiving dinner. Take them out of the noble language of the proclamation and put them in terms everybody can understand. . . . I got all excited. I knew it was the best idea I'd ever had.[72]

Mary was too sleepy to listen to Norman's idea and suggested that he go back to sleep. Excited, inspired, and wide awake, Rockwell wanted to call his friend, a fellow *Post* artist and neighbor, Mead Schaeffer. When he noticed the time, he changed his mind. He did not want to wake everyone on his party line. (At that time party lines were common and consisted of several households hooked up to the same telephone line. A call to one phone rang every phone. Each household knew when the phone rang for them by a special ring—long, short, long or maybe two shorts and a long.)

Because of the early hour Rockwell rode his bicycle to tell Schaeffer his idea. Schaeffer enthusiastically advised Rockwell to begin the project right away. In addition, Rockwell's idea stirred Schaeffer's patriotic spirit and he, too, began work on an inspirational painting for the war effort.

Rockwell planned to donate his paintings to the government for use in lifting national morale and selling war bonds. Once the sketches for the paintings were finished, he and Schaeffer went to Washington, where they contacted the under-secretary of war. With no success there they worked their way down to the Office of War Information, where they were told: "The last war you illustrators did the posters. This war we're going to use fine arts men, real artists."[73] As a further insult,

he then offered Norman Rockwell a job illustrating the Marine Corps calisthenics manual!

"Drop Everything Else"

The two dejected artists headed back to Vermont, with a stopover in Philadelphia. Rockwell had other sketches he wanted to show Ben Hibbs, the new editor at the *Post*. While in Hibbs's office, Rockwell mentioned he had been in Washington. As soon as Hibbs heard about Rockwell's *Four Freedoms*, he asked to see the sketches. Although Rockwell had lost his enthusiasm, the idea excited Hibbs. "Norman, you've got to do them for us," he said. "Drop everything else, just do the Four Freedoms. Don't bother with covers or illustrations."[74]

Rockwell regained his enthusiasm immediately and began work on the *Four Freedoms* on returning to his studio. Although he had the basic idea firmly in his mind and sketched on canvas, composing the final scenes proved to be a struggle. He painted *Freedom of Speech*, inspired by the town hall meeting, four times before he had the exact picture he wanted. Fortunately, *Freedom from Want*, a family enjoying Thanksgiving dinner, and *Freedom from Fear*, parents tucking their children in for the night, progressed quickly. He then wrestled two months with *Freedom of Worship*, which depicted people of different faiths praying in their own ways. Knowing that religion could be a touchy issue added to the difficulty in getting the final version exactly right. He later said, "A face in the picture would bother me, so I'd rub it out with the turpentine and do it over. I scrubbed so much on that painting—did

parts of it over so many times—that I was afraid I'd go right through the canvas before I finished."[75] Rockwell worked on the *Four Freedoms* for six months, seven days a week. "You know," he said later. "Those two pictures I had all the trouble with—'Freedom of Speech' and 'Worship'—are the ones I like best"[76]

With a clear and simple idea everyone could understand, Rockwell captured the essence of Roosevelt's four freedoms in the beauty and strength of these paintings.

Rockwell's *Four Freedoms* appeared on the inside pages of four separate issues of the *Post* in 1943. An essay written by a well-known author accompanied each illustration: Booth Tarkington on freedom of speech, February 20; Will Durant on freedom of worship, February 27; Carlos Bulosan on freedom from want, March 6; Stephen Vincent Benét on freedom from fear, March 13. The essays expressed the same sentiment Rockwell symbolized on canvas. Publication came at the perfect

Perhaps Rockwell's most inspirational works, the Four Freedoms *gracefully illustrated the freedoms set forth by President Roosevelt in his January 6, 1941, speech. (Right) In* Freedom from Want, *a fortunate family gathers at the dinner table, eager to sample the bounty of a Thanksgiving feast.*

Rockwell's *Four Freedoms*

Ben Hibbs, editor of the Post *when Rockwell painted the* Four Freedoms, *wrote in Rockwell's autobiography about the success of the series because Rockwell was too modest to write on his own behalf:*

"Requests to reprint flooded in from other publications. Various Government agencies and private organizations made millions of reprints and distributed them not only in this country but all over the world. Those four pictures quickly became the best known and most appreciated paintings of that era. They appeared right at a time when the war was going against us on the battle fronts, and the American people needed the inspirational message which they conveyed so forcefully and so beautifully.

Subsequently, the Treasury Department took the original paintings on tour of the nation as the centerpiece of a *Post* art show—to sell war bonds. They were viewed by 1,222,000 people in 16 leading cities and were instrumental in selling $132,992,539 worth of bonds.

Following the war, the original paintings—they are of heroic size—were hung in our offices. The two which I consider the finest of the four—'Freedom of Worship' and 'Freedom of Speech'—hang in my own office, and I love them. They are a daily source of inspiration to me—in the same way that the clock tower of old Independence Hall, which I can see from my office window, inspires me. If this is Fourth of July talk, so be it. Maybe this country needs a bit more Fourth of July the year around."

time for greatest impact, not only in America, but around the world. Allied forces were in trouble on all battle fronts, and the American people desperately needed encouragement and inspiration. As a result the *Post* received thousands of requests for reprints of the inspiring illustrations.

The Treasury Department took the original paintings on a sixteen-city tour, where they were viewed by 1,222,000 people and promoted the sale of $132,992,539 in war bonds. As the tour began, Rockwell left the privacy of his studio and small Vermont village to attend the opening banquet on April 26 in Washington, D.C. The next morning he autographed reprints of his *Four Freedoms* at Hecht's Department Store for people who bought war bonds. Late that afternoon Rockwell was asked to accompany the tour to fifteen other cities. Too exhausted to answer, he just scratched his head. Ben Hibbs stepped in to the rescue saying, "No. Norman's going to stay home and do *Post* covers."[77] Much to

Rockwell's relief the ordeal ended, and he returned to the comfort of his studio.

Ben Hibbs considered Rockwell's *Four Freedoms* great art. He wrote: "To me they are great human documents in the form of paint and canvas. A great picture, I think, is one which moves and inspires millions of people. The Four Freedoms did—and do."[78]

Rockwell's *Four Freedoms* were the triumph of his career. Seventy thousand people wrote to him to express their love for the paintings. They quickly became the best-known and most-appreciated paintings of that era. More than fifty years later these four paintings still enjoy popularity as they inspire yet another generation, not only in America, but around the world.

Rockwell put so much of himself into painting the *Four Freedoms* that he lost ten pounds. Drained and dazed with exhaustion after completing the massive canvases, forty-four by forty-eight inches each, he relaxed by doing a humorous April Fool's cover. He found working on the small *Post*-size canvas relaxing, with no worry about accuracy. He purposely included forty-five mistakes for the viewer to find, such as a man holding the wrong end of his fishing pole, wearing skis and earmuffs in summer, and using a lobster in a can for bait. One unintentional error would not make any difference.

Disaster Strikes

Early one morning in 1943, the day after he sent the April Fool's cover to the *Post*, Rockwell's studio burned to the ground. Too numb to comprehend his loss, in the following days he drew a cartoon of the events of the fire that would later appear in the *Post*. He also made a trip to Washington to redo some sketches that were lost in the fire. He needed them for a *Post* assignment about visiting the president. Upon returning to Vermont, reality set in, and Rockwell mourned his great loss. He wrote of the items lost in the fire:

> All my antiques, my favorite covers and illustrations which I'd kept over the years, my costumes, my collections of old guns, animal skulls, Howard Pyle prints, my paints, brushes, easel, my file of clippings—everything, the accumulation of twenty-eight years of painting, traveling, collecting.[79]

The loss would have been far greater, however, had the fire occurred a few days earlier. *Freedom of Worship*, the last in the *Four Freedoms* series, had been shipped to Philadelphia within the past week. The fire reduced an unrecorded number of Rockwell's original paintings to ash. As a result no record of his complete works exists.

The studio that burned had been an old barn Norman had outfitted for his workplace. When the Rockwells purchased their second home in Arlington, Norman had a new studio built from the ground up. While he waited for his studio to be built, he worked in the one-room schoolhouse on the village green, or common— a grassy area in the center of most New England towns.

Homecoming 1945

From his new studio Rockwell recorded the end of the war on canvas. He covered all three branches of the military in sepa-

rate homecoming covers. In one a marine shows a captured Japanese flag to his friends in a hometown garage. In another a sailor enjoys the hammock in the backyard of his parents' home. The most popular depicts a soldier being greeted in the backyard of his tenement house.

Two of Rockwell's homecoming paintings were honored by the Society of Illustrators at an exhibition held at Rocke-feller Center in New York in 1946. The marine and his friends in the garage received best of show, and *Homecoming*, the soldier arriving home at his tenement house, took third. Not only did *Homecoming* receive honors from Rockwell's fellow illustrators, but as the official poster selected for the eighth war bond drive, more than 300,000 copies went on display across the nation. Ben Hibbs considered

Homecoming, *one of Rockwell's most acclaimed* Post *covers, was selected to be the official poster for the eighth war bond drive.*

Homecoming, published on May 26, 1945, to be Rockwell's best. Because of Rockwell's modesty, Hibbs wrote about this painting in Rockwell's autobiography:

> The homecoming cover [the original painting] now hangs above my desk in my study at home and it has been borrowed many times for art exhibits, including at least one exhibit in the Metropolitan Museum of Art in New York. I regard it as the finest cover Norman has done; in fact, I have always felt that it is the greatest magazine cover ever published.[80]

Although *Homecoming* received acclaim from the art community, Rockwell's public upheld another work as their all-time favorite *Post* cover. In a poll taken by the magazine several years later, the cover for Thanksgiving 1951, *Saying Grace*, proved to be most popular by far.

This cover depicts a grandmother and grandson saying grace in a railroad station cafeteria, while other travelers pause to

The endearing aspects of Norman Rockwell's Saying Grace *have made it his most popular* Post *cover. The painting first appeared on the cover of the November 24, 1951, issue.*

Norman Rockwell painted portraits of numerous celebrities, ranging from Hollywood entertainers to Washington politicians.

watch. In portraying this simple act of worship in a public place, Rockwell touched the heart of America. As usual he paid close attention to detail, including the umbrellas inside and dreary weather outside the window. The table where the grandmother and boy sit with two other diners occupies the center of the painting. Only portions of other travelers are visible, giving the impression that they are entering and leaving. Rockwell draws the viewer into the picture with this sense of movement and quiet emotion as we share a moment of worship.

Celebrity *Post* Covers

By this time Rockwell was well established as America's best-loved artist. Throughout the 1950s he continued to paint his usual form of cover but added portraits of Hollywood celebrities, political candidates, and heads of state to his range of subjects. He painted President Dwight D. Eisenhower in 1952 and presidential candidates in every election through 1968.

In addition, Rockwell's portraits of Hollywood entertainers, including Bob

Hope, Jack Benny, and John Wayne, appeared as *Post* covers. Of all the celebrities Rockwell painted, Eisenhower was his favorite model. Rockwell later credited the president's appeal to his wide range of facial expressions. He wrote of Eisenhower's changeable expression:

One moment sort of a quiet melancholy and the next a radiant smile. And it's his wide, mobile mouth and his expressive eyes that do it. Watching him is like watching a diamond revolved in the sunlight, flashing colors and light. His face does the same thing; it's changing all the time, a real rubber face.[81]

When Rockwell painted a portrait, he composed a Rockwell portrait. That is, he captured the best of the person he painted. He even pleased President Lyndon B. Johnson with a portrait, while that of another famous artist, Peter Hurd, annoyed him greatly. Rockwell later commented that "Hurd, of course, had painted him as he was, while I had done him as he would like to think he is."[82]

The Other Side of Rockwell's Life

Although he illustrated the best side of life, purposely leaving out the bad, he could not do this in his own life. Throughout his career he rode the crest of success, only to soon dip into the valley of depression time and time again. Each success brought fear that he would never succeed again—that his current good idea would be his last.

He worked a full day, seven days a week, to produce a constant flow of paintings. Sometimes he felt he had painted everything in one location as many times as he could paint it. He then either moved or went on a long trip. The 1939 move to Arlington had resulted in a stockpile of ordinary people for models as well as new ideas. With this in mind, Mary and Norman decided to move to Stockbridge, Massachusetts, in 1953. Once again Norman hoped the change of scene would help him through the difficulties he was experiencing with his work. He did find help in Stockbridge, but of another kind. He wrote:

I sank deeper into the muck. I was dissatisfied, doubted my ability. . . . I got to talking with Erik H. Erikson, a psychoanalyst on the staff of Austin Riggs Center. Sort of casually to begin with, but pretty soon I found myself seeing him regularly. He helped me to understand the crisis. And I came through it rather more easily than I would have plodding along by myself.[83]

Throughout the 1950s Rockwell produced *Post* covers, story illustrations, advertisements, and calendars. In addition he and his son Tom wrote his autobiography, *My Adventures as an Illustrator.*

A Widower at Sixty-Five

A few months after Rockwell finished his autobiography in 1959, Mary went upstairs for an afternoon nap. With no warning, she suffered a heart attack and died in her sleep. Norman and Mary had been married twenty-eight years.

Left a widower at age sixty-five, Rockwell had fifty years of experience as an artist behind him and no intention to retire. As he mourned his wife, he lost himself in work. He painted a portrait of Mary. He tackled the *Triple Portrait* of himself looking in the mirror, painting a portrait of himself, for the cover of the *Post*, which would carry the first installment of his autobiography. In addition Rockwell and his son began work on the *Norman Rockwell Memory Album*, which was published shortly after the autobiography.

Despite his grief, life went on. In 1960 he attended the celebration of Grandma Moses's one hundredth birthday and helped the Boy Scouts of America observe their Golden Jubilee. He painted a special

Following the death of Mary, Rockwell immersed himself in his work. One of his paintings during this period was Triple Portrait, *which appeared on the cover of the* Post *on February 13, 1960.*

Boy Scout calendar that year and designed a postage stamp that commemorated fifty years of scouting.

The Golden Rule

Soon after Mary's death Norman again became inspired to illustrate a grand idea. He wanted to promote tolerance among the peoples of the world. Earlier he had completed the preliminary sketch for a ten-foot mural of fifty people representing the nations of the world to symbolize the United Nations. However, he received little cooperation from the American and British ambassadors. Discouraged, Rockwell lost interest in the idea and stored the sketch in a back room. In 1960, as he thought of illustrating the Golden Rule, Rockwell decided to fill a canvas with the faces from all over the world in an attitude of worship. He pulled out the old sketch of the United Nations and set to work. He chose several faces from the sketch and added others. The finished painting took five months of concentrated effort.

The *Golden Rule* appeared on the cover of the April 1, 1961, issue of the *Post*, and Rockwell received the Interfaith Award of the National Conference of Christians and Jews that year. He paid little attention to the many honors given him during his life and turned down most invitations to award banquets. He valued this one because the citation agreed with his philosophy of life and gave him meaningful recognition for

his dedication to the highest ideals of amity [friendship], understanding and

---

Presidential Portraits

John Mack Carter, editor in chief of McCall's *magazine, wrote in the January-February 1979 issue of the* Saturday Evening Post *about the political value of Rockwell's portraits of presidential candidates:*

"Every four years (Rockwell) would journey to the White House and then to the opposition camp to do the studies and then the portraits. What a vote-getter he was! Today I hear that television is such a powerful influence on the electorate that a 'smooth' actor might sweep into the top office of the land with few meaningful qualifications. But I say that television is nothing compared to one of Rockwell's portraits. Eisenhower twinkled as a grandfather to the world. Even LBJ didn't say that it was the ugliest thing he had ever seen. Perhaps his masterpiece in this genre was JFK—squared jaw, piercing eyes, heavy hair mopped to the side, looking absolutely vital. Kennedy knew a political resource if any man ever did, and he set out to win Norman over."

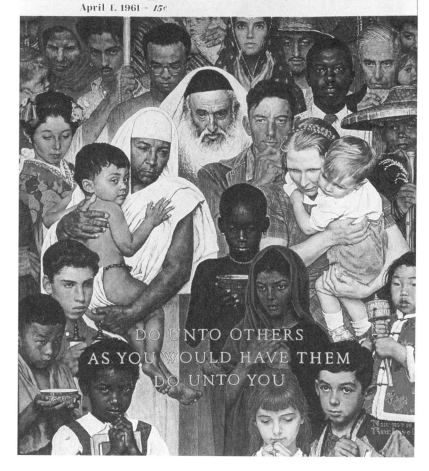

Rockwell's noble painting The Golden Rule *appeared on the cover of the* Post *on April 1, 1961. Rockwell received the Interfaith Award of the National Conference of Christians and Jews for helping to unite the peoples of the world.*

cooperation among men; and his artistic leadership in depicting with such exacting technique and unfailing humor the universal fact that all men, great and unknown, are members of the One Family of Man under God.[84]

Although the *Golden Rule* represents the people of the world, Rockwell found all the models within fifty miles of Stockbridge. Some were visiting and some were exchange students, while others lived in the area. The painting also includes his deceased wife Mary's face in the upper right corner, along with one of the Rockwell grandsons.

In September 1961 Rockwell surprised the family with the announcement that he planned to marry again. He and Mary L. "Molly" Punderson, a schoolteacher in Stockbridge, were married in October. Although this third marriage would bring him happiness, another kind of breakup lay ahead for Rockwell.

7 The End of an Era

The *Post* experienced changes over the years, and so did Rockwell. His first cover in 1916 focused on three characters done in black and white with a touch of red, centered against a plain blackground. In the following years Rockwell added more detail to his backgrounds, and the magazine began printing in full color. The *Post* changed the style of its logo, and Rockwell adjusted his illustrations to fit the new format. Although the magazine was being published long before Rockwell became a cover artist, the two matured together over their forty-seven-year relationship.

George Horace Lorimer

During this time Rockwell produced *Post* covers and story illustrations for six generations of editors. Rockwell had utmost respect for George Horace Lorimer, his first editor, and judged his other editors against Lorimer as his standard. With Lorimer, Rockwell always knew where he stood; the editor either accepted or rejected a sketch. When presented with five sketches, Lorimer routinely chose the three he liked best and never reconsidered a rejected idea. Once Rockwell understood how the editor worked, he began

including three good and two not so good ideas in each five sketches that he submitted. In this way Rockwell avoided having his good ideas rejected.

Norman Rockwell had the utmost respect for George Horace Lorimer (pictured), his first editor at the Saturday Evening Post.

Wesley Stout

When Lorimer retired in 1937 after being editor at the *Post* for thirty-seven years, Wesley Stout became editor. Stout never accepted a cover without making at least one small change. This style of editing contributed to Rockwell's insecurity for the next five years. Rockwell later wrote:

> In the past five years, ever since Wesley Stout had become editor of the *Post*, my feelings of insecurity had been aggravated. Under Mr. Lorimer I had always known, at least, whether or not he liked a cover. With Mr. Stout I was uncertain. Every time I submitted a cover he asked me to make some little change. . . . I wasn't able to paint a cover with any conviction because I knew, as sure as three came after two, that some little thing would be wrong with it. The constant nagging sapped my inspiration, made me unsure of myself.[85]

Ben Hibbs

In 1942 as the editorial staff again underwent changes, Rockwell heard rumors that the *Post* was in trouble. This worried him. As a result, when Ben Hibbs took charge as editor, Rockwell felt pressured to make a good impression. He presented nine of his best ideas. Rockwell expected Hibbs, like Lorimer, to choose the ones he liked best and reject the rest. Much to Rockwell's surprise Hibbs accepted them all. This made Rockwell doubt the new editor's competence and heightened his concern that the rumors of the *Post*'s impending doom were true.

That evening Rockwell told Mary, "Ben Hibbs is a wonderful fellow. But I don't think he'll last long. He accepted all my sketches, *all nine*. . . . It's wonderful but I don't think it's going to last. You can't run a magazine that way."[86] However, Rockwell was wrong. He confessed in his autobiography, "I'd been wrong before and I've been wrong since, but I guess that time I laid it over anything for pure white, out-and-out wrongness. . . . Ben took that magazine and nursed it back to health."[87]

Ken Stuart

A few years later further changes in editorial policy gave the art director, Ken Stuart, complete responsibility for *Post* covers, whereas in the past the covers had been approved by the magazine editor. Stuart allowed his artists more creative freedom and quickly became Rockwell's favorite editor. Rockwell wrote, "[Stuart] lets me do my own work, doesn't hold me back or try to paint the picture himself. . . . He gives me the feeling that he believes in me and only wants to help me realize my own ideas."[88]

In addition to allowing Rockwell more creative freedom than in the past, Ken Stuart stopped rotating the cover subjects between pretty women, dogs, and human interest. He dropped the women and dogs to focus on human interest—the type of covers Rockwell painted. Of course this suited Rockwell, king of human interest, or storytelling, covers. Now the *Post* would do fifty-two of them a year, and Rockwell painted his share. Rockwell enjoyed the bliss of this relationship until 1962 when the *Post* sank into deep trouble and Ken Stuart left.

Rockwell Breaks with the *Post*

At this time the editorial staff at the *Post* made drastic changes, almost completely eliminating the human interest cover in favor of portraits and photographs. Rockwell began traveling the world to paint portraits of foreign leaders, including Nehru, Nasser, and Tito, for the *Post*. The frequent travel left little time for outside work when other magazines, including *Look* and *McCall's*, offered him assignments.

The editorial staff at the *Post* changed again. The new editors decided not to publish Rockwell's portrait of Tito, citing technical difficulties as the reason. But Rockwell's son Tom thought it had more to do with not wanting a Communist on the cover. Much to Rockwell's dislike, the new editors wanted more control over his work. In fact, as he worked on a portrait of Jackie Kennedy, Jerrild Asger, the new art editor, came to Rockwell's studio and directed the brushstrokes! Although the portrait did not meet Rockwell's standards, the *Post* published it in the October 26, 1963, issue. This was the last work Rockwell did for the *Post*. His last cover appeared December 14, 1963—a portrait of John F. Kennedy that was pulled from the files and framed in black. This darkened version of the Kennedy portrait, which Rockwell had painted for the October 29, 1960, issue, appeared in memoriam to the assassinated president.

After forty-seven years and 317 *Post* covers, Rockwell severed relations with the *Post*. However, the magazine's most popular cover artist would be long remembered. The magazine suspended publication in 1969 and resumed again under new ownership in 1971. The redesigned and resized magazine frequently paid tribute to its most popular cover artist. In fact, Rockwell's art continued to appear on the cover and inside pages more than thirty years after he painted

his last cover and more than fifteen years after his death.

His Career Goes On

The era of Rockwell's America ended in 1963 when Rockwell left the *Post*. As the magazine industry changed along with the times, photographs replaced illustration. Magazines became specialized, directed toward the interests of a specific type of reader. As a result, the general-interest magazine disappeared. In fact, all the magazines Rockwell had worked with in the past ceased publication, at least temporarily, except *Boys' Life*.

Rockwell continued to get assignments, but they focused on issues that had little room for humor. Although this approach represented a radical change for Rockwell, it gave him the opportunity he had always wanted: to paint the grand idea. He said in a speech in 1963, "I am wildly excited about painting contemporary subjects—pictures about civil rights, astronauts, the Peace Corps, the poverty program."[89]

In this vein he portrayed the human side of integration legislation for *Look* in January 1964 with a painting of a young black girl being escorted to school by deputy marshals and again in May 1967 with a painting showing a slightly tense moment as white children meet their new black neighbors.

Norman Rockwell completed The Problem We All Live With *for the January 1964 issue of* Look *magazine. Rockwell relished the idea of tackling contemporary subjects like civil rights and integration legislation.*

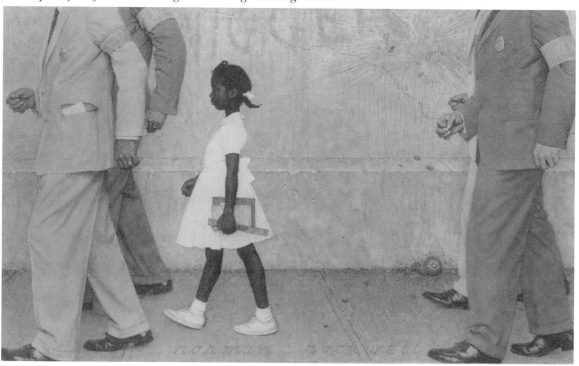

The Old Corner House Museum

The Old Corner House Museum in Stockbridge, Massachusetts, houses the Norman Rockwell Museum. Visitors can gaze upon Rockwell's many paintings, including the originals of the Four Freedoms.

As the United States made strides in the success of the space program, Rockwell gave us a peek into the future with a portrayal of an astronaut about to set foot on the moon in *Look*'s January 1967 issue. He later painted the *Apollo 11* space team for *Look*, published in July 1969, the same month the *Apollo 11* crew, including Neil Armstrong, actually landed on the moon. By the end of the decade, Rockwell's career encompassed an illustrated record of the American people from horse-and-buggy days to the moon landing.

In 1967 Rockwell and some of his neighbors in Stockbridge bought a large eighteenth-century Georgian house on the corner of Main and Elm. They restored the building and turned it into a museum of history of Stockbridge. The small town's historical exhibit attracted little interest until Rockwell offered to add some of his paintings to the display. Attracted by Rockwell's work, people came to Stockbridge from all over the country. A few years later, in 1973, Rockwell added the rest of his collection to the exhibit and donated his studio in 1976. The Old Corner House Museum in Stockbridge, Massachusetts, became a permanent home for Rockwell's work. The collection began with a donation from the Rockwells, and others added to it, even returning some of the paintings Rockwell had given away over the years. Most of the paintings were purchased with profits made from the sale of artist's proofs—that is, a certain number of prints, made in addition to the number to be issued for sale in a limited edition, that are given to the artist. In his later years Rockwell signed these prints, which were sold to raise money for the museum. Today the museum collection, which includes the originals of many of his *Post* covers and the *Four Freedoms*, represents a valuable legacy. For example, in May 1994 a study, (not the final painting) of *Freedom of Speech* sold at an auction for $407,000.

8 Another Town

Rockwell enjoyed art from the time he was old enough to hold a pencil until the day he could no longer control a brush. He never considered retirement but did slack off some in the early 1970s. In 1971 he said, "I work from fatigue to fatigue; . . . at my age there's only so much daylight left."[90] Although he was seventy-seven at the time, he still went to his studio seven days a week but routinely took a short nap after lunch. For further relaxation and exercise he took a five- or six-mile bike ride with his wife, Molly, every day.

Collector Plates and Lithographs

In his later years he had a good income from the work he had already done. Everyone wanted a Rockwell, and marketing experts made it possible for everyone to have one. Rockwell's work was reproduced in signed and numbered prints, or lithographs, many of which sold for more than Rockwell received for the original magazine assignment. Reproductions of his work on collector plates, silver ingots, and porcelain figurines became popular. His signature on these collector items increased their value. As signs of his age be-

gan to show in his painting, Rockwell spent much of his time signing these reproductions.

Rockwell adds the finishing touches to one of his paintings. The elderly artist continued to paint, never considering retirement.

A Bicycle Fall

In March 1974, shortly after Rockwell's eightieth birthday, Norman and Molly took a vacation to Little Dix in the Caribbean. One day while taking their usual bike ride, Molly rode ahead. As she neared the hotel, she looked back and discovered that Norman was not in sight. A hotel employee drove her back along the route they had taken. They found Rockwell sitting beside the road. He could not remember falling off his bicycle, and no one knows whether he fell accidentally or suffered a minor stroke. He seemed to recover, and the Rockwells returned to Stockbridge. A few weeks later he fell off his bicycle again. His son Tom wrote of this time in the afterword to Rockwell's autobiography: "He was still working, but much more slowly. When he was painting his portrait of John Wayne in 1974, he was distressed that he just couldn't seem to get things right, then he finished it and sent it off."[91]

The next year Rockwell was unable to complete a group of portraits he had started, and for the first time since he began his relationship with the Boy Scouts in 1913, someone else painted the Boy Scout calendar.

Hometown Honors

Stockbridge, Massachusetts, where Rockwell lived from 1953 until the day he died, paid tribute to their best-known resident. On Rockwell's eighty-second birthday, February 3, 1976, the eighty-five children attending Stockbridge Plain Elementary School, along with their teachers and principal, presented him with a large birthday cake. The cake came with a celebration, and everyone sang "Happy Birthday" and "For He's a Jolly Good Fellow." A few months later, on May 23, the citizens of Stockbridge staged an all-out celebration. Ten thousand visitors flocked to Stockbridge to watch a ninety-minute parade in honor of Norman Rockwell. Two thousand people participated in one hundred marching units, and twenty-five floats depicted Rockwell's America. The day was officially declared "Norman Rockwell Day, in appreciation of Norman Rockwell's contribution to the great American heritage," by committee chairman Charles Piggott.[92]

Molly and Norman enjoyed the parade from a flatbed truck. The elderly

In Stockbridge, Massachusetts, May 23, 1976, was declared "Norman Rockwell Day." The entire community gathered together to honor Rockwell (pictured), America's best-loved illustrator.

Norman Rockwell Day in Stockbridge

Frederic A. Birmingham wrote in the Saturday Evening Post *about researching old newspaper files that made him feel like an eyewitness to the parade on Norman Rockwell Day in Stockbridge, Massachusetts:*

"On May 23, 10,000 spectators and 2,000 participants gathered on Main Street to witness a 90-minute parade in Rockwell's honor, showing *Him* this time—via 100 parading units and 25 floats—the America he had so many times portrayed for them and the world.

What a day to remember! Among the marchers and watchers are many of the models who posed for the 317 Rockwell *Saturday Evening Post* covers. But perhaps most spectacular of all is the gigantic float reproducing in infinite detail and magnificent style the most famous Rockwell cover of all, *The Doctor and the Doll* . . . the cover of the March 9, 1929, *Post*. . . . And here come other Rockwell scenes, recaptured on floats: *Homecoming*, a serviceman's return; another medical scene, a little boy in a doctor's office for a backside injection; . . . the touching teacher's birthday party, staged by the Stockbridge Parents-Teachers Association."

guest of honor enjoyed the parade but sighed when it was over and said, "I'm tired but proud."[93]

Last Magazine Cover

In July 1976 Rockwell's last magazine cover appeared on *American Artist*. The cover, in honor of America's bicentennial celebration, pictured Rockwell himself wrapping a happy birthday ribbon around the Liberty Bell. In preparation for this cover Rockwell could not go to Philadelphia and have a photograph taken of himself wrapping a ribbon around the Liberty Bell. Instead he found a wooden barrel about the right size and posed for a photograph of himself wrapping the ribbon around the barrel. From this picture he painted himself and the ribbon, left the barrel out, and painted in the Liberty Bell from another photograph.

The Presidential Medal of Freedom

Rockwell's health continued to fail. By February 1977, when he received the Presidential Medal of Freedom—the nation's highest peacetime award—from President Gerald R. Ford, Rockwell used a wheelchair and required professional nursing

care. He still asked to be taken to his studio. Although he had lost the ability to paint, he could still do line drawings with pen and ink. Toward the end of his days, when he could no longer leave his bedroom, he continued to ask for drawing paper and a pencil.

Rockwell Dies

Norman Rockwell died November 8, 1978. Molly, his third wife, told reporters, "He died of being 84."[94] Some speculated that Rockwell might have suffered from Alzheimer's disease. However, Rockwell's

Norman Rockwell proudly displays the Presidential Medal of Freedom, an honor he received in February 1977.

friend and doctor, Franklin Paddock, disagreed. He said:

> Norman's last years were clouded. Certainly during the very last years of his life, his paintings were inferior, and his personality was almost totally nonreactive. After his death at 84, attempts were made to make his deterioration a focus for the study of Alzheimer's disease, but there was no medical evidence for diagnosis.[95]

Rockwell must have known before his career passed its midpoint that he would be driven to paint all his days. He put himself in a series of sketches as a babe in a cradle with a sketch pad in hand and in front of easels as a toddler, child, young man, mature man, and old man reaching out of a coffin to sign his final painting. The series ends with his familiar pipe resting in the grass near a tombstone. Rockwell was seldom seen without his pipe and often painted himself with it. The pipe appears in each of these sketches from the cradle to the grave.

Rockwell Moves on to Another Town

Norman Rockwell's funeral was held at Saint Paul's Episcopal Church in Stockbridge, Massachusetts. Those attending received a folder announcing "a service of thanksgiving for the life of Norman Rockwell." Boy Scouts and Cub Scouts lined the pathways to the church. They stood in solemn lines at first, but soon the boys began to behave as ordinary boys in one of Rockwell's paintings. Norman Rockwell was remembered as "a townsman, never a hermit, a part of town meetings, square

Rockwell's America

Ronald Reagan wrote about Rockwell's portrayal of America in the foreword to Norman Rockwell's Patriotic Times, *by George Mendoza:*

"The America in which young Rockwell grew up and launched his career was still mostly a Nation of small towns. Neighbor knew neighbor, farmers visited Main Street to swap tales at the barber shop, and Babe Ruth was just beginning to attract notice as a slugger. . . . The American people had tamed a continent, achieved prosperity, and secured peace for our Nation. They were a hard-working, churchgoing people, filled with spirit and faith. . . .

Our nation has changed profoundly since the days of the America that Norman Rockwell so skillfully portrayed. Yet the values that he cherished and celebrated—love of God and country, hard work, neighborhood, and family—still give us strength, and will shape our dreams for the decades to come."

dances, basketball games. His models became his ideals, and the town became the vision, the green hill far away."[96]

David Wood, director of the museum where Rockwell's paintings are on display, read from Rockwell's favorite poem, "Abou Ben Adhem."

"I pray thee, then
Write me as one that loves his fellow-men."
The Angel wrote, and vanished. The next night

It came again with a great wakening light,
And showed the names whom love of God had blessed,
And, lo! Ben Adhem's name led all the rest![97]

It was a beautiful day, and after the service the townspeople, most of whom had posed for Rockwell, continued about their business as though he had just "moved on to another town"—in the true spirit of a Rockwell painting.

Rockwell's Legacy

Norman Rockwell left behind a pictorial record of America that covered six decades. This span of time included two world wars, the Great Depression, the dust bowl, poverty, prejudice, and violence. Through it all, life went on. Some people fell victim to the times, others emerged as survivors, and some became heroes. Most were ordinary people making the best life they could for themselves and their families. Rockwell chose to record the best side of these ordinary people. In doing so he

Norman Rockwell stands amidst his many works. Rockwell's legacy, teeming with poignant paintings and lively illustrations, will continue to captivate and inspire future generations.

gave us hope for the future with a pictorial statement, in simple terms, that life goes on through the hard times and ordinary people make the best of it.

Robert A. M. Stern, an architect from New York who designed a new museum to house Rockwell's work in Stockbridge, put it this way:

> Rockwell's art mirrors our world—or at least an ideal, slightly lost version of that world. . . . Mom and apple pie are very good institutions, and so was Rockwell's America. . . . Rockwell was really a very fine artist. He captured in ways no one else has how America was, and how a large part of it wants to be.[98]

Although many of Rockwell's earlier paintings were lost when his studio burned in 1943, he still left a sizable legacy of creative work—more than four thousand originals. Many now belong to the Stockbridge museum's collection, but some still remain in the possession of art dealers. As more visitors came to the Old Corner House, plans were made to build a new museum on State Route 183 in the Berkshire Hills outside Stockbridge. The museum, opened in the spring of 1993, now exhibits about 150 of the approximately 500 Rockwell originals that it owns. The paintings are rotated in and out of the exhibit so that all are shown, but not at one time.

Rockwell's red barn studio was moved from the center of Stockbridge and now stands near the new museum. His easel, brushes, paint box, and all the things he collected remain as he left them—as though he has just stepped out for a moment and will return to finish yet another painting.

Although Rockwell's recognition as an artist was long in coming, his paintings have graced the walls of some of America's most prestigious museums, including the Metropolitan Museum of Art and Brooklyn Museum in New York, the Los Angeles County Museum of Art, the Corcoran Gallery, the Smithsonian Institution's National Air and Space Museum, and the National Portrait Gallery in Washington, D.C. These exhibits of his work stand as a silent declaration that Norman Rockwell did, indeed, create paintings of fine art quality. Rockwell never called himself anything but an illustrator; however, in his heart he knew the caliber of his work. In later years he said, "You know, there's a difference of opinion as to whether I am an artist or an illustrator, and when I find someone arguing that I am an artist, I always reply that I am nothing but an illustrator, but I always let my opponent win the debate."[99]

Still critics withheld their approval, viewing America's beloved artist as a dreamer who painted a lifestyle that did not exist. However, for ordinary people Rockwell captured moments of their own lives on canvases that became *Post* covers—the good part, feelings they would never forget painted by an artist they would long remember.

Notes

Introduction: America's Best-Loved Illustrator

1. Norman Rockwell as told to Tom Rockwell, *My Adventures as an Illustrator*. New York: Harry N. Abrams, 1988, p. 35.

Chapter 1: Young Norman Rockwell

2. Rockwell, *My Adventures*, p. 37.
3. Rockwell, *My Adventures*, p. 21.
4. Donald Walton, *A Rockwell Portrait: An Intimate Biography*. Kansas City, MO: Sheed Andrews and McMeel, 1978, p. 29.
5. Rockwell, *My Adventures*, p. 28.
6. Rockwell, *My Adventures*, p. 28.
7. Rockwell, *My Adventures*, p. 31.
8. Rockwell, *My Adventures*, p. 35.
9. Rockwell, *My Adventures*, p. 39.

Chapter 2: Education and Early Work

10. Rockwell, *My Adventures*, p. 43.
11. Walton, *A Rockwell Portrait*, p. 38.
12. Walton, *A Rockwell Portrait*, p. 38.
13. Rockwell, *My Adventures*, p. 48.
14. Rockwell, *My Adventures*, p. 49.
15. Rockwell, *My Adventures*, pp. 49–50.
16. Rockwell, *My Adventures*, p. 50.
17. Rockwell, *My Adventures*, p. 51.
18. Rockwell, *My Adventures*, pp. 59–60.
19. Rockwell, *My Adventures*, p. 58.
20. Walton, *A Rockwell Portrait*, p. 48.
21. Rockwell, *My Adventures*, p. 64.
22. Thomas S. Buechner, *Norman Rockwell: Artist and Illustrator*. New York: Harry N. Abrams, 1970, p. 38.
23. Rockwell, *My Adventures*, p. 64.
24. Rockwell, *My Adventures*, p. 65.
25. Rockwell, *My Adventures*, p. 65.
26. Rockwell, *My Adventures*, p. 68.
27. Rockwell, *My Adventures*, pp. 51–52.
28. Verlyn Klinkenborg, "Pyle and Rockwell—Totally American, Yet Not at All Alike," *Smithsonian,* July 1994.
29. Rockwell, *My Adventures*, p. 72.
30. Rockwell, *My Adventures*, p. 72.

Chapter 3: Rockwell Arrives

31. Rockwell, *My Adventures*, p. 112.
32. Rockwell, *My Adventures*, p. 74.
33. Rockwell, *My Adventures*, p. 74.
34. Rockwell, *My Adventures*, p. 78.
35. Rockwell, *My Adventures*, p. 94.
36. Rockwell, *My Adventures*, p. 94.
37. Rockwell, *My Adventures*, p. 98.
38. Rockwell, *My Adventures*, p. 106.
39. Rockwell, *My Adventures*, p. 106.
40. Rockwell, *My Adventures*, p. 107.
41. Rockwell, *My Adventures*, p. 108.
42. Rockwell, *My Adventures*, p. 108.
43. Walton, *A Rockwell Portrait*, p. 87.
44. Rockwell, *My Adventures*, p. 109.
45. Rockwell, *My Adventures*, p. 109.
46. Rockwell, *My Adventures*, p. 109.

Chapter 4: Rockwell the Illustrator

47. "What You See is What They Saw," in the *Saturday Evening Post, Norman Rockwell Memory Album.* Indianapolis, IN: Curtis Publishing, 1979.
48. Rockwell, *My Adventures*, pp. 114–115.
49. Rockwell, *My Adventures*, p. 115.
50. Rockwell, *My Adventures*, p. 119.
51. Rockwell, *My Adventures*, p. 119.
52. Rockwell, *My Adventures*, p. 122.
53. Rockwell, *My Adventures*, p. 130.
54. Rockwell, *My Adventures*, p. 130.

Chapter 5: How Rockwell Painted America

55.   Walton, *A Rockwell Portrait*, p. 106.

56.   Rockwell, *My Adventures*, p. 266.

57.   Rockwell, *My Adventures*, p. 270.

58.   Walton, *A Rockwell Portrait*, p. 123.

59.   Rockwell, *My Adventures*, p. 274.

60.   Rockwell, *My Adventures*, p. 279.

61.   Rockwell, *My Adventures*, p. 281.

62.   Helen K. Hawkins, "A Neighborly Look at the Artist Who Painted America," *The Saturday Evening Post*, January/February 1979.

63.   Rockwell, *My Adventures*, p. 203.

64.   Arthur L. Guptill, *Norman Rockwell: Illustrator*. New York: Watson-Guptill, 1946, p. 199.

65.   Rockwell, *My Adventures*, p. 114.

66.   Buechner, *Norman Rockwell*, p. 26.

67.   Rockwell, *My Adventures*, p. 352.

68.   Rockwell, *My Adventures*, p. 303.

Chapter 6: Losses and Triumphs

69.   Stuart Murray and James McCabe, *Norman Rockwell's Four Freedoms*. Stockbridge, MA: Berkshire House, 1993, p. 6.

70.   Rockwell, *My Adventures*, p. 349.

71.   Hawkins, "A Neighborly Look."

72.   Rockwell, *My Adventures*, p. 313.

73.   Rockwell, *My Adventures*, p. 314.

74.   Rockwell, *My Adventures*, p. 314.

75.   Walton, *A Rockwell Portrait*, p. 161.

76.   Walton, *A Rockwell Portrait*, p. 161.

77.   Rockwell, *My Adventures*, p. 318.

78.   Rockwell, *My Adventures*, p. 317.

79.   Rockwell, *My Adventures*, p. 324.

80.   Rockwell, *My Adventures*, p. 333.

81.   Rockwell, *My Adventures*, p. 359.

82.   Rockwell, *My Adventures*, p. 416.

83.   Rockwell, *My Adventures*, pp. 360–361.

84.   Walton, *A Rockwell Portrait*, p. 221.

Chapter 7: The End of an Era

85.   Rockwell, *My Adventures*, p. 306.

86.   Rockwell, *My Adventures*, p. 307.

87.   Rockwell, *My Adventures*, p. 307.

88.   Rockwell, *My Adventures*, p. 375.

89.   Landrum Bolling, "Norman Rockwell's Legacy," *The Saturday Evening Post*, May/June 1994, p. 5.

Chapter 8: Another Town

90.   Rockwell, *My Adventures*, p. 425.

91.   Rockwell, *My Adventures*, p. 429.

92.   Frederic A. Birmingham, "Stockbridge Becomes a Shrine," *The Saturday Evening Post*, January/February 1979.

93.   Birmingham, "Stockbridge Becomes a Shrine."

94.   *The Saturday Evening Post*, "Another Town," January/February 1979.

95.   Franklin K. Paddock, "The Norman Rockwell I Knew," *The Saturday Evening Post*, July/August 1988.

96.   *The Saturday Evening Post*, "Another Town."

97.   Rockwell, *My Adventures*, p. 419.

Epilogue: Rockwell's Legacy

98.   Bolling, "Norman Rockwell's Legacy."

99.   Paddock, "The Norman Rockwell I Knew."

For Further Reading

Books

Thomas S. Buechner, *Norman Rockwell: Artist and Illustrator*. New York: Harry N. Abrams, 1970. An overview, decade by decade, of Rockwell's work, by the director of the Brooklyn Museum. The book includes color plates of much of Rockwell's work, including *Post* covers, story illustrations, advertisements, and posters.

Arthur L. Guptill, *Norman Rockwell: Illustrator*. New York: Watson-Guptill, 1946. A biographical overview of Rockwell's work through 1946. Filled with color plates of Rockwell's illustrations and peppered with sketches and photographs of the artist. Also includes a detailed description of Rockwell's creative and technical procedure at that time.

Stuart Murray and James McCabe, *Norman Rockwell's Four Freedoms*. Stockbridge, MA: Berkshire House, 1993. The story of the *Four Freedoms*. Contains Rockwell's illustrations from World War II, including the *Four Freedoms*, and photographs of events surrounding publication of the paintings, as well as recent essays on what these freedoms mean today.

Donald Walton, *A Rockwell Portrait: An Intimate Biography*. Kansas City, MO: Sheed Andrews and McMeel, 1978. This biography offers a view of Rockwell's life based on the business association and friendship with Walton. They met when Rockwell accepted a commission to do a series of sketches for silver plates to be produced by the Franklin Mint and in-depth personal interviews. It contains Rockwell illustrations and photographs of Rockwell.

Periodicals

Allison Adato and Abe Frajndlich, "The People in the Pictures," *Life*, July 1993. Interviews with people who have posed for Rockwell's *Post* covers. They share their experiences and describe posing for Rockwell.

Sydney R. Kanter, "'The Black Eye.' Memories of Norman Rockwell," *The Saturday Evening Post*, July/August 1994. A photographer shares his memories of Rockwell's coming to his office for help in finding a child with a black eye to model for a *Post* cover.

Verlyn Klinkenborg, "Pyle and Rockwell—Totally American, Yet Not at All Alike," *Smithsonian*, July 1994. An article comparing Rockwell and his idol, Howard Pyle. Although there are many differences in their work, Rockwell admired Pyle for his dedication to his work and the authenticity in his illustrations.

Works Consulted

Books

Christopher Finch, *102 Favorite Paintings by Norman Rockwell.* New York: Crown, 1978. A collection of Rockwell illustrations accompanied by a short description and explanation of each piece. Includes illustrations from *Post* covers, Four Season calendars, inside illustrations, and advertisements.

———, *Reader's Digest Norman Rockwell's America.* New York: Harry N. Abrams, 1975. A biographical overview of Rockwell's work, filled with color and black-and-white illustrations. Contains the complete set of Rockwell *Post* covers plus other work.

George Mendoza, *Norman Rockwell's Patriotic Times.* New York: Viking, 1985. A collection of Rockwell illustrations with patriotic themes accompanied by essays and poetry of various authors. Includes an introduction by President Ronald Reagan.

Norman Rockwell as told to Tom Rockwell, *My Adventures as an Illustrator.* New York: Harry N. Abrams, 1988. An autobiography Rockwell wrote with his son. This story of Rockwell's life is the story of his career. Contains Rockwell illustrations and photographs of Rockwell.

Saturday Evening Post editors, *Norman Rockwell Memory Album.* Indianapolis, IN: Curtis Publishing, 1979. A collection of articles put together in remembrance of Norman Rockwell. Some focus on Rockwell as a person as well as on his career. Others tell about his funeral and Stockbridge after his death.

Periodicals

Frederic A. Birmingham, "Norman Rockwell: The Last Gentle Man," *The Saturday Evening Post,* January/February 1979. A biographical profile of Norman Rockwell published in the memorial issue of the *Post.*

———, "Stockbridge Becomes a Shrine," *The Saturday Evening Post,* January/February 1979. Contains information about Norman Rockwell and Stockbridge, Massachusetts, where he lived, his neighbors, and life in New England, and the tribute Stockbridge paid to Rockwell.

Landrum Bolling, "Norman Rockwell's Legacy," *The Saturday Evening Post,* May/June 1994. An article about the Stockbridge Museum, where much of Rockwell's work is now on exhibit. Includes a biographical sketch and information about the Rockwell collection at Stockbridge.

Esther Wach Book, "A Norman Rockwell at $407,000," *Forbes,* August 15, 1994. An article on collecting the art of illustrators popular during the golden age of illustration. The focus is artists Norman Rockwell and N. C. Wyeth, neither of whom ever gained the praise of critics but still remain popular with the general public.

Holly Miller, "Artists and Friends," *The Saturday Evening Post*, January/February 1979. An article about the friendship between Norman Rockwell and fellow artist and neighbor Mead Schaeffer.

Franklin K. Paddock, "The Norman Rockwell I Knew," *The Saturday Evening Post*, July/August 1988. Paddock, Norman's friend and doctor, writes about Rockwell and gives his view of Rockwell's work and outlook on life.

The Saturday Evening Post, "Another Town," January/February 1979. A memorial tribute to Norman Rockwell that describes his funeral and farewell from Stockbridge.

———, "Letters About the Artist," January/February 1979. A number of well-known people, including Jimmy Carter, Elizabeth Taylor, Erma Bombeck, and Senator Robert Byrd, paid tribute to Norman Rockwell in this issue of the *Saturday Evening Post* dedicated to the memory of Norman Rockwell.

———, "Strokes of Genius—The Artists' Legacy," January/February 1979. An article of short verbal sketches of illustrators Rockwell knew and admired and some who admired Rockwell includes: J. C. Leyendecker, Robert Charles Howe, Gene Boyer, and Robert Templeton.

———, "Sunday Always Follows Saturday Evening in the Post," January/February 1979. A look at how *Post* covers illustrated religion in America. Includes work by Rockwell as well as other *Post* artists.

Index

Credits

Cover photo: Springer/Bettmann

AP/Wide World Photos, 27, 79, 80, 84

Archive Photos, 21, 78

The Bettmann Archive, 11, 31, 48,

Brown Brothers, 59

Courtesy Peter A. Juley & Son; reproduced from the *Dictionary of American Portraits*, published by Dover Publications, Inc. in 1967; 28

Curtis Publishing Company, 39, 57, 60, 64, 68, 71, 73

Heritage Press/M.B.I. Inc., 52

National Archives, 67

Photo courtesy of The Norman Rockwell Museum at Stockbridge, 13, 14, 19, 30, 35, 43, 46, 54 (by Gene Pelham), 55 (by Louie Lamone), 77, 82 (by Louie Lamone)

UPI/Bettmann, 24, 33, 37, 38, 41, 50, 69, 74

Grateful acknowledgment is made to reprint quotations from *My Adventures as an Illustrator* by Norman Rockwell as told to Tom Rockwell. Published in 1988 by Harry N. Abrams, Inc., New York. Copyright © 1988 by the Estate of Norman Rockwell. All rights reserved.

About the Author

Deanne Durrett is the author of three other nonfiction books for Lucent—*Organ Transplants, The Importance of Jim Henson,* and *Angels.* In addition, she has published a middle-grade novel, *My New Sister the Bully,* published by Abingdon Press, and the nonfiction book *Healers,* which is part of the Facts On File American Indian Lives series. She has published stories and articles in magazines for adults as well as children and newspaper feature stories, commentary, and columns. She retired as San Diego regional adviser for the Society of Children's Book Writers and Illustrators in 1994 after serving five and a half years. She has been an admirer of Norman Rockwell for years and was born on his birthday.

21.19

```
--          Durrett, Deanne,
B              1940-
Rockwell
D           Norman Rockwell.
```

DATE